TWO-COUNTRIES

U.S. DAUGHTERS & SONS OF IMMIGRANT PARENTS

TWO-COUNTRIES

U.S. DAUGHTERS & SONS OF IMMIGRANT PARENTS

Flash Memoir, Personal Essays & Poetry

EDITED BY

Tina Schumann

Red Hen Press | *Pasadena, CA*

Cover art by Francis Picabia
Book design by Selena Trager & Hannah Moye

Library of Congress Cataloging-in-Publication Data

Names: Schumann, Tina editor.
Title: Two-countries : U.S. daughters and sons of immigrant parents : flash memoir, personal essays & poetry / Tina Schumann, editor.
Description: Pasadena : Red Hen Press, 2017. | The collection contains contributions from sixty-five writers who were either born and/or raised in the US by one or more immigrant parent. Identifiers: LCCN 2017011709 | ISBN 9781597096065 (pbk. : alk. paper) | ISBN 9781597095723 (ebook)
Subjects: LCSH: Immigrants' writings, American. | Children of immigrants—United States—Literary collections. | American literature—Minority authors. | Emigration and immigration—Literary collections. | American literature—21st century.
Classification: LCC PS508.I45 T86 2017 | DDC 810.8/09206912—dc23
LC record available at https://lccn.loc.gov/2017011709

The National Endowment for the Arts, the Los Angeles County Arts Commission, the Dwight Stuart Youth Fund, the Max Factor Family Foundation, the Pasadena Tournament of Roses Foundation, the Pasadena Arts & Culture Commission and the City of Pasadena Cultural Affairs Division, the City of Los Angeles Department of Cultural Affairs, the Audrey & Sydney Irmas Charitable Foundation, Sony Pictures Entertainment, Amazon Literary Partnership, and the Sherwood Foundation partially support Red Hen Press.

First Edition
Published by Red Hen Press
www.redhen.org

GRATITUDE

The editor would like to give special thanks and gratitude to Assistant Editor Jill McCabe Johnson for her invaluable insights, readings, editorial suggestions and moral support along the way. The same goes for Peggy Shumaker whose guidance, mentorship and generosity are world-famous for good reason. Big hugs to Julie Riddle who endured many a long email filled with whining and belly-aching, but nonetheless continued to restore my faith and cheered me on along the way. Many heartfelt thanks to the stalwart and dedicated staff at Red Hen Press. You never let me down and gracefully educated me along the way. Finally and always, lifelong love and gratitude to my own personal superhero, The-Amazing-Husband-Man, Paul Traeger. He knows why.

This collection is dedicated to my maternal grandmother, Maria Mélida Rivas-Sol (center) and her four daughters (clockwise from the top): Eva Antonia, Dora Maria, my mother Mélida Luz, and Ada Marina. You were all brave and you all made an impression.

CONTENTS

TWO-COUNTRIES

U.S. DAUGHTERS & SONS OF IMMIGRANT PARENTS

Tina Schumann

INTRODUCTION

When I was a child and strangers overheard my mother's accent they would sometimes ask her, "Where are you from?" Her standard reply was "Central America," unless the person asking was obviously another Latin and then she would get specific and say "El Salvador." I understood from an early age why she did this; the assumption that a majority of native-born Americans often make when called upon to instantly visualize a foreign country, particularly a country they most likely knew little about, often resulted in stereotypical images pulled together from an amalgamation of several different Latin countries. It seemed to my mother that in the perspective of most Americans, El Salvador was identical to Mexico and Mexico was interchangeable with Guatemala, Puerto Rico, Honduras, Uruguay or Cuba, and so on. It took too much effort to enlighten someone on the spot, so why bother? Because my mother's extended family immigrated from Spain and other parts of the globe (her maternal great-grandfather was Welsh) to El Salvador decades before she was born, my mother's physical features did not match what most Americans might have expected after flipping through the pages of a *National Geographic*. Current statistics show that about 1 percent of the Salvadorean population is purely indigenous.

My mother, Mélida Luz Sol (1926–2003), was born in El Salvador's capital city of San Salvador in 1926. She immigrated to the U.S. in 1940 at the age of fourteen when her single father, Narciso Sol, who worked as an importer with the United Fruit Company, suddenly died of a burst appendix. Her own mother had already immigrated to the United States and left her four daughters and husband in El Salvador several years earlier when it became clear the marriage was disintegrating. My grandmother joined her sister Carmen, as well as other siblings and cousins already living in San Francisco in the late 1930s. Upon her father's death, my teenage mother and one of her three older sisters, Dora Maria, made the trip gratis in the staterooms available on a United Fruit banana boat.

They traveled from San Salvador, through the Gulf of Mexico and finally into the harbor at New Orleans where they transferred to a train to make the week-long trip to San Francisco. My mother would return to the country of her birth several times over the course of her life, as much of her family continued to lived there.

I am the youngest of my mother's four children born and raised in the U.S., and as a middle-aged woman, I now appreciate the many complex elements that influenced my development as the American-born daughter of an immigrant mother and a U.S.-born, Anglo-American father. But as a child I not only took these facts for granted, as children do, but never thought to volunteer information about my mother's origins or the fact that half of my extended family spoke Spanish as their first language. One of my formative memories includes the time I brought home an elementary school friend and was shocked when she turned to me and said, "Your mom talks funny." All I could think was, *Really?* I hadn't noticed. To me, my mother's accent was such an integral part of who she was, it simply did not register with me. Nor did it occur to me that it was something I needed to forewarn the outside world about. I see now how unique (though perhaps more common than one might think) my family experiences were and are; how differently my mother and I viewed our roles as women, our expectations of life, relationships, careers and world views because of how, where and when we came of age. These differences were not just the result of a generation gap, but distinctions of culture, or more specifically, immigrant culture within a larger mixed culture. I also reflect on the many times when my mother's origins were pointed out to her and me in everyday life—what she went through in order to assimilate while maintaining her own culture, language and ethnic particularities.

While in her early thirties, my mother trained as a bank teller, and continued in that career for several decades. She once told me the story of the bank manager who dropped the keys to the vault on the floor in front of her whenever she requested them. The first few times he dropped the keys she assumed it was an accident, picked the keys up and went about her business. However, the next time he dropped them she knew it was no accident and asked him why he continued to drop the keys. The manager replied that he was not going to risk "touching a dirty Spic." I understand that this story is an example of what might be seen as discrimination *lite*. Others have certainly suffered far worse, but to my young, uninitiated ears this story was an eye-opening revelation, and just one example of how my mother and I might be viewed as different. I knew then with absolute certainty that my mother, and myself by extension, were going to be seen as something other than fully American. We were something that needed to be explained.

My father's ethnic roots stem from Ireland on his mother's side (she was a first-generation American) and Germany and Ireland on his father's side. He was born and raised in Jersey City, New Jersey, in a neighborhood made up of a wide range of ethnic cultures, from Polish and Russian Jews, to Italian and Puerto Rican immigrants. To say that he was raised in a melting pot is putting it mildly. He learned a smattering of Spanish from his Puerto Rican friends and learned how to cook from an Italian neighbor. He married his first wife, Tomiko Hiroki, while stationed in Japan during the Korean Conflict in the mid-1950s, and so I was raised with my siblings Pamela and Christopher, who are both half-Japanese. My father spent five years living in Japan and when he came back to the U.S. he opened a Japanese catering service in, of all places, Little Rock, Arkansas. As a result of my father's continued interest in Japanese culture and food, and the fact that two of my siblings are half-Japanese, I learned to use chopsticks at the same time I learned to use a knife and fork. Our backyard grill was never called a grill or BBQ, but a Hibachi. I was as familiar with *beni shōga* (pickled ginger) wrapped in steamed rice and seaweed as I was with my mother's rice and beans. When I was growing up my father often ate small cubes of firm tofu dipped in soy sauce as an afternoon snack while my mother was making *arroz con pollo* for dinner. It took me many years to realize that not every American kid was raised with this kind of ethnic blend, and exposure to other cultures.

My mother also had two children from previous marriages. My oldest brother, Ricardo, is full Salvadorean, and my brother Henry is half-Salvadorean and a mix of Native American, Scandinavian and Swedish. I suppose we might have appeared to be a motley crew to the outside world, but one accepts without question the family they are born into until the exterior world has an opportunity to point out the differences. I imagine all families are "different" in their own way; some differences are simply more obvious than others, especially in a culture that seems to be obsessed with ethnicity. I also realize now how lucky I was to have spent my formative years attending an elementary and junior high school in the Bay Area of the 1970s, which was what we would now refer to as ethnically diverse. My friends consisted of Chinese Americans, Filipino Americans, Guamanians, Mexican and African Americans, many of whom were first generation.

Looking back at my particular life circumstance and especially in light of my parents' passing, I came to a realization that I wanted to give voice to those "American" kids like me and immigrants like my mother. I assumed there must be many who shared similar stories. In several of the pieces contained here I heard very familiar narratives that reminded me of my mother's perspective and the situations that she and I faced because she was an immigrant. In Denise Valenti's flash memoir "Spanish" I recognized my own rejection of my mother's language. There came a point as a child when I simply did not hear it. Spanish was her language, not mine. My mother never attempted to formally teach me Spanish as Denise's mother did, but would translate songs and specific words if I asked. She would sometimes speak short sentences to me in Spanish and I always answered her in English. Now, of course I wish I were fully bilingual.

In Gabriella Burman's essay "Estela," I saw my own mother's propensities towards proper behavior, social rules and standards that appeared stogie and old-fashioned to me and my siblings. My mother demanded that I wear a dress to elementary school every day except Wednesday, when I was allowed to wear jeans like the other girls. How my mother looked when she left the house was of primary importance and a standard she tried to pass onto her growing daughter, but which often resulted in great conflict between us. If the world was going to judge her negatively by her accent, they certainly were not going to judge her for her lack of style. I remember my brother and I often giggled at my mother's mispronunciation of certain words ("Shits" when she meant "Sheets") as did Gabriella and her sister. I wish we hadn't.

There are pieces in this collection which I could not have anticipated when I began this project, but which I am so glad came my way; David Licata's "The Wolf Is in the Kitchen," Chris Wiewiora's "M-I-S-S-I-S-S-I-P-P-I," Sahar Mustafah's "The Arabians," and Mohja Kahf's poem "My Grandmother Washes Her Feet in the Sink of the Bathroom at Sears" for example. All of which made me laugh out loud and left me feeling a deep endearment for the children they were and the families they came from. Tina Chang's poem "The Shifting Kingdom" broke my heart in a million pieces and reminded me of the vast differences in the immigration experience my mother lived through and those being faced by families with far less resources, which often results in the loss of the innocent along the way. Children trapped between the desperation of adult lives, politics, economics, conceptual borders and the realization that a bright future may not be available to them on either side of that border.

Many of the pieces contained in this anthology served to enlighten me in unexpected ways regarding my own assumptions about the immigrant experience and those of their children. I was looking for corroboration, and in some cases received that, but I also learned that the relationships, degrees of understanding and negative versus positive parental influences are as varied as they are for any other segmented population, or families in general. To some extent, this resulted in the self-realization that my often-difficult relationship with my own mother may have had far less to do with her immigrant status and more to do with the fact that we were just two very different individuals, regardless of our origins.

During the submission period for this anthology, I received an email that contained the subject line, "A very serious question." The email, from a Latina-American writer, asked, "Do you consider yourself a *Latina writer*? If so, why and why not?" It's a fair enough question, but one that I have to admit set me on edge. Along with the ubiquitous "What are you?" inquiry asked far too often growing up, the need that seems to prevail in our country to immediately define others ethnically has always felt, to me, confining at best; and at worst implicates me in the American obsession with ethnic origins, as well as sexual and political orientation. I also have to admit that I never felt justified in claiming the full status of Latina since my father was American-born with Irish/German roots. In answering that question at all, I feel I am supporting our dependency on tidy and comforting classifications.

To be obliged to say to the world *THIS is what I am, you can relax now that I am in my proper box*, seems to me the worst kind of false acceptance, and never comes close to defining the whole person. Who defines that box and our need for the box at all seems to me the more interesting question. I replied to the question that I considered myself to be an *American writer*, though that again is hardly the whole story of me, the complex individual. I would not want to be defined by half of my ethnic origins any more than I would want to be defined primarily by my sex or political leanings.

When I was in my late teens and early twenties and first began applying for jobs, and thus filling out affirmative action forms, I immediately, and almost without thought, checked the "White" box every time. When I thought of my parents' skin color, it was white that came to mind.

I was naïve enough then to believe that was what the form was asking. This was in the early 1980s and I can recall only four choices being offered at that time: White, Asian American, African American and Native American. I remember my jaw physically dropping the first time I saw "Hispanic" on the form. "Pacific-Islander" and "Other" were a long time coming. The moniker of "Other" still gives me pause; what is "Other" anyway? Doesn't that include everyone? Aren't we all the product of some combination of chromosomes, cells and DNA molecules—a combination we ourselves may not be fully aware of?

If the affirmative action forms then (or now) had provided the option of marking half-Hispanic and half-White I would have been fine with that, but they did not, and over the years I became increasingly irritated at the odd and offensive supposition that the form implied; someone like me was simply not possible, and therefore not counted. So in my younger rebel years I began filling in a ½ symbol by Hispanic and a ½ symbol by White and thought, "Let them figure that one out!" In my recent research, I see that some of the now voluntary affirmative action forms online, while updated, still make someone of my particular ethnic mix not possible. The form I found on the website for, of all places, "The Society for Human Resource Management" starts with the choice "Hispanic or Latino" (*Latino*, by the way, being the *male* designation for someone who self-identifies as a person of Latin origins). The next choice offered is "White (not Hispanic or Latino)." So now I have been cancelled out three times over. I would not choose "Hispanic or Latino" as that is only half of what I am ethnically (and the last time I checked I was not male), nor would I choose "White (not Hispanic or Latino)," as that is not true either. The final zinger on this form is the last choice, which is . . . yes, you guessed it, "Two or More Races (*not* Hispanic or Latino)." You might be laughing at this point. I am.

I now opt out on affirmative action forms. If I am required to choose only one part of my heritage, then I would rather forego the choice altogether. I can only imagine that there are many other individuals in the U.S. whose ethnic blend has left them befuddled when faced with these forms.

My perceptions and experiences of what constitutes a person from El Salvador are unique to my family and my limited experience in that country (I traveled to El Salvador with my parents in 1972, when I was eight years old). Granted, there are general similarities such as language, food and tropical weather, but Salvadoreans are no more similar to each other than a person who was born and raised in Seattle, Washington is to a person born and raised in Madison, Wisconsin. Even the words they use in English to describe themselves vary, let alone their perceptions of what it means to be from El Salvador or their identity in the larger, global culture. Let's face it; the only box we all fit into is that of human being.

While I believe the claiming of and pride in one's culture is important, I wanted this collection to primarily illustrate our sameness as human beings. To say *Yes, we have differences, but look how similar we are.* Perhaps I am proposing a rather idealistic future where one's cultural and ethnic origins are not only present, but are so integrated and prevalent in our society that we no longer feel the need to speak of *tolerance* or *acceptance*, because we, without reservation, accept each other as is and take the intermingling of all cultures as one of the best aspects of American life, something to take pride in. Perhaps even something to claim as an American right? Some might say we are already there, and I have seen changes even in my lifetime. But I think the ethnic line is still drawn far too often in daily life and is usually presented in a derogatory or stereotypical manner. At other times the references point to a place on the spectrum where the culture in question is elevated to a politically correct, untouchable (and often false) standard that illuminates only a single facet of that culture. Nor does "the line" take into consideration the individual in question regardless of cultural or ethnic background. I realize this anthology itself may be seen as defining that line.

Perhaps I am asking too much? Perhaps I am asking for the human ego itself to change? Call me a pie-in-the-sky optimist, but I would like to live in a world where affirmative action forms are viewed as a long-dead social oddity we shake our collective heads over, to think we were ever that narrow-minded. If we are to realize true inclusion (dare I say *equality*), I believe our ultimate humane goal must be a society in which we no longer define the ethnic line, but celebrate the diversity.

I do realize that in the venture of creating an anthology that presents the voices of a select group of writers who were raised by immigrants, or who are immigrants themselves, in a sense contradicts the above statement. My thinking is this: since we are still in our infancy when it comes to truly accepting America as a melting pot, and not in the past, but in the present tense, I would like to chime in with evidence that illuminates our human elements over our individual languages, accents, features or skin color. I honestly believe *anyone* reading these essays and poems will relate on some level to the very human stories being told.

This volume is ultimately a celebration, a shout-out, and a raising of the flag that says the children of immigrants—and those in this collection who came to the U.S. at an early age (like my mother)—not only live and work in this country, but are most likely a neighbor, a co-worker, your students, their mothers and fathers, a Supreme Court Justice and even the President. We count. More importantly, here are the stories of our sameness, our human proclivities, our need and desire to be seen as legitimate members of the ever-changing human tribe that constitutes America, and the world. I am happily indebted to the talented writers who contributed to this anthology, to their bravery, their sense of self and their audacity in writing it down.

Tina Schumann
Seattle 2016

Do I contradict myself? / Very well then I contradict myself, / (I am large, I contain multitudes.)

—Walt Whitman

Elisa Albo

HERITAGE STATEMENT:

I was born in Havana to Sephardic Jews, and we emigrated to the U.S. when I was a year old. My parents were married the same year Fidel Castro ousted Batista. Over the next two years, they found the rapidly changing political situation intolerable and made plans to leave. Their plans became urgent when my father casually said something against the Castro regime one day at the hospital where he worked as a doctor, and someone renounced him. He got on a plane and came to Miami. My parents had honeymooned in Miami Beach and had friends and family in Florida. My nineteen-year-old mother, infant sister, and I joined him in Tampa a month later. We got out with the help of Hadassah and by way of Jamaica. We lived in Tampa for a year, in Pennsylvania for one winter, and finally settled in Lakeland, Florida, where I grew up and my parents still live. When they left Cuba, my mother says, they thought it would be "for a year or two."

AUTHOR BIO:

Elisa Albo is the author of the chapbook *Passage to America* (March Street Press, 2006). Her poems have appeared in journals and anthologies such as *Alimentum, BOMB, Crab Orchard Review, Gulf Stream Magazine, Interlitq, Irrepressible Appetites, MiPOesias, The Potomac Journal*, and *Tigertail: A South Florida Poetry Annual*. She recently completed *To Sweeten the Flesh*, a collection of food poems. She received an MFA from Florida International University and teaches English and ESL at Broward College. She lives with her husband and daughters in Ft. Lauderdale, Florida.

CARTOGRAPHY

after Neruda

I have no country.
My body is my map.
Myriad tributaries
flow in my limbs,
weave through twig
baskets of bones,
carry oceans of blood.

My nails are tiny barrier
islands, my hair seagrass,
eyes tide pools brimming
with sea creatures.
Shy snails inhabit
the shells of my ears.
Deer tread on the stones
of my wrists, the rocks
of my ankles.

When I breathe,
a gale fills my lungs,
a mistral, seasonal
siroccos. Rainwater
collects in valleys—
on the insides of elbows,
the back of a knee,
the hollow in my neck,
in ridges alongside ribs.
It spreads over banks,
floods into caves,
drips in rainforests,

wet fingers reaching
for the dusty edges
of deserts.

I have no country,
no familiar soil,
no sacred ground
in which to lay my bones,
no grandparents buried
in the country of their birth.
My parents will not lie
in theirs, nor I in mine.

My body is my map,
skin topography,
borders bending

with the fate
of the disinherited
who bear their resources
to wherever wars,
dictators, or circumstances
fling them on the globe.

On a clear day,
I can trace
where I was born:
on an island shaped
like a sweet tobacco
leaf, hand-rolled,

lit with a flame,
deeply inhaled,
savored, smuggled
out, set free
to toss and travel
on a western sea.

My body is my map.
Everywhere I journey,
my land journeys with me.

EXILE

She knows she can never return.
  The hole in the heart muscle
    releases a long, plaintive note
      but the mind, like water seeking
        its level, rushes in to fill the rent,

to soften and mute strings
  attached to the protected childhood,
    green plantains frying at noon, slow
      fans overhead urging Caribbean
        breezes through the many windows

of home. Gone, lost, even
  their shadows, except in the stomach
    and on skin—they too have memory—
      have learned to take in alien
        nourishment, reconfigure weather

patterns. In the new country, each
  move to a new house, each first
    night in a strange hotel, repeats
      the exile *sine qua non*—adapt and
        settle quickly—fill drawers, arrange

toiletries, place pictures, flood
  the streets the feet will know and
    swim. The palms' fronds overhead
      are clapping and the strokes—
        they too will become familiar.

Kazim Ali

HERITAGE STATEMENT:

My father's family moved to Pakistan from India in 1942 and so my parents were separated by that complicated national border when they were married. My mother joined my father in London where he had work. I was a home-birth, born on a cold Tuesday morning on Bingham Road in Croydon, U.K. When Pierre Trudeau opened the borders of Canada in the early 1970s my parents emigrated. We came to the U.S. about ten years later. It was the Reagan Years, but in our house a portrait of Ayatollah Khomeini hung over the fireplace. I never knew if I was Muslim or American or Canadian or Indian or some of those things or none of them. "Where are you from?" was the most complicated question you could ask me. "Where's home?" would usually follow, meant as a clarification.

AUTHOR BIO:

Poet, editor, and prose writer Kazim Ali received a BA and MA from the University of Albany–SUNY, and an MFA from New York University. Ali's poetry collections include *The Far Mosque* (Alice James Books, 2005), which won the Alice James Books' New England/New York Award, *The Fortieth Day* (BOA Editions, Ltd., 2008), and *Sky Ward* (Wesleyan University Press, 2013). His prose includes *The Disappearance of Seth* (Etruscan Press, 2009), *Bright Felon: Autobiography and Cities* (Wesleyan University Press, 2009), and  the forthcoming *Resident Alien: On Border-Crossing and the Undocumented Divine*. He is also the author of the novel *Quinn's Passage* (BlazeVOX Books, 2005), which was named one of the Best Books of 2005 by *Chronogram* magazine. In 2003 Ali co-founded Nightboat Books and served as the press's publisher until 2007. He has received an Individual Excellence Award from the Ohio Arts Council, and his poetry has been featured in *Best American Poetry*. Ali has been a regular columnist for *The American Poetry Review* and a contributing editor for the Association of Writers and Writing Programs' *Writer's Chronicle*. He is a former member of the Cocoon Theatre Modern Dance Company. Ali has taught at Oberlin College and the low-residency Stonecoast MFA program at the University of Southern Maine. He lives in Oberlin, Ohio.

HOME

My father had a steel comb with which he would comb our hair.

After a bath the cold metal soothing against my scalp, his hand cupping
my chin.

My mother had a red pullover with a little yellow duck embroidered
on it and a pendant made from a gold Victoria coronation coin.

Which later, when we first moved to Buffalo, would be stolen from
the house.

The Sunn'i Muslims have a story in which the angels cast a dark mark
out of Prophet Mohammad's heart, thus making him pure, though the
Shi'a reject this story, believing in his absolute innocence from birth.

Telling the famous Story of the Blanket in which the Prophet covers
himself with a Yemeni blanket for his afternoon rest. Joined under
the blanket first by his son-in-law Ali, then each of his grandchildren
Hassan and Hussain and finally by his daughter Bibi Fatima.

In Heaven Gabriel asks God about the five under the blanket and
God says, those are the five people whom I loved the most out of all
creation, and I made everything in the heavens and the earth for
their sake.

Gabriel, speaker on God's behalf, whisperer to Prophets, asks God, can
I go down and be the sixth among them.

And God says, go down there and ask them. If they consent you may go
under the blanket and be the sixth among them.

Creation for the sake of Gabriel is retroactively granted when the group under the blanket admits him to their company.

Is that me at the edge of the blanket asking to be allowed inside.

Asking the 800 *hadith* be canceled, all history re-ordered.

In Hyderabad I prayed every part of the day, climbed a thousand steps to the site of Maula Ali's pilgrimage.

I wanted to be those stairs, the hunger I felt, the river inside.

I learned to pronounce my daily prayers from transliterated English in a book called "Know Your Islam," dark blue with gold calligraphed writing that made the English appear as if it were Arabic complete with marks above and below the letters.

I didn't learn the Arabic script until years later and never learned the language itself.

God's true language: Hebrew. Latin. Arabic. Sanskrit.

As if utterance fit into the requirements of the human mouth.

I learned how to find the new moon by looking for the circular absence of stars.

When Abraham took Isaac up into the thicket his son did not know where he was being led.

When his father bound him and took up the knife he was shocked.

And said, "Father, where is the ram?"

Though from Abraham's perspective he was asked by God to sacrifice his son and proved his love by taking up the knife.

Thinking to himself perhaps, Oh Ismail, Ismail, do I cut or do I burn.

I learned God's true language is only silence and breath.

Fourth son of a fourth son, my father was afflicted as a child and as was the custom in those days a new name was selected for him to protect his health.

Still the feeling of his rough hand, gently cupping my cheek, dipping the steel comb in water to comb my hair flat.

My hair was kept so short, combed flat when wet. I never knew my hair was wavy until I was nearly twenty-two and never went outside with wet and uncombed hair until I was twenty-eight.

At which point I realized my hair was curly.

My father's hands have fortune-lines in them cut deeply and dramatic.

The day I left his house for the last time I asked him if I could hold his hand before I left.

There are two different ways of going about this.

If you have known this for years why didn't you ask for help? he asked me.

Each time I left home, including the last time, my mother would hold a Qur'an up for me to walk under. Once under, one would turn and kiss the book.

There is no place in the Qur'an which requires acts of homosexuality to be punishable by lashings and death.

Hadith or scripture. Scripture or rupture.

Should I travel out from under the blanket?

Comfort from a verse which also recurs: "Surely there are signs in this for those of you who would reflect."

Or the one hundred and four books of God. Of which only four are known—*Qur'an, Injeel, Tavrat, Zubuur.*

There are a hundred others—*Bhagavad-Gita, Lotus Sutra, Song of Myself, the Gospel of Magdalene, Popol Vuh, the book of Black Buffalo Woman*—somewhere unrevealed as such.

Dear mother in the sky you could unbuckle the book and erase all the annotations.

What I always remember about my childhood is my mother whispering to me, telling me secrets, ideas, suggestions.

She named me when I moved in her while she was reading a calligraphy of the Imam's names. My name: translated my whole life for me as *Patience*.

In India we climbed the steps of the Maula Ali mountain to the top, thirsting for what.

My mother had stayed behind in the house, unable to go on pilgrimage. She had told me the reason why.

Being in a state considered unacceptable for prayers or pilgrimages.

I asked if she would want more children and she told me the name she would give a new son.

I always attribute the fact that they did not, though my eldest sister's first son was given the same name she whispered to me that afternoon, to my telling of her secret to my sisters when we were climbing the stairs.

It is the one betrayal of her—perhaps meaningless—that I have never forgiven myself.

There are secrets it is still hard to tell, betrayals hard to make.

You hope like anything that though others consider you unclean God will still welcome you.

My name is Kazim. Which means *patience*. I know how to wait.

Dori Appel

HERITAGE STATEMENT:

I was born in Chicago in 1935. My grandparents emigrated to America at the end of the nineteenth century. Though all were Jewish, anti-Semitism was a much greater issue for my Polish grandparents than for their Hungarian counterparts. As in Vienna, Jews had a degree of freedom in Hungary during this period. I think my grandfather's leaving was due primarily to financial issues. "Stowaways" tells about my Polish grandparents, and though both grandmothers appear in "Legacy," the poem includes more details about my Hungarian grandmother. As the poem describes, she was reunited with my grandfather in New York early in the twentieth century, following a departure without her knowledge and a ten-year separation. (My mother was the "fortieth birthday gift" referred to in the poem.) I know very few details about the lives of my Polish grandparents before they came to America, though I do know that my grandmother Sarah rescued my grandfather from the Polish army barracks. Their first child was born in Poland, and four more sons, including my father, were born in America. My grandfather was a wagon-maker in Poland and worked in the garment trade on New York's Lower East Side.

AUTHOR BIO:

Dori Appel is the author of the poetry collection, *Another Rude Awakening* (Cherry Grove Collections, 2008). Her poems have also been widely published in magazines, including *The Beloit Poetry Journal*, *Prairie Schooner*, and *CALYX*. Publication in anthologies include *When I Am an Old Woman I Shall Wear Purple* (Papier-Mache Press, 2007), as well as several other Papier-Mache collections, *From Here We Speak* (Oregon State University Press, 1993), *City of the Big Shoulders* (University of Iowa Press, 2012), and *On the Dark Path*  (13 Moons Press, 2013). A playwright as well as a poet, three of her full-length plays are published by Samuel French and many of her monologues are included in anthologies. She was the winner of the Oregon Book Award in Drama in 1998, 1999, and 2001. www.doriappel.com

STOWAWAYS

In nameless villages
of Hungary and Poland,
those who stayed behind
waved goodbye and wept,
then disappeared.

My grandparents never spoke
of them, though faces
from the past shared their
small apartment, keeping watch
from tarnished silver frames.

The past is past, thank God—
we should be grateful to be here.

Since time and wars have
long since ground those
distant lives to dust,
it's foolish to ignore such
good advice. And yet,

In dreams I find myself
in rooms I've never seen,
unstitching hems
in search of wedding rings.

LEGACY

Goodbye Sharlotta
gold is running in the streets
send for you when I can
kiss the kids.

Is that what he said in his note,
my mother's handsome father,
when he left my grandmother in Hungary
to wait for him?
Well, something of the sort.

If my other grandfather
had attempted such a trick
my grandmother Sarah would have
gone after him in the wagon
and brought him home,
the way she did when they took him
for the Polish Infantry.

But my grandmother Sharlotta
drew her four children
closer to her knees and waited,
grateful that three of them were boys.
For ten years
relatives brought her groceries
by cover of night to save her shame,
and a borrowed servant
still called her *gnädige frau*.

When her littlest boy died
a relative wrote the sad news

to her husband in America,
since a fever in her girlhood
took with it most of what
Sharlotta learned in school.

Fever or no fever,
my grandma Sarah would have
written the letter in blood
and swum it herself
across the cold Atlantic,
demanding blood for blood.

But Sharlotta packed up
her three surviving children
when the boat fare came,
put on her good black hat,
and joined her husband
in New York.

This is where we find them,
in a modest fourth floor walkup
where he's given her another baby
for a fortieth birthday gift.
He doesn't seem to like her
any better than before,
but he comes home every night
(often late), and forgives her
many failings—her confusion,
helplessness, impatience
with the new little girl.

Her brain is weak, he sighs,
recalling the fever of her youth.
Sharlotta silently bites her lip,
but I make a different choice.

You did this, I tell him,
in my grandmother Sarah's voice.

William Archila

HERITAGE STATEMENT:

Both of my parents, Rolando Archila and Margarita Alfaro, were born in Santa Ana, El Salvador. In November of 1980, when I was twelve years old, I left my native country of El Salvador. I left the war that tore that country apart. Without having read enough Salvadorean history, I arrived in Los Angeles with many questions unanswered and conversations unfinished. I had to learn a new language and culture. I became part of the growing immigrant community. Twelve years later in 1992, a peace treaty was signed between the left and right wing parties in El Salvador. I decided to go back, hoping to find a home, but in my own native country, I was a foreigner, a stranger. I searched for something that no longer existed, a quality remembered from my childhood, a sense of belonging to a country and a language that had changed. I also had changed. I returned to Los Angeles feeling not quite at home. Here I realized that home is neither here nor there. However, the need for a sense of home as base, a source of identity, grew deep inside of me. I began to understand that homelessness and its loneliness are the identity of the exiled writer. And as an exiled writer you try to rebuild your home in your work.

AUTHOR BIO:

William Archila was born in 1968 in Santa Ana, El Salvador. He earned his MFA in poetry from the University of Oregon. He is the author of *The Art of Exile* (Bilingual Review Press, 2009), which won an International Latino Book Award in 2010 and was honored with an Emerging Writer Fellowship Award by The Writer's Center in Bethesda, Maryland. He has published his poems widely, including in *AGNI*, *Southern Poetry Review*, *Copper Nickel*, and *The Georgia Review*, among other journals and anthologies. His book was featured in "First Things First: the Fifth Annual Debut Poets Roundup" in Poets & Writers Magazine. His second book, *The Gravedigger's Archaeology*, published in 2015, recently won the Letras Latinas/Red Hen Poetry Prize.

CAFFEINE

Sometimes it's a full orange hanging in the skyline
a road full of guitars and cigars

or a raindrop sliding down my mother's eyebrow.
My father, on the fire escape, reads

the black grounds collapsed in his cup.
"It's one in the morning somewhere in Central America,"

he says, "I sit in the hospital bed next to your mother,
San Juan de Dios, September 9, 1968.

You're wrapped in my arms
as she dips her finger in coffee, rubs it on your lip.

Drop by drop, a map spreads in your belly."
This could be true, and I want to believe it,

the whole weight of a nation that gathers
in the distant blue tropics, its whole weight in a cup.

The two of us watch the smog fill this sprawl of LA,
headlights and taillights pouring into the freeway.

It's the same story that drags me to work,
my head bobbing as the bus hisses, exhales exhaust,

song that unloosens me when I come home
tired, fall like coins on the dusty floor,

away from sinks filled with dishes and pans,
when I am with him drinking that mud, I dissolve

into the place of my birth, a slip of land by the shore.

THE DAY JOHN LENNON DIED

I come down the thrashed mountain
repeating, "The lord is my shepherd. I shall not want,"
my mother's hand over mine, the moon on guard,
wind slapping my face, smell of rain and trees
as we enter the states, fog rolling out
at daybreak, suburbs glazed in light—
a load of refugees coming out of the ravine
across streets, hiding behind parked cars
dripping with mist, bodies low and close,
creeping on the ground like soldiers over puddles.

My mother in her best clothes—Lee corduroy
Jacket, Levi's Jeans—carries a newspaper
close to her chest, the picture of a man
from Liverpool shot in front of his house.
I am eleven, running toward a father
who had become a kitchen helper, pots and pans
burned black, the slow drag of chain smoke
as he waited for the bus, the cold breath
of the American pavement on his back.

I never expected the next morning, grey and damp,
watching my father coming out of the wooden house.
I want to take the boy, who lost his dad in a gun blast,
say, here is mine, a man who left a country rift in half.
Here he is, defeated, this Salvadorean I will outgrow,
this one with the wet apron and yellow gloves.
I say nothing, not a single word, not even a sound
as he touches my head, my arms around his waist.

F.J. Bergmann

HERITAGE STATEMENT:

I was born in Madison, Wisconsin, in 1954 and grew up partly in Janesville, Wisconsin, and partly in France, where my father's job had taken him. My father, Franz Walter Matthay, was born in Köln, Germany, in 1911, and at nineteen was encouraged to immigrate to the U.S. by visiting relatives who wanted to rescue him from an abusive stepmother. He changed his first name to Frank, received an MBA from Harvard, and eventually became the vice president in charge of foreign sales for the Parker Pen Company, which sent him on many trips abroad. He died from Alzheimer's complications in 1979.

AUTHOR BIO:

F.J. Bergmann is the author of the books *Aqua Regia* (Parallel Press, 2007), *Sauce Robert* (Pavement Saw Press, 2003), and editor at *Star*Line*, the journal of the Science Fiction Poetry Association (sfpoetry. com). She is also poetry editor at *Mobius: The Journal of Social Change* (mobiusmagazine.com). Her work has appeared widely in journals such as *Asimov's Science Fiction*, *Beloit Poetry Journal*, *Hotel Amerika*, *Main Street Rag*, *Margie*, *Mississippi Review*, *North American Review*, *Rattle*, *Southern Poetry Review*, *Sow's*  *Ear Poetry Review*, and *Weird Tales*. She is the winner of the 2012 Rannu Fund for Speculative Literature Poetry Award. Her most recent chapbook is *Out of the Black Forest* (Centennial Press, 2012). She is the recipient of several writing awards including the 2011 Heartland Review's Joy Bale Boone Prize, the 2010 Wisconsin Fellowship of Poets Triad Prize (both eligible categories), the 2010 Atlanta Review International Publication Prize, 2009 Tapestry of Bronze Demeter Prize, 2009 Tattoo Highway 18 Contest, 2008 Science Fiction Poetry Association Rhysling Award for the Short Poem, 2007 Atlanta Review International Publication Prize, 2007 Tattoo Highway 15 Contest, 2006 Mary Shelley Imaginative Fiction Award, 2004 Pauline Ellis Prose Poetry Prize and the 2003 Mary Roberts Rinehart National Poetry Award.

FINITE LOVE

Savor a second glass of wine, something to read or write;
let's see what we can fish out of the river of smoke.
Whatever brings you here, my darling little cabbage?
walking in your sleep, desperate to wake
before your parents' pale dreams,
voiceless on the wrong side of the mirror,
can eat you whole. *Medium rare.*

The oldest stories tell us what it's like
to be accepted as a woman:
to be blamed for apples, to feast on sausages,
to hide your knowledge.

Father, set apart with the German mark clawed upon him
like frostbite. Inside that unhealing wound
the maggoty past eats him alive. Sinking back
into the earth, see how frightened he is;
his webbed hands wave silver as grain,
no longer human. *Goodbye.*

Mother, whose soul is hidden under a rock,
her voice compressed: grammar, not rejected sense.
I would we were. Hold me as I am holding you.

Some kinds of trauma can purge or geld us.
It doesn't matter—see what we reserve
for ourselves: the absolution of language,
to loose our powers and send the craft
scudding over the blue-deep Sea of Crises,
while we sleep on a bed of ice
encircled by guttering candles,
waiting to be born.

TRAVELOGUE

From the pages of my father's book sifts
the natron-scented sand he shook from his shoes
onto the carpet of the Luxor hotel room.
Later chapters are stained with urine
and have small wormholes.

Random signatures are missing.
Between pages 78 and 79,
where I pressed his shriveled husk,
his eyes, still open, stare wildly,
a ring of white around the desperate blue.

When I ruffle through the leaves, I hear the regular mutter
of the first commercial propeller plane to cross the Pacific.
A receipt flutters downward; the sales slip for the camera
confiscated by Japanese customs: "Military! Spy! Contraband!"

There is an earlier photo of him standing
next to a Jivaro tribesman with whom
he traded his rifle for a shrunken head.
The head is still in its box, wrapped in tissue paper;
the flocked cheeks have been eaten away, leaving nothing
where tiny teeth should gleam, sharp as needles.
Its eyes, thankfully, are closed.

Richard Blanco

HERITAGE STATEMENT:

Richard Blanco's mother, seven months pregnant, and the rest of the family arrived as exiles from Cuba to Madrid, where he was born on February 15, 1968. Forty-five days later, the family emigrated once more to New York City. Only a few weeks old, Blanco already belonged to three countries, a foreshadowing of the concerns of place and belonging that would shape his life and work. Eventually, the family settled in Miami, where he was raised and educated. Growing up among close-knit Cuban exiles instilled in him a strong sense of community, dignity, and identity that he'd carry into his adult life as a writer.

AUTHOR BIO:

Richard Blanco is the first Latino-American gay poet to be chosen to write and present a poem for a Presidential inauguration. His poem "One Today" was read on January 21, 2013, at the second inauguration of President Barack Obama. His acclaimed first book of poetry, *City of a Hundred Fires*  (University of Pittsburgh Press, 1998), explores the yearnings and negotiation of cultural identity as a Cuban American, and received the Agnes Starrett Poetry Prize from the University of Pittsburgh Press. His second book, *Directions to the Beach of the Dead* (University of Arizona Press, 2005), won the Beyond Margins Award from the PEN American Center for its continued exploration of the universal themes of cultural identity and homecoming. A third collection, *Looking for The Gulf Motel* (University of Pittsburgh Press, 2012), was published in 2012. His poems have appeared widely in literary journals including *The Nation*, *The New Republic*, *Ploughshares*, *Michigan Quarterly Review*, and *TriQuarterly Review*, and several anthologies including *The Best American Poetry*, *Great American Prose Poems*, *Breadloaf Anthology of New American Poets*, and *American Poetry: The Next Generation*. Blanco is the recipient of two Florida Artist Fellowships, a Residency Fellowship from the Virginia Center for the Creative Arts, and is a John Ciardi Fellow of the Bread Loaf Writers' Conference. A builder of cities as well as poems, he holds a BS in civil engineering and an MFA in creative writing.

AMÉRICA

I.

Although *Tía* Miriam boasted she discovered
at least half-a-dozen uses for peanut butter—
topping for guava shells in syrup,
butter substitute for Cuban toast,
hair conditioner and relaxer—
Mamà never knew what to make
of the monthly five-pound jars
handed out by the immigration department
until my friend, Jeff, mentioned jelly.

II.

There was always pork though,
for every birthday and wedding,
whole ones on Christmas and New Year's Eve,
even on Thanksgiving Day—pork,
fried, broiled or crispy skin roasted—
as well as cauldrons of black beans,
fried plantain chips and *yuca con mojito*.
These items required a special visit
to Antonio's *Mercado* on the corner of 8th street
where men in *guayaberas* stood in senate
blaming Kennedy for everything—*"Ese hijo de puta!"*
the bile of Cuban coffee and cigar residue
filling the creases of their wrinkled lips;
clinging to one another's lies of lost wealth,
ashamed and empty as hollow trees.

III.
By seven I had grown suspicious—we were still here.
Overheard conversations about returning
had grown wistful and less frequent.
I spoke English; my parents didn't.
We didn't live in a two-story house
with a maid or a wood-panel station wagon
nor vacation camping in Colorado.
None of the girls had hair of gold;
none of my brothers or cousins
were named Greg, Peter, or Marsha;
we were not the Brady Bunch.
None of the black-and-white characters
on Donna Reed or on Dick Van Dyke Show
were named Guadalupe, Lázaro, or Mercedes.
Patty Duke's family wasn't like us either—
they didn't have pork on Thanksgiving,
they ate turkey with cranberry sauce;
they didn't have *yuca*, they had yams
like the dittos of Pilgrims I colored in class.

IV.
A week before Thanksgiving
I explained to my *abuelita*
about the Indians and the Mayflower,
how Lincoln set the slaves free;
I explained to my parents about
the purple mountain's majesty,
"one if by land, two if by sea"

the cherry tree, the tea party,
the amber waves of grain,
the "masses yearning to be free,"
liberty and justice for all, until
finally they agreed:
this Thanksgiving we would have turkey,
as well as pork.

V.

Abuelita prepared the poor fowl
as if committing an act of treason,
faking her enthusiasm for my sake.
Mamá set a frozen pumpkin pie in the oven
and prepared candied yams following instructions
I translated from the marshmallow bag.
The table was arrayed with gladiolus,
the plattered turkey loomed at the center
on plastic silver from Woolworths.
Everyone sat in green velvet chairs
we had upholstered with clear vinyl,
except *Tío* Carlos and Toti, seated
in the folding chairs from the Salvation Army.
I uttered a bilingual blessing
and the turkey was passed around
like a game of Russian Roulette.
"DRY," *Tío* Berto complained, and proceeded
to drown the lean slices with pork fat drippings
and cranberry jelly—*"esa mierda roja,"* he called it.
Faces fell when *Mamá* presented her ochre pie—
pumpkin was a home remedy for ulcers, not a dessert.

Tía María made three rounds of Cuban coffee
then *Abuelo* and Pepe cleared the living room furniture,
put on a Celia Cruz LP and the entire family
began to *merengue* over the linoleum of our apartment,
sweating rum and coffee until they remembered—
it was 1970 and 46 degrees—
in *América*. After repositioning the furniture,
an appropriate darkness filled the room.
Tío Berto was the last to leave.

LOOKING FOR THE GULF MOTEL

Marco Island, Florida

There should be nothing here I don't remember . . .
The Gulf Motel with mermaid lampposts
and ship's wheel in the lobby should still be
rising out of the sand like a cake decoration.
My brother and I should still be pretending
we don't know our parents, embarrassing us
as they roll the luggage cart past the front desk
loaded with our scruffy suitcases, two-dozen
loaves of Cuban bread, brown bags bulging
with enough mangos to last the entire week,
our espresso pot, the pressure cooker—and
a pork roast reeking garlic through the lobby.
All because we can't afford to eat out, not even
on vacation, only two hours from our home
in Miami, but far enough away to be thrilled
by *whiter* sands on the *west* coast of Florida,
where I should still be for the first time watching
the sun set instead of rise over the ocean.
There should be nothing here I don't remember . . .
My mother should still be in the kitchenette
of The Gulf Motel, her daisy sandals from Kmart
squeaking across the linoleum, still gorgeous
in her teal swimsuit and amber earrings
stirring a pot of *arroz con pollo*, adding sprinkles
of onion powder and dollops of tomato sauce.
My father should still be in a terrycloth jacket
smoking, clinking a glass of amber whiskey
in the sunset at The Gulf Motel, watching us
dive into the pool, two boys he'll never see
grow into men who will be proud of him.
There should be nothing here I don't remember . . .

My brother and I should still be playing *Parcheesi*,
my father should still be alive, slow dancing
with my mother on the sliding-glass balcony
of The Gulf Motel. No music, only the waves
keeping time, a song only their minds hear
ten thousand nights back to their life in Cuba.
My mother's face should still be resting against
his bare chest like the moon resting on the sea,
the stars should still be turning around them.
There should be nothing here I don't remember . . .
My brother should still be thirteen, sneaking
rum in the bathroom, sculpting naked women
from sand. I should still be eight years old
dazzled by seashells and how many seconds
I hold my breath underwater—but I'm not.
I am thirty-eight, driving up Collier Boulevard,
looking for The Gulf Motel, for everything
that should still be, but isn't. I want to blame
the condos, their shadows for ruining the beach
and my past, I want to chase the snowbirds away
with their tacky mansions and yachts, I want
to turn the golf courses back into mangroves,
I want to find The Gulf Motel exactly as it was
and pretend for a moment, nothing lost is lost.

Gabriella Burman

HERITAGE STATEMENT:

My mother was raised in La Paz, Bolivia. She is of Polish-Jewish extractions and emigrated from Jerusalem to the U.S. in 1970, after she became engaged to my American father. I was born and raised in Southfield, Michigan, a suburb of Detroit.

AUTHOR BIO:

Gabriella Burman is the communications director for bigtentjobs.com and an award-winning journalist who resides in Huntington Woods, Michigan, with her family. Her nonfiction appears or is forthcoming in *Skive Magazine*, *Prime Number Magazine*, *The Bear River Review*, and *Joy, Interrupted: An Anthology of Motherhood and Loss*. Gabriella Burman's collection of essays, *Michaela* (CreateSpace Independent Publishing Platform), was published in 2015. Follow her on Twitter @gabriellaburman.

ESTELA

My mother, a tall woman with short, blonde hair that is always perfectly coiffed, was raised in Bolivia (not *Bulgaria*), and has always had particular trouble with two words in the English language: *vocabulary*, in which she emphasizes the third instead of the second syllable so that it comes out, "vocaBUElary," and *subtraction*, which she pronounces "subStraction," no matter how many times my younger sister, Naomi, and I, as children, giggled and tried to correct her.

My mother's name is Estela, and her earliest memories are of La Paz, a city deposited in a valley 13,000 feet above sea level, and hugged on either side by the country's two tallest mountains, which are snowcapped all year round. Forty years ago, she was transplanted to flat and suburban Michigan by my father, Matthew, an American doctor from New York City, who was then completing his residency in ophthalmology at a Detroit hospital. They had met in Jerusalem a year before they married, when the owners of a summer camp his sisters had gone to as children introduced him to their visiting niece, Estela.

The story goes that she wasn't interested in him at first. He pursued her anyway, showing up on his Moped uninvited to parties she was attending, until she finally relented. She had dreams of a career as a translator at the United Nations, where she would use her Spanish, the English and French she had learned attending a Mennonite school in La Paz, the Yiddish of her youth, and the Hebrew she learned at college in Israel. But after my father's residency, my parents never returned to New York. My father purchased an ophthalmology practice in Detroit, and apart from a two-year stint in San Antonio—where my father served in the United States Air Force, my mother worked as a teacher in a Hebrew school, and I, as a toddler on an outing, toppled over a fence into a horse's trough—Southfield, Michigan became her home for good.

Estela stood apart from her Midwestern peers not simply because of her accent, which my friends liked to imitate, but also because she retained a formality that no amount of American casualness could dent. She had been raised by her stern Polish-born father to call the workers in her parents' clothing boutique, "Don Fermin," and "Donna Rosa," and similarly, she was known as "Mrs. Burman" by the employees at my father's office, where she managed his growing practice, and by all of my friends, no matter whether they had known her a day or a decade.

The way she dressed also reflected her sense of decorum. Although I saw photographs of my mother wearing bell bottoms, it seemed to me that Elvis, the Beatles and Janis Joplin had made little to no impression on her, that they had simply wafted over her head. Her blouses were always precisely tucked into her skirts, her clothes organized in neat squares of color in her drawers. She remained slim by counting calories, and measuring her food on a scale. The only time she has ever looked momentarily disheveled is after her once, or perhaps twice-daily workouts, which are as important to her as the Steinway grand piano in the living room, which she plays for hours without interruption on Sunday afternoons, and which she claims will serve as her coffin when she dies.

My mother is fastidious not only about her health, but punctuation, and not imposing on anyone at anytime, anywhere. Her house is spotless and she doesn't hoard; rather, she *collects* Lladró figurines which no one is allowed to touch. If this environment sounds oppressive, it was not without some levity. My sister and I were innocents. We traveled, we danced, we played outside in the copious amounts of snow that fell each Michigan winter. But, as I came of age, listening to Top 40, and daydreaming about celebrity boys, I began to cleave to friends who talked about sex, and whose mothers encouraged me to call them by their first names. I began to drift away from my mother's clutch. Where she imposed order, I left clothes in disarray on the upholstered bench at the foot of my bed. When she wasn't looking, I switched the radio station in her station wagon from WQRS, Detroit's classical music station, to Top 40 stations so I could crush on Duran Duran.

Estela's own childhood in Bolivia had been mostly full of order. While her parents sold coats and dresses to society ladies, indigenous cholas (Latin American Indians), in their elaborately colored shawls, wide-hipped skirts, and bowler hats, tended to her and her two younger sisters, prepared meals, and kept their home immaculate. As such, Estela grew accustomed to dust-free surfaces, and carpets that looked as new as the day they were laid.

As I have grown older, however, I have come to better understand my mother's preoccupation with perfection. It has less to do with built-in household help, and more to do with the psychological makeup of second-generation Holocaust survivors.

My grandparents kept the concentration camp numbers branded onto their forearms covered with Band-Aids, but revealed the atrocities of Auschwitz to friends, most of whom were also survivors, around the dinner table on late evenings, in a haze of cigarette smoke, after my mother and her sisters, Sarita and Lily, went to bed. Who knows what snippets of conversation my mother overheard. She must have absorbed enough to steel herself with this one resolute thought: Never complain about the bitterness of adolescence, the frustration of siblings, or the clothes she didn't like, because her parents, having suffered the almost complete annihilation of their respective families, had borne more heartache than she could ever dare to feel.

And so she became infallible and invulnerable, an A student, a dutiful older sister, and years later a dedicated daughter to her aging parents. She was a prim and proper wife and mother who never had to apologize for making a mistake, because, in her mind, she never made any. On the rare occasion when she did act out as a youngster, my *Zaide* (Yiddish for grandfather) had to only chase her once around the dining room table in order for her to regain her composure.

Estela recalls many happy memories in her family's apartment in La Paz, largely, in my estimation, because my grandmother, Lonia, whom we call Baba, had been saved from the gas chambers as much by her cunning as by her uncontainable sense of humor. Her laughter peals lovelier than the sound of any bell, even today, in this new century, in which she has just turned ninety-one. When we are together, she watches videos of classic Yiddish songs on YouTube, holding my iPhone in her hand like some kind of exotic fruit.

In one family story, my mother and her more rambunctious younger sisters, who grew up an arm's rather than a wrist's distance from the tragedy of their parent's history, were making a racket in the apartment. The owner of the apartment above was so unnerved that she jabbed a broomstick on the floor, its rhythm a warning to my mother and aunts. They, in turn, took a broomstick and jabbed back on the ceiling, until they bore a hole, and the owner's slipper showed through the floor.

I don't know if this story tells you more about my mother, or about Bolivian construction circa 1955. It serves, however, as a rare example of childhood raffishness. Such shenanigans never took place in our own spacious two-story colonial in Southfield. Rather, I lived in fear of setting my mother off, if and when I left dirty dishes in the sink, or the newspaper askew when she hadn't yet read it. Once I slid down the banister and accidentally toppled over a large plant at the bottom of the staircase; I don't recall the punishment as much as her ire over my having made an inconsiderate mistake.

And then, just after her fifty-seventh birthday, came the most disordering event ever, a failure beyond that of her goal to work at the United Nations, or, subsequent dreams of working as an editor, or, fleetingly, going to law school. Her first grandchild, my oldest daughter, Michaela, was born in 2003 with brain damage to her motor center, having been deprived of oxygen during labor and delivery after an uneventful full-term pregnancy in Atlanta, where my husband Adam and I were living while he pursued his MBA, and I worked as an editor at a weekly newspaper, in a career through which my mother could live vicariously.

My mother flew down immediately to the hospital where Michaela was born, and stayed with us as we transferred our baby to the nearby children's hospital for the next three weeks, until her seizures were (temporarily) brought under control, and Adam and I learned to feed my breast milk through a small tube that went down her nose into the back of her throat and into her stomach, since she lacked the coordination to simultaneously suck, swallow, and breathe. I remember collapsing into my mother's arms. The distance between her formal elocution and my "hey, guys" vernacular no longer mattered. We were on task, together, without any language necessary, to care for a child for whom spoken words would never come. We measured, together, the volumes of food and medicine that we pushed through a syringe into Michaela's feeding tube. We followed, wordlessly, the instructions shown to us for how to administer CPR, which, thankfully, we never had to use.

Privately, my mother grieved. I understand from my father that she took antidepressants for a time, but she never discussed the matter with me, not what drove her to the medication, nor her decision to stop taking it. Whatever interior journey she was on, she never showed it to me, or to the world.

Outwardly, she was enormously helpful, and, when Adam and I eventually bought a house near Detroit to be close to my parents, she felt duty-bound to babysit on call, run to Sam's Club to stock our pantry with paper goods and diapers, and to puree Michaela's beef stew and chicken into four-ounce portions which she would freeze and store, and which served as Michaela's lunch at school every day, as she practiced eating by mouth.

The food itself, however, has never had any Latin flair. Like Woodstock, Bolivian cuisine did not penetrate my mother's exterior. Estela has never prepared *salteñas* or *buñuelos*, and she does not use chili peppers when she cooks. Other than the green salad that accompanies every meal, her cooking retains a Polish stockiness: meat, starch, and cooked vegetables, fragranced with nothing more than garlic and onion, and very little in the way of fresh herbs. This repertoire serves my carnivore father well, and was nutritious for Michaela, a growing child.

But while tasty, the dishes bore no connection to the Andes, as though Estela herself was sealed, hermetically, from any exploration of her past. As such, I can hardly tolerate the heat from a jalapeño, or any spice that sears my lips. The Spanish language, however, filtered in, as did the Yiddish phrases of my youth. Michaela, and our two younger daughters, were, by turns, *"mamita linda," "querida,"* or *"preciosa,"* words we interchanged with *"bubbeleh," "mammaleh,"* and *"maideleh,"* as fluidly as my mother changes languages in mid-sentence when on the telephone with her parents and sisters. She doesn't even notice when she does it; I was, and remain, transfixed by the music of a sentence spoken in at least two languages, and I have learned to decipher a conversation's meaning from my own rudimentary understanding of both.

When I was growing up, Estela chose not to speak to us in Spanish, and it is a decision I regret to this day, for it muzzles me in terms of the depth of a conversation I can have, say, with my grandmother. There is only so far out into the water she and I can tread before her teeth break on the English that she reads better than she speaks, and we return to the shallow remarks we have made to each other for years. She wishes me health and *"mazel,"* and she thanks *"Dios"* for everything she has. You see, two languages. Just like that.

Shortly after I got married, I lost a job and found myself with time to spare. I left Adam in New York City, where we had met and lived as newlyweds, and flew to Fort Lauderdale, to the two-bedroom condo on the golf course to which my parents had moved my grandparents after they retired from the store. They were nearing eighty; they had been in La Paz for fifty years. Their children had all left for Israel or the United States, and the community of Holocaust survivors in Bolivia, once numbering in the thousands, had dwindled to the low hundreds. There was no reason for them to stay in their adopted home. Come to think of it, there was no reason for them to live on a golf course in Florida, either. I spent a week there with my grandparents, a tape recorder, and an English-Spanish dictionary, upon which I dutifully relied to ask them questions about the war. Because my Spanish is so mediocre, I did not understand all of their answers, and as a journalist, I knew I was missing crucial information that would have led to follow-up questions that would have revealed even more details. My mother's decision to not speak to me in Spanish stung again. She had not refrained from passing on the language because, as I recall her saying, my father's Spanish wasn't "good enough," and we would learn "mistakes." She had refrained, I believe, because when she wrapped the telephone cord around her body, and pressed a finger to her opposite ear during long-distance calls to Bolivia, the language was the one thing she could preserve for herself.

My mother did allow for the introduction of a few new aspects to her life—she learned to clean a feeding tube, guide Michaela through her physical therapy exercises, and lather her granddaughter's hair with one hand while supporting her posture with the other, and she performed these tasks with a sense of duty for the ones she loved: Michaela, whom she adored, me, whom she wanted to unburden. But whereas Michaela became my life's purpose, my mom never extrapolated from her experiences with Michaela that engagement with the disabled could become her great calling. She remained, in essence, an immigrant, and would not budge again.

As a child, I only once saw her undone. I found her crying late at night when my father still had not returned from his office in Detroit, a city that had not been safe since the 1960s. Perhaps I only watched her from the bedroom door left ajar. Perhaps I walked in, and tried to console her. Either way, I wonder now what she was really crying about. Was she scared for my dad's safety, as I understood her to be, or was she crying because she was an isolated mother, alone in the house, in a city and country far from her parents, her childhood friends, her language and her sisters?

I wish I could see some of that vulnerability now. But I never do, not even after Michaela's sudden and unexpected death on May 23, 2009, at age five-and-a-half, during a routine sleepover at my parents' house two weeks after the birth of our third daughter, Maayan. My mother has simply not permitted herself to collapse. She has not shown herself to be flung from the stars of the elevated existence we all led, nurturing our beloved Michaela. She is not willing to accept the resulting chaos of what I refer to as our own Holocaust.

On the dreadful, sunny morning when the worst thing imaginable materialized, she cradled Michaela's body and spoke to her in the gibberish terms of someone who has rightfully lost her mind. But by later in the day, she had changed from her robe into a skirt to greet the visitors streaming into the house, and served cold chicken for lunch, insisting that I, a lactating mother, had to eat. Shock, you say. Yes, I know. But while I am still dazed, three years on, I don't think Estela is in shock anymore. She continues to keep order, in the house, at work, and in her own routine of manicures, work, piano, and the gym. Whereas she once cooked mashed food for Michaela, she now cooks whole food for Ayelet, our middle daughter, and for our then-youngest, Maayan. Estela acts like nothing has changed. She won't cry in front of me, she won't rail at the skies, she won't talk about the catastrophe of burying a child. She has refused to cross the threshold onto our new planet of grief, one generally inhabited by both parents and grandparents, who grieve doubly: for their grandchild, as well as for their own child.

Instead, the facade holds. And, after many futile and heartbreaking attempts on my part to poke holes in her shield built on logistics, wherein I try to share an emotion that snaps back in my face with the sting of a rubber band, I have come to accept that she wins. In order to keep her in my life, I must validate her stoicism, and resilience, and not confront her with my grief. I know that turmoil is coiled up inside her, and I know from my own experience, that the post-endorphin benefits of exercise are only temporary. Sometimes I fantasize that my mother, who claims she wants nothing for herself, has decided to run away to Italy, to learn yet another language that will come easily to her. If she did so, I would be happy for her. Perhaps then she, and I, would be free.

Lauren Camp

HERITAGE STATEMENT:

My father was born and raised in Baghdad, Iraq; my mother grew up in the Midwest. As a child, I observed and shared Iraqi rituals and foods with my father's extended family frequently. Somehow, those customs and language didn't seem odd. I understood that they were part of me, though no one else in my class had any familiarity with them. In the past few years, I began writing poems to capture some of the culture. The manuscript is called *One Hundred Hungers*, and it is both a portrayal and an envisioning of my father's childhood in Baghdad in the 1940s, and my childhood interacting with those customs and rituals.

AUTHOR BIO:

Lauren Camp is the author of three volumes of poetry, *This Business of Wisdom* (West End Press, 2011); *The Dailiness*, which was selected as the winner of the National Federation of Press Women's 2014 Poetry Book Prize and chosen as the Editor's Pick by *World Literature Today*; and *One Hundred Hungers*, which was selected as the winner of the 2014 Dorset Prize from Tupelo Press. Lauren is editor of the poetry blog *Which Silk Shirt* and co-winner of The Anna Davidson Rosenberg Poetry Awards for 2012. Her poems have  appeared in *Cæsura*, *The Comstock Review*, *Beloit Poetry Journal*, *Ekphrasis*, *Spoon River Poetry Review*, *Cave Wall*, *RHINO*, and others. She has also guest-edited special sections for *World Literature Today* (on international jazz poetry) and for *Malpaís Review* (on the poetry of Iraq). On Sundays, she hosts "Audio Saucepan," a global music/poetry program on Santa Fe Public Radio. You can find Lauren online at www.laurencamp.com and follow her blog at http://laurencamp.com /whichsilkshirt.

LETTER TO BAGHDAD

Even if my father never speaks a word of it, I will know
he brought a candle, a cough and the occupied side of his heart.
I will know the trees held him, that they rose above rooflines,
and where they met, he climbed and saw roads paved only with praises.
The sun he carried across oceans turned copper at his window.
I saw it too, on the grey edge of my childhood,
and I was marked when each day awoke. He devoured the silence,
the parts that could not be cured, and when he was hungry for it,
I swallowed the silence, his self-portrait of confession.
When I found an old shawl and silver teapot in the oven,
and he pretended he didn't know what they meant,
I remembered bitter lemons had moistened his mouth.
What he inhaled from his copious memory
left his tongue empty then full, and somehow I know
his tongue will always be brushed with the leaving.

One day we were talking about beginnings, and I had begun.
I wasn't at the center anymore, and we kept letting in a little air,
and he showed me a word for the boy he once was
and he showed me this Arabic word and in this way I knew
this was the most authentic mourning I would ever see.
And I saw it and he said it again,
and we were covered with it. Entirely covered. This was his home, he said,
as he gave me the address, the place
where the first time and the spurned and the color
and the milkmaid stood in the alley. And even though he didn't tell me
about yesterday and the day and the day and I never saw
any other way to tell it I never saw
heaven or the land that was black, one day I knew enough
to take the word from him and drink my fill
of everything every little thing every steeped thing

and there were many trees and not enough cold and we sat by the river that curves in every direction and our hearts lifted up to the birds.

PAUSES

My father filled with pauses so long he forgot how clear the river ran
and the screen of light through the Nabq trees;

many things must have gone wrong, many things, whether every night
or when someone pulled up the white tapestry of home,

pressed and folded. And the singing pots—what if they sang
to desolate sand as men with boxes began the work of stooping over,

and others walked past holding scalloped red pieces of worry? Could a person
leave behind stalls of lemons, honey and wool, leave the lithe lines

of sun in a city grown to the cadence of water? If they were taking it away,
he took what he could in his body: on his thick arms, the turmeric sun,

the hum of the water, his dark eyes like scars. He can't wake up now
in that place where elders spoke gravel and each sweet sound

of orange. Three times it was fractions and tangles, then common
laconic laments repeating themselves. What he wanted

was waiting, was staying in the "to" of the future, tomorrow—
For what is salaam when you're leaving your city sun-creased

and hunting? These uncertainties have always been part of his body;
once he was a boy with whooping cough. He walked through the wall

and door of absence and the sky gathered days. Goats and cows stood foolish
and heavy in dirt, but across the world, he didn't turn around

into that unpredictable ending; instead, he consented to many
slow steps and strange punctuation, and now when he opens his palm,

it's still filled with edges, still filled with dates.

VARIATION (LET'S PRETEND)

Let's pretend you tell me what happened.
How you lived in the city two streets from the river.

Let's suppose you begin speaking and you speak
until all the colors and empires
of Baghdad tumble from your mouth.

Your words take me to Karkh and back to Rasafa,
to Abbasid Palace and Kadhehemiah, the center of business.

And now I can see the people who were neighbors,
the ruined brick of Khan Murjan
and the eggshell designs of Mustansiriya Madrasah.

You run your fat fingers through my dark hair
as if in the deep muscle of a temporary sleep.

I will quiet for centuries to eat and eat details.
And as night is falling you tell me
how Farhud sauntered past in its dark coat and boots,

and you didn't see it. Let's agree that I know something
was wrong, that I've figured that much out,

that I've read those articles you keep sending
about the coups against Jews, the invasions.
Your gaze in the background is hazy.

You name a street and a corner. Who took you to school.
Tell me the cycle of daybreak the month of isolation

the year you were six. You pull out old photos with arches
in the city of suggestions under the cardamom trees.
Give me the terrible excitement, your warm salty truth,

the glass cup, the testimony Grandpa hid from his children,
the spayed useless sky, the doorpost, the wardrobe.

Because I need it, you tell it:
the habits, the scarring, the shuffle of leaving
your home. You won't make me keep waiting.

Let's agree that you'll tell me the details.
Please. You have to remember every flake
of the air and the furrows of danger.

Tina Chang

HERITAGE STATEMENT:

Tina Chang was born in 1969 in Oklahoma to Chinese immigrants who had met in Montreal, where her mother was working as a nurse and her father was earning his doctorate in physics. The family moved to New York when she was a year old. She was raised in New York City. During her younger years, Chang and her brother were sent to live in Taiwan with relatives for two years.

AUTHOR BIO:

The current Brooklyn Poet Laureate, Tina Chang is the author of *Of Gods & Strangers* (Four Way Books, 2011), *Half-Lit Houses* (Four Way Books, 2004) and co-editor of the anthology *Language for a New Century: Contemporary Poetry from the Middle East, Asia, and Beyond* (W. W. Norton, 2008). Her poems have been published in *American Poet, Indiana Review, McSweeney's, The Missouri Review, Ploughshares, Quarterly West,* and *Sonora Review,* among others. She has received awards from the Academy of American Poets,  the Barbara Deming Memorial Fund, the Ludwig Vogelstein Foundation, New York Foundation for the Arts, Poets & Writers, and the Van Lier Foundation, among others. She teaches poetry at Sarah Lawrence College.

THE SHIFTING KINGDOM

after Brigit Pegeen Kelly

The coyote is bristled with the pelt like an armored
wound, and I am the girl in the sewn coat

camouflaging fiercely, a runaway in caravan
but I have no artillery and my coyote will guard

no one. Now, there are only the cactus
and the desert blossom unfolding their soft garments,

and the twilight road along whose crossings
dolls are strung in nettles, over whose skulls

prayers pass like a procession carrying
cups of wreckage. I had not thought enough

of arrival, of entering the portal of my mother's dream,
of rising from sleep with my cape of leaves

and my mouth open—like Jesus's robes—to bells
and rampage, trumpet and siren, and that song

the horizon wails just before dawn, bodies
left behind and the loss of it forgotten. Now our hides

are the coyote's gift, darker in our disappearance,
and if we lose it is to the angel and the blood

of all his feathers. Not the angel entire, but the pity
of a wing. And though my coat does not quite fit,

and though the bleating ram will never leave me alone,
there is only *God keep you* in all this, and *safe keeping.*

My fear is like the unfurling road, with headlights searing
and no sleep in sight. It is a back that bends to the gruel

of my ancestor's song, and a country that is only a splinter
of a shelter, a reminder of kitchen hands like dying coal.

The roof blows away in the heat as barbed wire cuts
night wind. Here the girls lie down at your tied ankles.

Here everyone obeys the coyote so you don't know where to call,
in whose belief to softly wade. And there is always

in this desert sand the tale my grandmother spoke to me,
but now her voice floats over this worn pelt, a coyote's hide,

which no longer runs and shivers at his sound. What I
wished for is not as I understand it to be; I have still

not seen a savior, unless that warm wind passing beyond the fences
when my coyote went for a walk was one. And though

there are no exits here, no doorways or openings, there is also no way
to enter—no way in this coyote's den to rise up to do so.

*Note: Noemi Álvarez Quillay attempted to journey 6,500 miles from the southern highlands
of Ecuador to New York City where her mother and father lived. Accompanied by coyotes—hu-
man smugglers—and one month after her departure, she was picked up in Mexico by the au-
thorities and taken to a children's shelter. A few days later she was found hanged from a shower
curtain rod. Authorities ruled it a suicide. She was twelve years old.—New York Times*

Viji K. Chary

HERITAGE STATEMENT:

I was born in Chennai, India, on July 1, 1968. Two years later, my father, an engineer, was offered a job in San Francisco and our family immigrated to the U.S.

AUTHOR BIO:

Viji K. Chary completed her undergraduate degree in genetics at the University of California, Berkeley and an MA in public administration at California State University, Hayward. Her stories have been published in *Highlights for Children*, *Ladybug Magazine*, *Hopscotch for Girls*, and many more. Her first book *Porcupine's Seeds* received the prestigious *Mom's Choice Award*. Viji currently writes for children and her publishing credits can be found at www.vijikchary.com.

LAYING A FOUNDATION

After an eighteen-hour flight from San Francisco to Singapore, my exhausted family checked into a room for transit passengers. Everyone claimed a bed and dropped off to a deep slumber. A few hours later, one by one, we awoke and showered.

My mother disappeared into the bathroom wearing wrinkled casual dark pants and a plain knit top. Fifteen minutes later she emerged draped in a blue-green sari. A bindi between her eyebrows, a black beaded necklace, and golden earrings and bangles were the mark of a properly dressed married Indian woman. She was ready to meet our family in India.

"Amma has made her usual Singapore transformation!" I announced.

"Why don't you change at Thatha's house?" asked my younger sister.

"Because your grandparents feel like I'm still a part of their family when I arrive in a sari," explained Amma. "This is how I dressed when I lived in India. Besides, I see them once in four years. Why not make them happy?"

I was plagued with many questions. Didn't she want to be her own person? Shine in her own individuality? Not conform to society? Did she really want to give up her identity to make someone else happy?

Even when family visited us in California, my mother would dress in traditional attire and serve three traditional Indian meals. "Yes, it's more work. But we need to make our guests feel like they're at home," she would say.

On my sixteenth birthday, Amma threw me a party with family friends. I gushed at all the new clothes I received. During the following months, whenever we were invited to one of the guests' homes, Amma reminded me gently to wear the clothes they'd given.

"They'll see that you appreciated their gift," she said. "It's a small gesture."

But what about being who you really are? Wearing and eating what you want? Being true to yourself?

Amma's actions laid a foundation where both parties' customs and identities met. They had common ground from which to begin conversations and build relationships. From there, it was safe to express independent opinions and views.

Dressed in a sari and having established an initial rapport, Amma felt comfortable talking to her Indian cousins about her work as an accountant, pursuing higher education and later, her job as a CPA. Her female cousins were intrigued about her life in the U.S. None of them had dreamed of continuing their education. None of them had worked outside the home.

Years later, when I married, my husband was not particularly traditional. My father-in-law however, was orthodox and began his prayers at four a.m. Not only was he a vegetarian, but he did not eat garlic, onions, store-bought pickles, or "new world" vegetables like cauliflower. He ate only home-cooked meals. For me, vegetarian cooking was simple but not without garlic and onions. I learned to cook new dishes and relishes. Without realizing it, I was laying a foundation for my relationship with my father-in-law. From here, I was able to go about my day-to-day activities without alienating him.

Was I doing what I wanted? Was I being true to myself? Yes. I wanted a secure base so that I could be free to be myself.

A few years later, my husband and I lugged two children to India. As we were in our transit hotel in Kuala Lumpur, I changed from my blue jeans and sweat shirt into a chudidhar and khameez. A bindi between my eyebrows, black beaded necklace around my neck, dangling golden earrings and bangles jingling on my wrist, I was ready to meet my family in India. I was ready to lay a foundation.

Angie Chuang

HERITAGE STATEMENT:

I was born in San Francisco, California, to immigrant parents from Taiwan. My father, Tien-Yuh Chuang, was born in Fujian, China, immigrated to Taiwan by boat with his family when he was five, and then again to the United States in the 1960s, during the post-Sputnik push for foreign engineering grad students. He married my mother, Ling-shin Chen, born in Taiwan, after he completed his PhD at the University of California, Berkeley, and brought her back to San Francisco's East Bay area suburbs, where I grew up. I was raised bilingual and bicultural, speaking Mandarin before I spoke English. I went to Saturday Chinese School every week from first grade until I graduated high school.

AUTHOR BIO:

Angie Chuang is a writer and educator based in Washington, D.C. Her work has appeared in *The Best Women's Travel Writing 2011* (Travelers' Tales, 2011), *Tales from Nowhere* (Lonely Planet, 2006), *The Asian American Literary Review*, *Washingtonian* magazine, and other venues. She is on the journalism faculty of American University School of Communication. She was a journalist for thirteen years, as a staff writer for *The Oregonian*, *The Hartford Courant*, and *The Los Angeles Times*. She is working on a nonfiction book centered on her relationship with an Afghan-American immigrant family and travels with them in Afghanistan.

"Six Syllables" is adapted from *The Four Words for Home* (Aquarius Press/Willow Books, 2014), a braided memoir which weaves her family's immigrant story with that of an Afghan immigrant family with whom she traveled to Afghanistan. She is now working on a second nonfiction book about choices, regrets, and roads not taken.

SIX SYLLABLES

The gap between being an outsider and belonging can be much narrower than we fear. In Kabul, we napped every afternoon, a two-hour siesta that made up for rising before dawn with the mosque loudspeaker's first call to prayer. As with most things in Afghanistan, naps were easy to enter, difficult to get out of. The soft breathing of the women beside me kept time; their headscarves lay neatly folded next to them and their black hair tumbled over their pillows. Late-afternoon light filtered through gauzy curtains. The slide into sleep was liquid, unknowable. Waking was another matter. The women tried to rouse me gently: a soft nudge on the shoulder. My name, in Pashto-accented English, as if murmured through cotton batting. By then the nap never felt right, like I had gotten either too little or too much sleep. A dizzying chemical taste in my gummy mouth reminded me that I was on malaria pills. I always forgot where I was. Was I really in Afghanistan? Or at home? Where was "home," exactly?

In Pashto, "home" is not a single word, but four. There is a word for home that means "house," another that means "country," still another that means "birthplace," and a fourth that means "homeland." No wonder I had begun to feel—in a land that had endured invaders, occupations, war, and the displacement of its people, many times over—that feeling at home had become elusive. The dissonance between home and homeland had been written into the very language.

I had traveled here from my own home at the time, in Portland, Oregon, with members of an Afghan immigrant family I had befriended there. Just as the Shirzais had welcomed me into their own house in the fir-lined hills alongside the Willamette River, their relatives in Kabul—particularly two young women named Nafisa and Nazo—had made me feel safe and nurtured from the moment I arrived in this compound-style abode. The sisters-in-law had attended to my every need and treated me like one of their own. Nafisa had mournful brown eyes and a naturally downturned mouth—except for when her husband, Nazo's older brother, was around, in which case her face turned all coy and giggly. That, in turn, would make the unmarried Nazo roll her green eyes and tsk-tsk at her sister-in-law. Nazo had wild, curly hair that was always escaping the confines of her headscarf, or *chador*. The two were inseparable and I, joining them, became one of three: We cooked together, stayed up late talking, and laughed until we couldn't catch our breath. But outside the home's walls, I felt very different.

The city was hard on the senses and psyche, a swirl of dust, diesel residue, odors from the open sewers. Amputee landmine victims and dirt-caked, sickly children begged on every street corner; widows in filthy blue burqas silently extended hands out from under the veils. High school–aged boys, giddy with post-Taliban freedom, harassed women in the streets: *Marry me, beautiful. Please marry me.* Even the catcalls still had oddly fundamentalist overtones.

The disorientation of waking from lariam-riddled naps, in a place that felt startlingly unfamiliar all over again, made me wonder what I was doing in Afghanistan, with the Shirzais. I wanted to be more than a hanger-on or a war tourist. I hadn't come to Kabul to gawk at the destruction and misery of a quarter-century of war. But why *was* I here? And why could I not, just once, wake from a nap and know where I was?

Then one day, I did.

It was a voice, not Nafisa's or Nazo's, that brought me out of sleep that afternoon. It was faraway, male, chant-like in cadence. It got louder, then softer, then louder again. He sang the same six syllables over and over again. What was he singing? Why had I not noticed this voice before? It sounded utterly new yet completely familiar at the same time.

I had forgotten to wonder where I was. It didn't matter now. Nafisa and Nazo stirred, looked at me quizzically through sleepy eyes. Somewhere between quietly getting up, wrapping my headscarf around my head, finding my shoes in the pile outside the bedroom, tiptoeing across the courtyard, and cracking the courtyard door open to sneak a peek, the thought—*Oh, right, I'm in Kabul*—flickered across my consciousness. The voice grew louder. He was coming around the corner. In time with the chanting, cart wheels squeaked and strained. Something made a whipping sound, like sails in the wind.

Then, licks of blue, gold, fuchsia, and white teased the dusty sky and dun landscape like flames. And he was on our street. A pushcart full of fabrics—billowing from poles, folded in neat rows, nearly engulfing the wiry man behind it all.

"*Chador au chadori . . . Chador au chadori.*"

He was selling *chador*, headscarves, and *chadori*, burqas. On each corner of the cart, a post held a *chadori*, striated by dozens and dozens of tiny pleats, billowing in saffron, snow white, and dusky blue, the most commonly worn shade. The veils filled with hot Kabul air to assume the ambiguous forms of their future wearers. I studied the oval mesh face-screens at the tops of each one, as opaque and inscrutable as they were when actual women were behind them. The borders of the screens were embroidered with repeating floral patterns, works of delicate craftsmanship. Then the wind picked up, and the hanging ghost-women evaporated as the veils became flags, horizontal in the breeze.

"*Chador au chadori . . .*"

The walnut-skinned man wore a white prayer cap. His baritone was languid, his Rs liquid, and the rising and falling notes of his tune so familiar. Had I heard him before, in my sleep? As he approached, I slipped behind the front door—a scarf and veil salesman surely would expect female modesty. But just after he passed, one more look.

"*Chador au chadori . . .*"

As he disappeared from sight, the voice faded. I *had* heard the tune before. It was not in my sleep, and not here in Afghanistan. From the time I was a child, I regularly visited my grandparents in Taoyuan, a mid-sized city in Taiwan's north. The United States was the only home I had known, but with repeat visits to Taoyuan, the city—the damp, tropical air; the people who spoke Mandarin with accents like my parents'; and the bitter scents of Chinese greens and ferric waft from organ meats at the outdoor market—had become a part of me.

For as long as I can remember, every morning in Taoyuan the same chant rang out over and over, carried by a tinny amplifier, often muffled by rainfall. The voice was female, and I can't say if it belonged to the same woman for all those years. But the words and the tune were always the same:

"Man to bau, man to bau . . . Man to bau, man to bau . . ."

The woman pushed a cart full of *man to*, steamed rolls, and *bau*, stuffed breads, around the perimeter of the outdoor market. Her deep voice rose and dipped, stretching out the round vowels. The chant faded and grew as she made her way around the neighborhood. I saw her once, a woman in a conical straw hat and a weathered face the color of weak Oolong tea. Her cart was packed with round, stacking stainless-steel containers full of those creamy white rolls, each as big as a fist. The steaming dough trailed milky-sweet clouds in her wake.

"Man to bau, man to bau . . ."
"Chador au chadori . . ."

The six-syllable, rising-and-falling cadences of her cry and his chant were echoes of each other. Different languages, different products; same song, same notes. Was it just that these two countries, in their varying trajectories toward modernity, still had economies that supported chanting, cart-pushing street vendors? Perhaps. But when I heard that chant in Afghanistan, I felt at home there for the first time. I heard the scarf and veil salesman a few more times, always upon waking from my nap. Once, I peered out the front door to get another glimpse of him; the other times, I just languished, half-asleep. For the rest of my time in Afghanistan, I never again woke up feeling dislocated. "Through metaphor," Cynthia Ozick wrote, "we strangers imagine into the familiar hearts of strangers."

Those six syllables had rendered the differences between the four words for home irrelevant. A week ago, this house had been foreign to me, filled with strangers who welcomed me with open arms and hearts. Now, I had a little bit of birthplace, country, and homeland wrapped up inside this compound, with its fig trees in the courtyard and rooms lined with pomegranate-hued rugs—and with Nafisa and Nazo.

Note: Names of Afghan and Afghan-American family members have been changed for their protection, as some of them have been threatened for cooperating with an American journalist.

Jeanie Chung

HERITAGE STATEMENT:

Both my parents immigrated to the United States from Korea, leaving their entire families, most of whom remained in North Korea. Growing up, I never appreciated the enormous sacrifices they made for my sister and me, for example, speaking mostly English at home, and always to us, so that we would enter school fully fluent. Fully burdened with the expectations of raising their children to be perfect Korean kids—minus the language—and also successful American kids, they often faced twice as many struggles as most parents. This essay began as a meditation on my own difficulties growing up Asian in an almost completely non-Asian community, but looking back, it's equally about my parents' attempts to negotiate in that same world.

AUTHOR BIO:

Jeanie Chung is a former sportswriter for *The Chicago Sun-Times* who made the switch to fiction seven years ago. Her stories have been nominated for the Pushcart Prize and have appeared in *Timber Creek Review, The Madison Review, Hunger Mountain* and *upstreet*, as well as the anthology *The*  *Way We Knew It: Fiction from the First Twenty-Five Years of the MFA in Writing Program at Vermont College (1981–2006)*. Her journalism and interviews have appeared in *The Writer's Chronicle* and *The Chicago Tribune*, among other publications. She lives and works in Chicago.

CUTS AND FOLDS

Blepharoplasty comes from the Greek words "blepharo," which means "eyelid," and "plasty," which means "shaping." It's so nice to have a mother who can help out with the troop for an afternoon, the Brownie leader says. And what an interesting activity. Origami. The girls don't have many opportunities to make crafts from other cultures. Origami is funny, though. It can get confusing if you're not careful: you fold and unfold, turn the paper sideways, over, upside down. It's so easy to get all jumbled up. Disoriented.

"No, honey," my teacher would say, interrupting me in the middle of drawing my hair, taking the yellow crayon out of my hand and using it to make an oval for my face. "You're supposed to draw *you*."

Blepharoplasty comes from the Greek words "blepharo," which means "eyelid," and "plasty," which means "shaping," or "intense, searing pain in the service of beauty." But pride must suffer pain. It's also called "Asian eyelid surgery." Much simpler. It says exactly what the problem is and how to fix it. Like "wart removal." What I didn't know then was that, according to Japanese legend, if you fold a thousand paper cranes, your heart's desire will come true.

"It's too expensive," my dad says. "When you become a doctor," my mom says, smiling, "you'll know lots of other doctors, and one of them will be able to do it for you for free."

The important thing is to start with the crease. That's where you'll put the dark eyeshadow, when your face heals. Once they've made the crease, they cut off some fat—they call it subcutaneous, which means "under the skin"—and some muscle. This tissue is the epicanthic fold, meaning, "extra skin that makes your eyes slanted." Removing it involves an incision just above the lashes, so they won't be hanging under that skin any more. More teeny, tiny stitches close the wound. It takes about an hour. There's another way, where they sort of sew the eyelid into place without any cutting. Then there are some people—women, mostly—who just use special glue and this little fork to mold their eyelids into place every morning. What a pain.

There are pictures. A red, angry line runs below the eye socket bone. Then, glistening—What is it? Fat? Muscle? Subcutaneum? Is that even a word?—above the lashes, where the doctor tightens up the eyelid. The naked, glistening tissue where the fat and muscle have been removed isn't gross at all. Have you ever seen a picture of a cocoon, right before it opens, the way it's all wet and glossy and shot through with veins? That's what the photos remind me of. Or of a baby being born. Kind of goopy, sure, but shiny and brave with new life. Then the stitches.

From the picture, you'd think someone hit the girl in each eye with a bottle. Well, pride must suffer pain.

There are slightly differently styles of origami cranes, but in general, a crane has its wings extended, as if it were flying. Other than that, though, it looks kind of like a swan. Of course, the most famous swan might be *The Ugly Duckling*. He had big feet, his head was too big, his eyes were shaped funny, but then he grew up to be a beautiful swan. All he had to do was give it time. That story is supposed to make girls like me feel better.

My friends and I start wearing makeup on a regular basis in sixth grade. The magazines tell us to put the darkest shade of eyeshadow "in the crease of the eyelid." They have creases; all I have is a shallow dip.

"Huh," my friends ask each other. "What's she supposed to do now?" But they don't have any answers. They let me stand at the mirror and let me try to figure it out, giving me just a tiny bit more room than they did before, watching as I try to "contour" my eyes by wiping a dark smear across my flat eyelid. They've never seen anything like it before, not up close like that.

How will they insult me properly, if they can no longer pull their eyes into slants? I'll still look different enough. There was the girl, in fifth grade when I was in fourth, who called me a nigger. Kids are creative that way. They've never seen anything like it before, not up close like that.

All the girls want to look like Farrah Fawcett. The only Asian woman you see speaking English on TV is the lady on the laundry commercial who declares, full of pride, "Ancient Chinese secret!" No one thinks of her as pretty, though she probably is. But Asian girls aren't pretty, are they? With the slanty eyes and all?

Of course, origami isn't Korean. But when my mom was in school, she and her friends spoke Japanese. They learned Japanese history. They even learned Japanese paper art. My mom never knew how to be a proud little Korean girl either.

They say it'll hurt. Please. Someone cuts off some skin and sticks a needle in my eyelid a couple times? So what? Plenty of things hurt more.

What I didn't know then was that, according to Japanese legend, if you fold a thousand paper cranes, your heart's desire will come true. And if I knew, I'd have said: what's folded can be unfolded. To change something, you have to cut.

Everyone tells me to be happy with who I am. That I'm beautiful on the *inside*, and isn't that what's important?

You know how sometimes you keep staring and starting at your face in the mirror, and you notice every pore and every bump and every freckle? Like standing really close to a pointillist painting. After a while, you can't tell what's beautiful, what's ugly. You can't tell what's you. You're no longer there.

My parents actually think doctors do free surgeries for their friends. They don't know anything about this country.

When the surgeon pulls off the extra skin, if he keeps pulling, pulls hard enough on the eyelids, I wonder if he could turn someone all the way inside out. Upside down. And if he did, I wonder what he'd see.

Me, I hate origami. But then I never was much of an artist. In my first pictures—standard kindergartener scribblings of a family and a pointy-roofed house underneath an orange, spider-legged sun—I'd give myself blonde hair and blue eyes.

"No, honey," my teacher would say, interrupting me in the middle of drawing my hair, taking the yellow crayon out of my hand and using it to make an oval for my face. "You're supposed to draw *you*."

That same guy who wrote *The Ugly Duckling*, Hans Christian Andersen, wrote *The Little Mermaid*. The mermaid wanted to be like people—like regular people—and so she had a witch get rid of her tail, cut it into two legs. And with every step it was as if she were walking on knives, but it was worth it. She said, "Pride must suffer pain."

My parents don't ask: what is the matter with the way you look now? You don't think you're beautiful? Can't blame them, I guess. Why should they be the first?

What I didn't know then was that, according to Japanese legend, if you fold a thousand paper cranes, your heart's desire will come true. And if I knew, I'd have said: what's folded can be unfolded. To change something, you have to cut.

It's easy to change something like your eyes, or your hair, or your legs, or your stomach, or anything about the way you look. But your heart's desire, deep down, that won't ever change.

In the end, I didn't do it. Because it's easy to change something like your eyes, or your hair, or your legs, or your stomach, or anything about the way you look. But your heart, your heart's desire, deep down, that won't ever change.

Nancy Bwerka-Clark

HERITAGE STATEMENT:

While both my parents were full-blooded Ukrainians, my mother was born here. My father emigrated in the early 1920s and was extremely reticent about discussing his life, but he brought his love of the land with him. Even though he became an insurance agent and was a jazz violinist and drummer in a big band for more than forty years, he loved fruit trees and gardening.

AUTHOR BIO:

Nancy Bwerka-Clark has been a professional writer and editor for many years, and has been published as a playwright, short story writer and essayist. Her poetry has appeared in *The North American Review*, *Tattoo Highway*, *Flashquake* and *Orchard Press Mysteries*. Poems are also included in the anthologies *Beloved on the Earth: 150 Poems of Grief and Gratitude* (Holy Cow! Press, 2009), *Regrets Only* (Little Pear Press, 2006), *Visiting Frost: Poems Inspired by the Life and Work of Robert Frost* (University of Iowa Press, 2005), *Nurtur-**ing Paws* (Whispering Angel Books, 2011) and *Hope Whispers* (Whispering Angel Books, 2009). In 2012 her work was named a finalist in the Thomas Merton Poetry of the Sacred Contest.

MY FATHER'S ORCHARD

Apple trees in villages
all speak the same tongue,
a buzz and bumble
of hot pollination
at spring's cool core.

Bearing shadows
on your shoulders
of rooted men,
and women,
and trees—

you left the rolling hills
of Western Ukraine as a boy,
alone, to find a hillside
in New Hampshire
that looked just like home.

You graft, splitting
the branch and fitting it
to a slit in the bark, binding
the cut until the transplant
stands up for itself.

Pink veins the new buds;
they open
        like falling snow.

The shelter is always the same—
cool, dull green of the heart-like

leaves, when even the voices
of bird and wind speak
the language of apples.

UKRAINIAN LESSON

What do I bring to the table?
A shoebox found in the back of a closet
with letters opened after the war—every
war's cold there—written in lavender ink.

What news, now history, do they carry
of aunts, uncles, cousins, the family
my father never saw again?
Who knows, until the code's cracked.

"Consider what is big, *bolshoi,*
in thick Cyrillic syllables.
We must learn to slip the
glottal bolts and barricades."

In the alphabet, one character
bellies up to consonants complex
as cathedrals. The Trappist monk
of tongues, the squat configuration
is a *makisnyak,* seen but not heard
in almost every word.

"The tongue must suck against the teeth
like a hungry peasant's, then double back
like a soldier camouflaging tracks in snow.
Da svidanya means good day, it is a farewell."

Da svidanya, my dear *makisnyak,*
Friar Fatso, *bolshoi* comrade
quiet as a cabbage. This purple prose

is more a maze than a Czarist bibelot
in its construction. I'll keep my words
by Webster, and read between the lines.

Liz Rose Dolan

HERITAGE STATEMENT:

My mother was born in Tullaree, Kilcoo, in 1905; my father was born in Castlewellan in 1901, both in County Down, Northern Ireland. Single, they both arrived in this country in 1930 just in time for The Depression. It's called the luck of the Irish. My four siblings and I were born and raised in The Bronx, New York City, thank God, as the opportunities for higher education were rich and we were not.

AUTHOR BIO:

Liz Dolan's poetry manuscript, *A Secret of Long Life* (Cave Moon Press, 2014) was nominated for the Robert McGovern Prize. Her first poetry collection, *They Abide*, was published by March Street. A six-time Pushcart nominee and winner of Best of the Web, she was a finalist for Best of the Net 2013. She has received fellowships from the Delaware Division of the Arts, The Atlantic Center for the Arts and Martha's Vineyard. Liz serves on the poetry board of *Philadelphia Stories*.

THE MAN FROM GOD KNOWS WHERE

Central Wrap hummed like a steam engine as I tossed the brown packages wrapped with twine onto the conveyor belt during the 1958 Christmas season at Stern's Department Store, around the corner from the lions in front of the New York Public Library on 42nd Street. I was sixteen. Occasionally, I threw a package over the head of a favorite co-worker, a wavy-haired, cobalt-eyed, well-built young man named Gerard Guilfoyle. His dark good looks were matched by the deftness with which he caught the flying surprise that almost clipped his right ear, "Guess I'll have to ride home with you tonight, Liz, just to get even."

Although Gerard lived in lace curtain Pelham Bay Park, and I lived in the working-class South Bronx, we both took the Lexington Avenue Local home. As we approached Cypress Avenue, my stop, Gerard, swaying to the undulation of the train, grabbed the overhead leather strap, "I'll walk you to your building, Liz."

"That's really nice of you, Gerard, but not necessary," I lied, "besides tomorrow's a school day, you have a long ride ahead of you." As the doors of the train slid open, Gerard cradled my elbow in his hand and we ascended the dingy IRT stairs to the street where the crispness of the winter air stung my nostrils. Orion the Hunter and The Pleiades smiled down on us as Gerard caressed my shoulder, pushing up the collar of my navy blue Chesterfield to warm me.

I shivered when Gerard shattered my crystal reverie, "Sure are a lot of bars in this neighborhood, colorful names, too."

"Never paid them much mind," I said, inching away from him. I never had but Gerard was right, there were too many bars on this street and every one bore an Irish stamp: The Shannon View, the Rose of Tralee, The Eire. As I was attempting to change the topic, who should emerge from the bowels of The Eire but the ruddy-complected Mr. Slattery, known to all as Scatter-ation. He doffed his frayed tweed cap, swept it across his waist and bowed when he saw me.

There was no avoiding his elfin self as he always scurried across busy 138th in the middle of the street directly in front of the triple oak doors of St. Luke's, our parish church, as he had explained to me too many times before, and as he explained again to Gerard and me.

"You never know who's been bribin' who to get a driver's license these days or what ijit might be careening down our fair thoroughfare terminatin' the life of an innocent like myself. And should I suddenly be needin' a priest, aren't they right there in the rectory countin' the two and three dollars that every decent parishioner donates each Sunday in the yellow envelope. Elizabeth, Elizabeth," he said to me, "my girl, you're growin' grander every day."

"As you are yourself, Mr. Slattery, how are you?"

"Fair to middlin', fair to middlin'. And who is this stout buckadah protectin' ya from the cold?"

"My friend, Gerard Guilfoyle."

"It's a firm handshake ya have, Mr. Guilfoyle. I knew a Cornelius Guilfoyle when I first came to this country. Are your people from Leitrim?"

"I really don't know where my people are from; my parents were born in Manhattan."

"Your grandparents then?"

"I don't know, Mr. Slattery."

"A narraback, are ya? 'Tis sadness itself when those glorious blue eyes and that glossy thicket of black hair have lost their Celtic lineage. You'll never know where you're goin', Gerard, until you find out where you've been, never know your heart 'til you find its home place. There's no denyin' what you've come from, my boy, no denyin' it." He reached up to pat Gerard on the shoulder and shook his head in sympathy.

"I'll try to find out, Mr. Slattery, I'll ask my folks."

"At your right hand there is a great Irish girl herself, her parents sprung from the magical mists of the Mourne Mountains in County Down, even if it is in the God-forsakin' North."

"Not as magical as Mayo, even if it's in the God-forsakin' South, Mr. Slattery," I said. "And those County Down parents are wondering where I am right now."

"Right you are, right you are, my girl. I'll be dodgin', myself, s'been a pleasure meetin' yourself, Gerard. Guilfoyle, 'The Man from God Knows Where.'" Mr. Slattery turned and disappeared into the dark night like a banshee. Gerard laughed as we approached my building.

"He's had a few, Gerard. 'The Man from God Knows Where' is a poem we recite at family parties."

"A nice man," Gerard said, "a very nice man."

Gerard was very nice, too, and as we dashed across the street in the protective shadow of St. Luke, I prayed that Gerard would traverse that street again but somehow I knew that Loughery's and the Shannon View and even the rapscallion Mr. Slattery scared away The Man from God Knows Where. Not even St. Luke, the physician, could heal the schism of an ocean and centuries of mysticism and mythology.

In the South Bronx we were a breed apart. We still identified ourselves by the parish that baptized, married and buried us just as my mother told she was from the lush green hamlet of St. Malachy's in Tullaree, Kilcoo. We still drank tea with milk instead of the ubiquitous American Maxwell House. We still blessed our throats with candles on the feast of St. Blaise to ward off the winter chill (God forbid we couldn't talk). We still bore the dust of the earth on our foreheads on Ash Wednesday to remind us from what we came and to where we would return. We crossed ourselves when we passed a church. In so doing, we paid tribute to the Father who had dug the potatoes in the fallow fields of Kilcoo, to the Son who navigated the ocean to the land of heaven knows what and to the Holy Ghost who imbued us with the Spirit that made us what we were, and no matter how far we strayed and took on fancy American airs, what we would always be.

Vickie Fernandez

HERITAGE STATEMENT:

Before Castro's regime, my family had no desire to leave their country. They changed their minds once the quality of life began to deteriorate and they were faced with job losses and inhumane food rations. My great-grandmother and my uncle were the first to flee. Once established, my uncle began the arduous process of bringing his sisters and their families to the U.S. In 1969, my grandmother and her two children were the first to arrive. They flew to Miami and were welcomed into La Casa de la Libertad, a halfway house for Cuban refugees that provided food, shelter and clothing until they got on their feet. When given the choice to stay in Miami or join my great-grandmother and uncle in New Jersey they chose New Jersey. In spite of the fact that life in Florida was easier for new arrivals, they wanted to stick together. Grandma, an artist and entrepreneur, worked ceaselessly at a factory to save up for her own business, a successful flower shop in Elizabeth, New Jersey. I once asked her why she loved flowers and she said, "*Las flores* are like life *mi amor*, you have to appreciate them in the moment. Because like you and me and everybody else, they start to die the minute they get cut from the thing that they came from." Though they missed their homeland, they appreciated their new life and lived very much in the moment. Roots intact, they sowed new seeds and made a life here in the States.

AUTHOR BIO:

Vickie Fernandez is an award-winning writer whose work has appeared in *The Rumpus, Metropolis, Carnival Lit Magazine, The Rusty Nail Literary Magazine* and in a number of publications you've probably never heard of but should check out. She was the recipient of the 2011 Judith Stark award for nonfiction and a finalist in *Hunger Mountain*'s 2010 competition for creative nonfiction. When she's not working on her memoir and wrangling new unruly tales into submission you can find her performing her stories in dive bars, well-lit

coffee houses and improv theaters all over Philadelphia. She hopes to someday move to Mexico and live in a brightly colored house with plenty of room for her pet monkeys, Frida Kahlo shrines, and disproportionate collection of cowboy boots. To learn more about Vickie go to www.vickiefernandez.com.

CUBAN MEDICINE

It's a hot, sticky day and the air conditioner is on the fritz. The car stinks of fowl and Mom is wearing the bobbed wig that never sits right on her head. Sweat beads run down her cheeks as she sings along with Billy Joel about the good dying young. She smells bad, the floral accents of her perfume fail to mask the metallic toxins that push through her pores. She stops mid-chorus, hunches over and throws up into a plastic shopping bag. She used to be statuesque, she used to wear purple and go to Prince concerts. She used to be my mother. Now she's only cancer.

Ever since Mom decided to quit chemo, Grandma's been on the scramble for a cure. On weekends, instead of watching cartoons, I amble up and down the aisles of health food stores that smell like wet earth and grain. Grandma plucks small fortunes' worth of organic goods from shelves into shopping baskets. All of which Mom will consume raw, except for the kale, that has to be steamed quickly to kill the hundreds of gray aphids that blanket the stuff.

I'm in the back seat with the chickens. They stare up at me from the small cage that once housed my pet rabbits. I was told they ran away—dug a tunnel under the vegetable garden to freedom. I am told lies.

Mom's the only adult who tells the truth. When she first got sick, she sat me down in the beige foyer of her hospital room and told me that she was going to die—the words evaporated between us before I could get a grip on them. I sat there, eight years old, mouth agape and nodding. Death was something that happened to old, gray people trapped beneath the cellophane of photo albums, not to my twenty-eight-year-old mother. For months after her diagnosis, afraid of waking up to find her gone, I'd make Mom hold my hand until I fell asleep—our arms a bridge of flesh between twin beds.

We arrive at the Santeras' house that sits ensconced between trees on a dead-end street. I help Mom out of the car while Grandma grabs the birds from the back seat.

Grandma grabs hold of my arms, raising her arched brows over her glasses, "*Pórtate bien*, or no TV tonight. Okay, *niña*?" Grandma communicates in hisses and threats these days. I don't intend on misbehaving but mumble, "I promise to be good," and jerk free from her grip. I want to run away. I want to be a kid. I want to hug my mom but the last time I did, I was afraid I'd break her.

I watch as Mom hobbles down the walkway. She looks old, her limbs delicate as dry leaves.

I think about how just two years ago, I sat on the itchy blue carpet in our bedroom, braiding the pink mane of a My Little Pony, while mom worked out.

Her legs swooshed through the air, long and muscular. She wore her black curls pulled up into a fuzzy bun that flopped around as she did jumping jacks; eyes sharp, face red, blood coursing through her thick blue veins. The thought of that version of her makes the ground feel loose under my Keds so I push it away.

Once inside the strange house, I choke on the scent of frankincense. It reminds me of church, which we have stopped going to. We've stopped doing a lot of things. There are candles everywhere. The kind with the saints on them that you light and can't blow out, they have to burn to the wick, die out on their own—like a life. In the kitchen, herbs are strewn across the countertops, so thick they look like moss. The kitchen table is cluttered with prayer cards and seashells. Insects swarm around rotting fruit and red wine in dollar store goblets. A statue of St. Lazarus stares up at me, dogs at his feet, lapping at his wounds with their pink tongues as he leans on his crutch.

There's a book on saints among the clutter. I flip through to St. Teresa of Ávila, my saint. I skim to a paragraph that reads: patron saint of bodily ills, headaches and loss of parents. I put the book down because it reads true. The soles of my sneakers stick to the linoleum as I pace.

Mom grabs hold of my hand and I feel her pulse in my palm like a chant. We are both buzzing with something beyond fear as an ageless woman appears in the doorway. She's wearing white from head to toe and a scarf is wound around her head like a snake. From her long neck hang a million tiny beads. My grandmother hands the woman two crisp one hundred dollar bills. The Santera tucks the money into her turban and lights a thick cigar from the flame of a candle that sits on the counter. She narrows her black eyes at me and winces.

"The girl . . . must not see!" she whispers and blows a sour cloud in my direction.

Mom lets go of my hand and the three women disappear down rabbit hole steps to the basement. I wonder what other children do on Saturday mornings.

I'm going to be ten years old in a few months and I don't even care. I've stopped wishing for things like presents and themed birthday parties with friends. I still believe in God and every night, hands clasped, elbows sinking into my mattress, I pray. I used to pray for Mom to get better and now I pray for her to fall asleep and get carried off to Heaven by a fleet of angels.

I sit alone and wait in the low-ceilinged kitchen while the strange woman in the turban tries to fix my mom. A thin-winged hope flutters inside of me as the room pulsates with too many wishes. I'm gnawing on a hangnail when the screaming starts. I look over at the basement door as one of the now-headless chickens pushes through. It runs in circles then collapses at my feet.

My mother stands in the doorway, covered in blood, eyes wide. For a moment, I see everything as if she's made of glass. The beast that's slowly consuming her insides slithers up and down the length of her, its tentacles at her throat. I look away—this is what I mustn't see. The Santera stands beside her, small and defeated.

While mom washes the chicken blood from her chest and face in the sink, the woman pulls the two hundred dollars from her headdress and squeezes it into my grandmother's trembling hand.

"*Perdoname señora*, but this curse, it is too deep," she says.

In the car, on the way home, Grandma is so hysterical she has to pull over. Mom rubs her back—cuticles still caked with blood from the useless chickens—as grandma cries and bangs her fists against the steering wheel. Mom is always consoling people. When friends and family come over and break down at the sight of her, she offers them tea and assures them that everything will be okay. I wonder who consoles her.

I miss the chickens as we get back on the Jersey Turnpike. Within the reverberating lull of motion, I stare at the back of my mother's head. The hairs at the nape of her neck spool like tiny tornados and my heart begins to thump in its blue nest of veins. The truth ruptures in my chest and spreads slowly like lava—my mom isn't going to die on some faraway day in the future—she is dying, right now, in front of me. My mouth opens like a wound and I let out a deep cry that bleeds into the song playing on the radio. I realize that I'm not ready to surrender her to Heaven or angels. I make the sign of the cross with my small, sweaty hand—forehead to heart, heart to left shoulder, and then the right—and I pray. I pray like hell for my mother's life.

Gloria Frym

HERITAGE STATEMENT:

My father, Bernard Frym, was born in Lublin, Poland. He was the youngest child of a Talmud scholar, Henoch, and his wife Ester. Henoch died when my father was nine. Ester tried to raise her four children among her large and deeply religious extended family. Ester was persuaded by her eldest brother, who had already immigrated to Brooklyn, to join him in America in the mid-1930s, find a new husband, and send for her children later. She was married off to an older man, who set up the necessary sponsorship and created bank accounts of $2,000 for each of her children. When they reached Warsaw, my father's favorite sister, Hencha, was denied a visa because she failed to count backwards in Polish. She perished in the Holocaust, as did the majority of my father's family. My father's eldest sister Alice and my maternal grandmother Dina, a Russian-émigré widow with a teenage daughter, met in night school where they were studying English. They arranged a meeting between Bernard and Claire. Once married, my parents settled in Brooklyn, where I was born in 1947.

AUTHOR BIO:

Gloria Frym's most-recent books are *Mind Over Matter* (BlazeVOX [books], 2011) and the chapbook *Any Time Soon* (Little Red Leaves, 2010). Other works include *The Lost Poems of Sappho* (Effing Press, 2007) and *Solution Simulacra* (United Artists Books, 2006). A previous book of poems, *Homeless at Home*, won an American Book Award. She is the author of several volumes of poetry and two critically acclaimed short story collections: *Distance No Object* (City Lights Books, 1999) and *How I Learned* (Coffee House Press, 1992). She is a recipient of The Fund for Poetry Award, the Walter & Elise Haas Creative Work Fund Grant, the San Francisco State University Poetry Center Book Award, and several California Arts Council grants. She teaches writing and literature at California College of the Arts.

A LITTLE HISTORY

I was five years old, and it was during summer, perhaps July, because I remember that it was very hot, the air was thick and salty. This was not in the story, but outside it, like blankets, like sheets on a bed. In the bed of I.

My family was staying at the beach, as many families of the middle class did to flee the heat of New York. Such heat was left to those who came from hot climates, as though they could bear it better. The beach was right outside the bungalow. The beach is right outside the story, outside of history, though history has been made on beaches, but not this one or this history. I remember I was sick, very sick with a fever and sore throat. One morning I awoke and the shades were drawn and the room was darkened. *Why is the room so dark?* I asked my mother. She was part of this history, her story intersects though is not significant to this event. *Because you have the mumps*, she said, *and your eyes are very sensitive. How awful*, I said, not conscious of any other eyes than my own and why they should be called sensitive. I could not get up, I could not play, and I could not read.

Our family was part of a larger extended family who rented the bungalow for some part of the summer, the rent was expensive, and the families that comprised the larger family were close, though only by necessity not by choice. Each adult took turns reading to me the same story, "Thumbelina," a story of a beautiful little girl so small that she fit in a spoon. Thumbelina suffers the classic trials of women of her day—she is a gentle girl who loves flowers and birds, and every male she meets wants to capture her, and most of them are ugly and awful. One strong contender is a rich, middle-aged mole who never sees the light of day. Having fallen from a lily pad and lost her way home, Thumbelina is desperate and almost goes through with the wedding.

A maternal field mouse takes her in. "If you wish, you can stay with me for the winter, if you'll keep my parlor nice and clean and tell me stories—I'm so fond of stories!"

One tribulation after another forms the narrative.

"Marry the Mole," the field mouse says.

"Marry the Mole," the mole says.

In the end, with the help of a white swallow, Thumbelina does find her equal, a man, a flower's angel, the prince of them all. She does seem to live happily ever after. She becomes queen of all the flowers. She meets her match. My father and mother were not well matched. They were not equals. They did not live happily then or after.

My father and my mother's brother would make the long drive to the beach together over the weekends after they had worked all week to pay the exorbitant summer rent on the bungalow plus the rent on our regular apartments. I remember my uncle reading "Thumbelina" to me. This is the best part of the story, when history is lovely. He was a little deaf from the war, the history that preceded my little episode by a mere handful of years. There is always a war to be born before, during, or after. He was a little absent-minded by nature, but so very sweet, that his baby blue eyes seemed to belong to a child, and he read with such animation and expression, such drama, that "Thumbelina" became completely mine. I could tell it to you now, the whole story, scene by scene, were it truly pertinent to this story.

Then my father took his turn. He was a recent immigrant. On the boat over, so he could order breakfast, he repeated to himself the only American words he would speak upon landing: *apple pie and coffee, apple pie and coffee, apple pie and coffee . . .*

He spoke with an accent. What a story that is, full of hope and privation, loss and sorry. I couldn't know then what he suffered, only that he said "ahppills" for apples. And he could not for anything pronounce the "th" in "Thumbelina." As he read, he kept saying "Tumbelina, Tumbelina."

It was terrible to my ears, which perhaps were as affected as my eyes, at age five, just after hearing my uncle read so perfectly, so emotionally, to listen to my father mispronounce and read in the flat, uninflected, halting voice of a man unused to reading aloud, this most beautiful and romantic of fairy tales.

My uncle too had suffered. He left Europe in a potato sack. But this is not the point of the story, nor did I know anything about that. Only that after my father repeated "Tumbelina" about five times, after he stumbled, aware that one of the letters of this name, this extremely foreign word, would not, no matter how he tried, wrap itself around his tongue, I burst into violent tears, thrashing in my hot little bed, throwing off the sheet my mother had covered me with. *Stop, stop, stop!* I cried, *Bring back my uncle because he can read so much better.*

My father shut the book. The pages slapped against each other. He stared at the shadows on the window shades. And then he stared at me. He stood up and left to get my uncle.

This has never been a distant memory, but a permanent refraction, a little history of fracture, now a story.

Melissa Castillo-Garsow

HERITAGE STATEMENT:

I grew up in Ithaca, New York, where I was raised with Spanish as my primary language. My father immigrated to the United States at age twenty-two from Mexico City where he worked in a cheese factory in Green Bay, Wisconsin. He decided there was no future in factory work and enrolled in the University of Wisconsin–Stevens Point. There he met my mother, who is of German-Polish-Native American descent, born and raised in the Green Bay area on a small family farm, and the first in her family to go to college. She also had recently returned from a year of study in Colombia and was one of the few people in the area who spoke Spanish. They supported each other in attending Cornell University in Ithaca, New York, where my brother and I were raised spending summers in Mexico City, celebrating Mexican holidays and speaking Spanish, whether we wanted to or not.

AUTHOR BIO:

Melissa Castillo-Garsow is a Mexican-American writer, journalist and scholar. She completed her BA at New York University in journalism and Latin American studies, her Master's degree in English with a concentration in creative writing at Fordham University and is currently pursuing a PhD in American studies at Yale University. Melissa was awarded the Sonoran Prize for creative writing at Arizona State University and was a finalist for *Crab Orchard Review*'s 2009 Charles Johnson Student Fiction Award. She has had short stories and poems published in *Shaking Like a Mountain*, the anthology *A Daughter's Story*, *The Acentos Review*, *The Minetta Review*, *The 2River View*, *Hispanic Culture Review*, *The Pacific Review* and has a forthcoming novel with Augustus Publishing. She also has forthcoming articles in *The Bilingual Review*, *Women's Studies*, and *Words.Beats.Life: The Global Journal of Hip Hop Culture*. Her first novel, *Pure Bronx*, was released by Augustus Publishing in 2013. To learn more visit www.melissacastillogarsow.com.

POEM TO THE WHITE MAN WHO ASKS ME AFTER OVERHEARING ME SPEAK SPANISH WHERE TO FIND THE BEST MEXICAN FOOD AND THEN IS SHOCKED TO FIND OUT I AM MEXICAN

I see myself in you
and I don't recognize anything,
but a fading Arizona tan that becomes
a Caribbean beach against
your chalky exterior when you smell
cocoa hair & vanilla-scented
canella margaritas and a
hidden tumble in the sand—
whispered words you can't
understand
and I would never say.
Because I was twenty-four before I ever tasted mofongo
and knowing the difference
between one cuisine and another
does not make it exotic,
it means I paid attention
and I can do it with Italian food too.
I watch my reflection in you,
see-through tights and long black liner, dark thick hair
and an occasional affinity
for high heels—I don't apologize for
being sexy or occasionally loving
my body, I apologize for
letting my guard down
thinking you could see more than
a green, white and red-ribboned package.
Because growing up bilingual
doesn't make me sexy—it makes me like most people
I know and it certainly does not make me

your tour guide to tacos or your
trophy for the night.
So stop looking for beaches.
I see what you see;
Eva and Jennifer—beautiful
women I look nothing like
and am nothing like because
I speak Spanish but mostly because
I won't be an object of study
or teach you about "culture" or
translate the untranslatable.

Because if for once you could just look
past the *Macarena* soundtrack
and Brazilian model dreams
you'd probably realize your last girl
was the burlesque dancer
and I only dance salsa every six months or so
when I meet my Venezuelan-Spanish professor best friend
who first fills me in on his Seventeenth-Century History graduate class.

TÚ

Dedicado a mi prima Edna, nineteen, whom I never met, porque fue asesinada el 19 de julio de 2010 en Ciudad Juárez, México.

Tú eres diferente
      from me.
You had to:
      cross the border everyday
      take out your passport and
      sit in traffic, staring at
the barbed wire
to remind you of tu Mexicanidad.

I

Thousands of miles away
I never knew your border.
Mine was different:
      piñatas and enchiladas
      Mariachis and flan
      la Virgen above my bed
bright pink cheeks when my friends said
"I can't understand your dad."

We

We used to wear matching bracelets
      "best friends forever."
We promised we would never become
      "just primos"—
separados por un país that makes
      "nosotras" sound wrong.

Vosotros

is a word we never use
and don't know how to use.
You lived in Tijuana
I lived in translation.
Vosotros is a word we don't want to use.

She

She has a border too—
In a state where I tell her to carry ID everywhere she goes.
        Colombian-Mexican-American
        Revise: Mexican Colombian-American.
        Chimichangas, cactus, cumbia.
Half-sister. Three passports.
Answering only en Inglés.

They

can't tell the difference.

CUANDO SUEÑO CON ARIZONA

When I think of Arizona,
I don't think of SB 1070,
I think of my little sister:
Gabriela Citlali Londoño Castillo.

> Gabriela because my father let me name her
> like my brother named me.
> Citlali because we are Indians and
> to honor our Abuela.
> Londoño because her mother is different
> from mine (una Colombiana)
> and Castillo because she is my sister—
> she is one of us.

When I think of Arizona,
I don't think of teachers stumbling
over her name like they did mine,
although I know they will.
I don't think of when other kids
make fun of her for being an immigrant,
although I know they have.
Or the Rudyard Kipling poem
she had to memorize.

> Sueño con the Arizonian after eight years
> she considers herself to be.
> Copper-toned and pencil-shaped,
> sitting at the table with her colors,
> while I remember a young woman:
> Gentle enough to tame a rat she names Lou,
> strong enough for rock-climbing nationals,

focused enough to play Mozart for hours.
Mi Columbian-Mexican-American inocente.

Cuando sueño con Arizona
I don't want to think of SB 1070.
I can't. Ahí está mi lápiz
and too young to be broken.
Gabriela so it can be said in Spanish y Inglés
      Citlali because our bisabuelo spoke Otomí
           Londoño porque es Colombiana y
                 Castillo from el DF like our father.

So I name her to me, bring
      her closer than the safest neighborhood:
      mi lápiz, drawing her world and me,
      trying to (under)stand for us both.
      Writing what history.

Ana Garza G'z

HERITAGE STATEMENT:

My parents met and married in Mexico. They came to Central California in the mid-1960s, hoping to save enough money to buy a home in Mexico. They did farm work, mostly in grape, cotton, almond, and tomato fields. In the early 1970s, my dad started working in a winery, where wages were good enough for them to buy their first home in Earlimart, California, where I grew up. In the early 1990s, after their three children had finished college and trade school, they moved to Fresno, California, working in fruit-processing plants until they retired. Fresno is still where my dad does mysterious things in the backyard while my mom does magical things in the kitchen, and it's where I work as a community interpreter and translator.

AUTHOR BIO:

Ana Garza G'z has an MFA from California State University, Fresno. Fifty-nine of her poems have appeared in various journals and anthologies, with two forthcoming in *Breath & Shadow* and *Intimacy*, a Jacar Press anthology. She lives in Central California, where she teaches at Fresno State and works as a community interpreter.

PA GRAFTS TREES

"I weighed 155 pounds
this morning," Pa says, slicing a limb
the size of a pork sausage off
the peach. "Then I took a dump,
and I weighed 160."

He blows his nose into his hand and cuts
the scar left by the severed branch. "Doesn't make sense—
unless it's air I'm getting full of."

I pick up the limb and hand
him an apple shoot, a slender thing
like chicken bones. "Or maybe it's the Garza
kicking in and filling out the extra colon space," I say.

He laughs. "Five pounds of Garza filled with shit," and ties
the surrogate with builder's tape. "Just wait
till this one catches on." He pats the bark
around the notch. "I'll have a Goddamned bucket
of apples," and rests his hand beneath the shoot so I can
test the knot and measure the angle

with my index finger and thumb. "Just need you a book
to be immortal," I say, following him
past the avocado with two varieties, the rose
with miniatures and cabbage blossoms, the dahlia
with the tapered petals and exotic color, the hybrid
quince with apple-tasting fruit, the citrus
with limes, lemons, oranges, grapefruits, and tangelos
toward the plum with the apricot branch he put in last week.

"A book," he says,
   and we pause at Ma's hydrangeas, which he secretly sprinkles
   with ammonium phosphate to turn them blue, and poke
   around the pomegranate, which I don't tell him Ma bathes
   with bleach. "Books only live if you open them and know
   to read," he says, hunkering down and squinting.

He adjusts the irrigation drip to shift the water
   closer to the tree. "Mostly it's dead wood." He spits into
   the flowers, crawls along the garden trim, and stretches
   for the peach limb I've been holding like a staff.

"If we get it to sprout," he says burying
   the fat end of the limb, "I can slice
   a peach and eat it.

Can't nectar up your fingers
in a book," he says. "Can't feel
the sugar punch of living
sun inside your mouth and blood
or turn a leaf to find your hands
tucked in exactly like a fruit, or bind
yourself in something different to make you
someone else's arms."

PINTO BEAN MEDITATION

Like God, I touch each
and every bean in the pot, pinch
the dry seeds to pick out
the halved, the wrinkled, the lumpy
from life about to be, drop
them into a cup to be emptied
over garbage, leaving
the oval and smooth for a bowl
of the chosen, and hope
the Lord sorts sloppily for soup.

Melody S. Gee

HERITAGE STATEMENT:

My mother escaped to Hong Kong from rural China in 1959, at age twelve, just before the Great Leap Forward. She came to Sacramento, California, in 1966. My father was born in California in 1940, and was raised by his two immigrant parents, also from Guangdong, China, in their family's take-out restaurant. I was born in 1981.

AUTHOR BIO

Melody S. Gee is the author of *Each Crumbling House*, winner of the 2010 Perugia Press Book Prize. She received her MA in poetry from the University of New Mexico. Her essays and poetry most recently appear in *Blackbird*, *Connotation Press*, *failbetter.com*, and *Fox Chase Review*, among others.  She teaches writing at St. Louis Community College and lives in St. Louis, Missouri, with her husband and daughter.

ONE YEAR EXTRA

The story again, MaMa. How you lied about your age
      to escape Guangdong,
how Ah-Hoo sold her jewelry to buy you
      a younger child's visa.
How now you want to change the date on your driver's license,
      bitter you must work

an extra year before retiring. Again you pour out the decades
      in white gold rings,
your mother-in-law's wedding chain, and jade carved in the year of the boar.
      Again you count them
the way you count change at the market, relieved to find
      every coin and year.

When Ah-Hoo shells pistachios with me, she peels back 1959
      and the Great Leap Forward
as Mao snaked through the country toward your village,
      how close they came
to turning Li-Hong Lei into a commune. That year, you asked a fortuneteller
      if you would ever leave China.

This year, I will know roads the width of a bicycle tire, and
      your every beginning.
That shade of green—there where the rice splits its reed—that is what green
      means to you.
With his good eye on you, the fortuneteller said you were destined
      for the ocean, for sidewalks

off the mainland the width of fifty bicycles. When you take me to meet
      your missing year,
we are both foreigners. At this river, you are eleven—no, twelve—

stepping the rhythm of fishermen's oars
as if they had followed you to California and all the way back. Then suddenly
    you pull off your socks.
We skip the years like the stones you throw, breaking the water
    to reach the other side.

WHERE WE ARE GATHERED

My mother sprayed our yard with seeds
gathered in Hoi-Peng. *Lai-ah*,
she urged them, *come up*.

Fingers of green onion, snow pea vines
fisted around wire, bitter melon
tight as a belly. Their names
I can't remember now, and could not

say when I did remember.
When she called, they offered her
their tenderest parts.
She gathered.

But what do they, stretching from
the hot grip of loam toward
decapitation, know of names?
What do they know of *daughter*

being more a name than my own?
What of water for the dead come
too late and too much?
I cannot gather words like seeds,
or drink her voice like water to offer,

in return, myself. In loose folds of earth,
my mother's words are sewn into new
squash blossoms, their white,
silent faces breaking open.

Danusha Goska

HERITAGE STATEMENT:

My parents were peasant immigrants from Eastern Europe. My mother, Pavlina Kerekova, was born in Slovakia, the country that sent the most immigrants, per capita, to the U.S. during the massive wave of immigration between 1880 and 1924. Pavlina had not met her coal miner father until she arrived in the U.S. at eight years old in 1929. My Polish father, Anthony Goska, grew up in the anthracite-mining region of Throop, Pennsylvania.

AUTHOR BIO:

Danusha Goska, PhD, is a writer and teacher living in New Jersey. Her work has won the New Jersey State Council on the Arts grant, the Eva Kagan Kans Award, and the Halecki Award. Her essay "Political Paralysis" appears in the anthology *The Impossible Will Take a Little While* (Basic Books, 2004). Her book *Save Send Delete* (Roundfire Books, 2012), about her yearlong debate and love affair with a prominent atheist, is available on Amazon. Of *Save Send Delete,* Larry Dossey, MD, said, "Danusha Goska is a lyrical, forceful writer with a huge heart and talent to burn. Her inspiring observations embody the best vision of which we humans are capable. Goska deserves widespread attention." She teaches at William Paterson University.

SILENCE

It was a summer afternoon and I was napping on a tour bus in Poland, weary from working to internalize the Polish language, the only natural barrier in that invader's nation of choice. I had had to start from scratch, with "My name is . . ." As I drifted off to sleep, I suddenly felt I was a tiny child snoozing on a spiral rag rug. I felt safe within a field protected by a goddess who held the fierce shield of Athena. She sat at a secretary, calculating figures. I heard her whispering over and over the numbers "*jeden, dwa, trzy.*" I knew they were words for numbers, and I, an adult, could hear the women in the bus seat in front of me repeating these numbers out loud, and I recognized these words, because of the sudden jolt of a memory of my mother doing household accounts. I didn't know before that moment that I knew those foreign words. I did not even consciously remember sleeping next to my mother when she did her figures. Apparently some part of my memory does not speak English.

I grew up in a house where Polish and Slovak were spoken daily. My parents doggedly resisted my prodding for lessons and translations. Though I sometimes felt like the only immigrant born in America, I could not speak a word of their native tongue.

Those among us who couldn't speak English were different, old and dying out. There had been some catastrophe; they couldn't reproduce. When I was born, Aunt Tetka was old and she's old now. When my elder brother was a baby, she was old, when he was a grown man, "strong like bull" and respected in town, she was old. Now he's dead and she's still old, still speaking Slovak, a one-woman ethnic enclave in Bayonne, New Jersey.

My siblings and I felt a polite pity for them, combined with repressed ridicule. Realizing that we shouldn't make fun, and didn't, was one of our first opportunities to act grown up. But making fun would have been superfluous. We couldn't mock something that obvious, something that so clearly communicated everything that needed to be understood.

Sometimes, when I was far from home, on a Girl Scout trip, maybe, feeling that current in the soles of my feet and palms of my hands that new situations caused, a passing stranger speaking some Slavic language would sound so alluring, so intimate. I would follow, struggling to make eye contact, to produce the secret handshake that would indicate our kinship, to possess some kind of comfort. The rich luxury of words and syllables would flow over me like warm dill soup and I would be pricked by that common, maddening experience of a word being right on the tip of my tongue.

The meaning of those familiar sounds seemed just a moment's mundane concentration away, like the message of a half-forgotten dream.

When in fact I would have no idea what their words meant, no notion in my fingers of what collaboration the coins in my pocket might have to the requirements of the price tag staring me right in the face. I would literally have nothing to say.

So I was forced to skip past the essential words, and rush to my heart, believing that when I heed my feelings, somehow it is right. I knew what those people were saying, I heard them with the third ear my multilingual household gave me. They turned; they smiled. Their eyes were as blue as my cousins' eyes. An American passed, and, suddenly, I blurted, "I'm sorry. I thought you were someone I knew," and scurried to rejoin my troop.

However it may have sounded to me, we knew what a Slavic accent meant in America. Cartoons, movies and national news villains spoke like our uncles. Because of men like Khrushchev, Grandpa and Boris Badenoff, America had to keep making nukes. I never let my father forget that he couldn't pronounce "th." "North," I nagged, relentless, fanatic. "Not 'nort,' 'north.'" I wanted to cool my shame. I wanted to make him a better person. I wanted to diffuse him.

I know the fear and envy saved for the stranger in your own backyard, or snoring on your living room couch. Can they speak of something in a language that you can't? Is there some piece of reality they, like physicists, can lay claim to with their strange words, and grammar? And if this isn't so, then why do they break off in the middle of a perfectly good English sentence to pile on these impossible syllables? All the uncles and aunts suddenly, solemnly, nodding, saying, *"Ai, tak,"* *ah, yes*, in dense agreement, and maybe even breaking into song. In an impatient answer to my nagging my mother gives me one word to say and I try to repeat it and she explodes: "No, *no!*" Somehow, some way I said one sound, or didn't, and it is breaking my mother's heart. It betrays her. There must be some sound in there that I don't hear, all part of the secret society they make and keep with their tongues.

When your parents speak a language you don't, they can orchestrate your life with the switchback drama of a Washington sex scandal. They can, for example, wait for the most vulnerable teen years of self-definition to reveal that your grandfather may not have been an itinerant shepherd come up from Hungary after all, but the village priest, a fact they'd been discussing right under your nose all along.

I envied them. They seemed more sophisticated and yet somehow more innocent.

The photos that Soviet bloc censors let through stunned me. My cousins: hard-jawed hunters, slung dead boars over their shoulders; ice-eyed nymphs on skates. Ice skates were something we couldn't afford.

English, then, seemed to vitiate us the better we learned it; America was now defined as the purgatory where we paid with being poor, fat, and lost for the crime of abandoning our home.

They never talked of their home in front of us; they bit their tongues. Having this language meant crucifying their organs of speech.

There was a day I was supposed to remember because it changed the hearts and minds of my generation forever; but no, I was appreciating the nice black horsy on TV and my father said, "They've got to stop talking about JFK. Momma said that if you talk about somebody after he dies, he sticks around to listen and misses his chance to get into Heaven."

This statement galvanized me. Finally some news of these people, in words I could understand! I held my breath, marshaled every cell in my body as one giant recording machine. I lay there pretending to sleep. This was how I acquired most data in my home.

"Shut up, Tony," barked my mother. "I don't want you talking that Skunk Hollow crap in front of the kids. They'll pick it up."

I'd show them. I'd go to the library and to school . . . but no, apparently teachers, publishers, the town fathers, were all in on the conspiracy. The maps of Europe in my textbooks stopped at Germany. The year's new teacher would, when calling roll for the first time, act is if my name were a Communist plot. Our town library's admittedly meager card catalogue didn't have a single entry under "Poland" or

"Slovakia." At bookstores I became acquainted with the responding little laugh. "No, we don't have books on . . . *a ha* Poland," "Oh, so you're *a ha* Polish?"

The jokes were unequivocal in their assessment of what it meant to be me. "How do you know your house has been robbed by a Polak? The garbage can is empty and the dog is pregnant." "How do you know if a Polish girl has her period? She's only wearing one sock." "What is the pile of manure for at a Polish wedding? To keep the flies off the bride."

I claimed defunct ethnicities: Austro-Hungarian; Prussian. I felt no immediate loss. I wondered if anyone Polish had ever done anything good. I wondered if my German classmate was right, and we were a subspecies. I wondered if my parents had made it all up, just to be perverse. No matter what I tried, they wouldn't talk. My father gave me family names to research; years later my mother would reveal these to be fictitious.

I wondered if they felt that I was calling them liars. Wanting their language in my mouth impugned their myth: that we were in training, waiting, stoic, to be something else, something better. My hankering for their language showed that what they were had its own value, and was missing from this world they thrust me into, with such expectations.

In this vacuum of vocabulary I sensed terrible secrets, terrible shame, an invisible leprosy that made us different from other people, from those winners called Americans.

I concluded that Poland and Slovakia are ever shrouded in some dense fog, as plump, white, clotted and shifting as Aunt Tetka's upper arms, that people there walk with heads tucked into collars and only speak cryptically, and never above a whisper. When fingering the arc of my globe I pictured days that clocked dawn and dusk but no noon; I pictured mountains of impossible pitch that limit all communication to cuneiform tablets hammered at great effort, carried once a year by masked runners who'd had their tongues cut out.

This was one mystery, the other was sex. Somehow they became one in the deep reptile root of my brain. The foreign tongue: a fearful thing, a cause of shame, something that must feel good and of which I was deprived. I looked upon my first Slovak-English dictionary the way I looked at my first sex manual: the mechanization of the last great mystery, a Promethean act. We'd all just better lay low and wait. I soon found both volumes to be inaccurate and incomplete. I said to myself, "Of course."

My paternal grandfather, a ready surrogate parent, out in the garden, up to his hips in vines, huge, suspendered, with his blunt and booming syllables, trailing fruit-scented smoke like a winter chimney, brought the folds and mountains of Slovakia with him to America. He must have found it hard to move about freely here. He didn't last long in the mines.

I have perfectly clear memories of my Slovak grandmother, his wife, all in crisp black and white, uncompromising colors. A smart black dress, a white lace collar (copied and stitched after a few minutes perusal of a downtown plate glass window), all haloed in silver luster, like of a Remington blade or Ansel Adams print. Confronted with a newspaper in Hungarian (their particular oppressors at that time), she'd read aloud in Slovak, never missing a beat, and she'd clobber her kid brother on the head when he was slow in picking up this linguistic trick. He died, seven decades later, of a brain tumor.

I remain in breathless admiration of her spare peasant musculature, for which any task, from finger-cracking walnuts to reaping twenty hectares of wheat, seemed easy.

I smell her cologne, brisk, no-nonsense, from Paris. I see her seated before the TV, also black and white, slicing up the apple in her lap, urging on Saturday night wrestlers. I feel her knotted fist pummel my thigh during palm-sweating, gasp-inducing scenes in movies. I live in fear of her temper and in gratitude to her example. I know that there is simply nothing in this world tougher than she, and all I need do is claim her in my hour of need. Of course, we never met. She died before I was born.

My father's mother was a bootlegger who spoke only Polish and refused unto death to speak of Poland, a peculiarly Slavic vow of silence. The only sentence I know with certainty that she ever spoke was, "Because the czars burned our books," in answer to the question, "Why did we come to America?" This tiny woman hid in a wagon under a pile of blankets and cabbages to cross a border bristling with police; she did this to get to books, books she'd never have the luxury of learning how to read.

Crossing the water, in my early teens for a few short weeks with my mother and aunt, didn't help. I mostly remember the dizzying, oceanic effect of heavy fields ripe with grain and my flint-muscled uncle who lived hard next to them. He was a tight-lipped communist who could finger queen bees and find baskets of mushrooms where I saw only brown leaves. He denounced the priests as *bla-zons* and lunatics. He worked his own schedule from dawn to dark on meals of smoked pig fat and fistfuls of raw hot chilies.

We asked about their lives *now* and our own flesh and blood would look in four directions and hiss, terrified, "No. The secret police." We asked about their lives *then* and the wailing would begin. We were told of the Cohen boy next door who once rescued my mother, drowning, out of the River Nitra; he died in the camps. That wonderful blonde who was raped repeatedly by Russians and became a timid spinster. The emigrants who left and never wrote. Slovaks who guarded prisoners for the Nazis, and were paid with sandwiches. A skinny, black-clad aunt who spanked hungry collaborators with her broom. "But, Tetka! They feed us!" Jozho in the bar who just last year stood up and sang, "I was born Slovak and I'll die Slovak" and was taken away never to be seen again.

I could not talk with them. Thank God for my fat, greasy cousin, who pinched me when no one was looking and played the fiddle like a devil, for the gooseber ries, the dumplings, and the booze. And I remember my mother and my aunt suddenly stopping on a street corner, and staring at a little black-haired girl in a flounced white dress saying something to a rounded blond boy in red overalls. And I remember my mother and my aunt looking at each other, with the same stunned expression, gasping and crying.

I pulled at their sleeves: "What? What?" What story prompted these shared tears? My mother turned to me and said "Children. Speaking Slovak."

Back home, I wrote a high school report on immigration. I found in the *En-cyclopedia Americana* that the year my mother entered this country, Congress, under great pressure from all sectors, including scientists, passed The Emergency Quota Act to keep us out. We were racially inferior. This was a law on the books in my lifetime.

I went to my parents and asked more questions.

Yes, they were beaten, by racists, teachers, even their own kind, who wanted to save them from these languages they brought with them, these languages they could not get off of their tongues, these tongues that betrayed them. If only they could escape them, if only they could abandon memories of their own grandmothers who were clever or sturdy or wild enough to survive, who may have had their own tricks to better my grandmother's with the newspaper. If only they could replace their music, its rhythms Western scholars couldn't even write down, their unique internal metronome, their proverbs, their prayers, their memories, their instincts, their desires. If only they could replace their every word, said or dreamed or imagined, with silence. They can live with their grief and shame, their own terror that with one false move, one wrongly said word or misplaced laugh, they'd expose themselves, they'd lose what the journey across the water had brought them and hurtle back into being landless, hungry, hunted, owned.

I thought that that profound silence, the absence of songs, costumes, rites, that void, was all my parents had passed on to me. They—so frequently absent from me as they worked maybe two full-time jobs in factories, cleaning, carrying bags in country clubs—assumed that I was somehow absorbing how to be a good American. Until my twenties, when I actually met WASPs and the American middle class, I guess I thought so too. But when I was with people who threw food away, who bought their clothes, who did not share, I, too, practiced *the silence*. "Real" American culture, reminiscences, experiences, perceptions, expectations, the very meanings of their words, were puzzle pieces, which, if I listened to carefully and patiently, I would gather the pieces to create a complete language of who I should be. In comparing myself to them I found that what I valued, what I found beautiful, what made me laugh or cry or angry, were foreign. I thought that those things were what made me wrong, and that I needed to get rid of them. "Real" Americans concluded from my silence not that I was different, but that I was a failed version of themselves.

I left America, again and again.

While living in Africa and Asia I felt a comfort I never felt in America. I had an accent; I was apparently different. Folks were willing to learn about me. In answering others' courteous questions, their humble hesitance to presume acquaintance: "What do you do? See? Think? Believe?" I became acquainted with myself.

I chose to spend a year in Poland, a year of chilblains and food lines and not earning any money. The night I came back, my parents' first and only question was: "Were they good people?"

"They were bitter and difficult," I replied, without hesitation. "They were moody and obsessed with their suffering. And no matter where I went, I knew, even if I didn't have a dime, that I'd be safe, and have a place to sleep, and something to eat."

My parents nodded and looked at each other. "They were good people." My father lifted my backpack, stuffed with poppy seeds and plum liquor and sausage thrust on me by people who expected me to be as clever evading customs laws as they. "*Ona jest bardzo mocna,*" he said to my mother.

For the first time I understood the words shaped in my father's voice, in his mother tongue. There is no word to describe what I felt. Suddenly it wasn't a random code my parents had devised on their own, out of a perverse eccentricity, to torment and exclude me; suddenly I was part of it, and it stretched back for centuries. Suddenly I wasn't crazy or peculiar or possessed, or worse, random; suddenly I could lay claim to my thoughts, my feelings, in my own legitimate tongue, which, if I kept speaking it, would make sense to somebody. And, suddenly, a wall fell, to be replaced by a frighteningly vibrant connection between them and me.

"Yes," I said. "I *am* very strong." My parents looked at each other, paled and red-speckled, open-mouthed. The spell was broken.

"She understands."

One day, when I was a kid, my mother had pulled me aside to teach me how to iron a man's shirt. It was my father's, gotten, as we got all our clothes, from great, black plastic garbage bags donated by rich people. I don't know how many people had worn it before my father, or with what degree of care.

My mother lifted it; it was limp, sky-blue, short-sleeved; you could see through it. "It may be just an old rag," she said, "but it is what your father has to wear. Treat it with care, as if it were a rich man's shirt." My mother knew how to iron rich men's shirts.

She showed me where to start, how to point the iron, how much to spray it with my fingertips, after dipping them in a bowl of cool water she kept nearby. She placed the shirt carefully. In the end, to me, it looked perfect. I felt very proud.

I know now that in that lesson, in hearing her leave for work before dawn, day after day, never calling in, walking on legs that were as veined as maps, in my father's feeding us on berries and mushrooms and bread-and-butter leaves—he could find provisions for a family of eight on any patch of land, on a highway margin—my parents taught me more, silently, about my culture, than I will ever be able to shake, in order to become the successful American some part of them wanted me to be.

Andrei Guruianu

HERITAGE STATEMENT:

My parents left Romania shortly after the Revolution of 1989. Much was un-certain in terms of the country's future at that point, and with a chance to leave the country for the first time after the fall of communism my parents took the opportunity to come to America and pursue a better life for themselves and for me and my sister. In the transition, much was sacrificed—friends, family, and possessions all left behind. And with those sacrifices came less tangible ones—language, culture, identity—the kind that are hard to anticipate and often the most difficult to bear. Admittedly, much of my early writing deals with memories of Romania, of "home," and though I feel that I have moved away from direct engagement with the topic in recent years, it was nonetheless a formative and exploratory period of narrative, autobiographical writing that helped me under-stand a personal history that was changing faster than I could imagine.

AUTHOR BIO:

Andrei Guruianu was born in Bucharest, Romania. He immigrated to Queens, New York, with his par-ents at age ten. He currently lives in New York City where he teaches in the Expository Writing Program at New York University. He is the author of a memoir and several collections of poetry. In the past he has served as editor and publisher of the literary journal *The Broome Review*, *Parlor City Press*, and as guest editor of the internationally distributed magazine *Yel-low Medicine Review*. In 2009 and 2010 he served as  Broome County, New York's first Poet Laureate. More of his work can be found at www.andreiguruianu.com.

FROM MOTHER TONGUE TO BORROWED TONGUE:
THE WRITER AS PERPETUAL FOREIGNER

My own language has become foreign to me. I can't tell you exactly when, whether it has taken months or years to come to this, lost in its cadence coming through as noise. Maybe it has always been this way, and I am only now aware of how adrift one could feel, even when tucked in a cradle of sound, pre-birth and pre-suffering, that umbilical thread to the unconscious that defines us more than any utterance passed through the sieve of experience. I can't recall anymore when I have felt otherwise. Were there days that, as a child, I felt the language given to me was mine, was of my own making? Was it ever as natural and as beautifully ordinary as drawing in a breath and holding it in, sharp with the sting of mountain air and pine? Were there days when instead of distance, instead of a separation there was an intimacy with language, a lover's knowing without having to see in the dark, knowing before it becomes knowledge?

I do know that with each year the rift between mother tongue and the borrowed tongue grows deeper. I stumbled once through the catacombs of this new language that I now impose on you because I cannot see it as anything less than an extension, a limb, sometimes a feather and sometimes a bludgeon. Through it we might suffer together, you and I and all of us, or exalt for a moment in the vertigo of flight, we might choke on the dust of the whole edifice coming down, crumbling. Words as tools, blunt objects for learning how to see and think; these are not the tools of emotion. Utilitarian hammer and nail. Letters fastened together to make sense and maybe a little more. Again, I ask, was it ever otherwise? Or did I look at myself always speaking from a distance, pausing to understand, to translate, to interpret me for myself?

I like to think there were days when the artifice was a beautiful construction, whatever fissures existed patched up and closed, that it would have been difficult to pick up the flaws with the naked eye, to tell apart in a crowd. Age has made those fissures more visible, maybe not larger, but clearer in contrast. Everywhere I look there are foreigners, speakers who speak versions of themselves, who speak versions of me. In dialects of the mother tongue I hear the echoes of the bludgeon trying to break through the walls of a new life, for a new language amounts to that—a built-from-gathered-parts-kind-of-life, a making of consciousness. There is violence in this act, in the building and rebuilding, in the movement across lines of knowing, even more so across lines of feeling. Fissures that grow, the way water and ice can tear at the earth, a simple violence we hardly pay attention to anymore until the hole in the ground grows to the point where it swallows us and we're standing in it, life-sized, unable to see past the edge of what we've been digging.

The mother tongue has never been mine; this I can now say for certain. I do not possess it, and it does not possess me. But it is not that simple. To use language to speak of language makes you a slave to metaphor, to cliché, to kitsch. Language is our Sisyphean task; it is the burden that owns us. The weight we cannot fully abandon by the side of the road, however much we'd like to get on with the business of the road. For the writer, it is an honest mirror, merciless, boulder-heavy. It is the awareness of a craftsman who dabbles in tchotchkes to put bread on the table. He knows what he's doing. He knows he's not doing anything; that the art is ultimately meaningless, will not save souls, and yet he makes it beautiful. He takes pride in knowing he can, at least for a little while, get your attention. He lives within a language of base pleasure and beauty, that language of the easily understood. He speaks the language of barbarians so that he himself would feel as they do—a part of something, a momentary belonging.

Barbarian craftsmen. Beautifully destructive. Dwellers of no-man's-land where a false step, one careless syllable can wound. I count myself among the destroyers and the builders. I resort to metaphors of violence because no others will do. Those who seek solace in words, in language, are looking in the wrong place for the wrong thing, for the wrong reasons. I mean here a different kind of violence than is expressed when we say, for instance, language is power (or knowledge is power, for they are intertwined). I don't mean the language of overt political discourse, language that is used for and against real or perceived outside forces. I am referring to every utterance, every attempt to voice, to make heard, to use language as means of expressing, as a violent act, an act of severance.

With every word, whether born into a language or inserted into another, we separate ourselves, we cleave the self into many, so many that it becomes impossible to gather them all back into the fold. Language, therefore, by its very nature creates separation from self. The claim that through it we come to know ourselves, that through language we come to understand ourselves is only part truth, mostly myth. With every utterance we inhabit a world outside of the self, a world that is foreign. It is a world that is not ours—we are not of it and it is not of us. The transactions we mediate through language only serve to enforce this separation. The world will never be the language we have for it; we can never be the language we have for ourselves. How then, to not feel always a stranger, always a foreigner as soon as you are born?

I am lost, irredeemably lost; this also I can now say for certain. I cannot hear myself think with the language of the soul (if we might allow for sentiment when speaking of the "mother tongue," tipping sweet to saccharine), and I cannot write that soul into existence as much as I try. And I've tried, only to see myself each time from afar, the outlines of what I believed in growing faint, the emptiness of the space left behind the only thing that I could point to and say, "See, there it is, that's where a part of me lived, briefly, thinking it knew how to live; that's where a part of me died, looking for answers."

And now, not even that. It is becoming harder to lie to myself and believe in it. The artifice too shallow. This language, which I've bartered with my time and my breath, which I've butchered time and again and which has butchered me is all I have, is only flesh on blood, temporary housing, an illusion, always a dying thing. And it can be a hollow kind of pretty, or hauntingly beautiful, and in its rhythm I can lose you as I lose myself—around corners, in the moonlit alleys I favor because the stillness has not yet been torn from itself; is at peace. Listen to the silence there carve out a space; listen as a howl enters in the predawn darkness of the woods, rattling the bones, a chill that rips down the spine and buries itself to hilt in marrow. It thinks it knows who I am, simply wandered too far, too long, and it calls and I answer; I break the silence each time to say "Yes, here I am," though I'm already split and scattered, though I should know better by now; I get no reply, and this is what I have to show for it.

John Guzlowski

HERITAGE STATEMENT:

John Guzlowski's parents met in a slave labor camp in Nazi Germany. His mother Tekla Hanczarek came from a small community west of Lviv, in what was then Poland, where her father was a forest warden. John's father Jan was born in a farming community north of Poznań. John was born Zbigniew Guzlowski in a Displaced Persons camp in Vienenburg, Germany, in 1948, and changed his name to John when he was naturalized as an American citizen. His parents, his sister Donna, and he came to the U.S. as DPs in 1951. After working on farms in Western New York State to pay off their passage to America, they eventually settled in Chicago in the city's old Polish Downtown in the vicinity of St. Fidelis Parish in Humboldt Park.

AUTHOR BIO:

John Guzlowski earned his PhD in En-glish at Purdue University in 1980, and is now retired from Eastern Illinois University, where he taught contemporary American literature and poetry writing. He has authored two books of poetry: *Lightning and Ashes* (Steel Toe Books, 2007) and *Third Winter of War: Buchenwald* (Finishing Line Press, 2007). These books continue the story of his parents that began in his chapbook *Language of Mules*, which was republished as *Język Mułów i Inne Wiersze*, a Polish-English edition of this chapbook and other poems, and published by Biblioteka Śląska in Katowice, Poland. His poem "What My Father Believed" was read by Garrison Keillor on the Writer's Almanac program. Other poems have appeared in a number of periodicals in the U.S., Poland, and Hungary, including *Margie*, *Nimrod*, *Atlanta Review*, *Crab Orchard Review*, *The Chattahoochee Review*, *Slask*, and *Akcent*.

GROWING UP POLACK

My dad spent four and a half years in Buchenwald concentration camp in Nazi Germany. My mother spent two and a half years as a slave laborer in various camps there. When the war ended, she weighed 125, he weighed 75. After the war they couldn't return to Poland, so they lived in refugee camps till they received permission to come to the U.S. They made the trip in June 1951 on the *General Taylor*, a troop ship.

Recently, I found photos in *The New York Times* archive of that same ship taken the day my parents arrived.

My parents weren't in the pictures, but they must have brushed against the people who were. They must have stood in line with them, waited for food with them, closed their eyes and prayed with them. Together they worried about what it would be like in America.

My parents and the others on the *General Taylor* were all displaced persons; country-less refugees, who had lost their parents and grandparents, their families and their homes, their churches and their names. It had all been left behind, buried in the great European graveyard that stretched from the English Channel to the Urals and from the Baltic Sea to the Mediterranean. Yet here they all were on this former troop ship, coming to start a new life in America.

After working in the farms around Buffalo, New York, to pay off the cost of their passage, my parents settled in Chicago, in the Humboldt Park area with a lot of other Poles, displaced persons, refugees, and survivors. One of the things they soon found out was that they weren't Poles and they definitely weren't Polish Americans. I never heard those words growing up. What I did hear in the streets, at school, and in the stores was *Polack*. My parents were Polacks and so was I.

We were the people to whom nobody wanted to rent a room or hire or help. We were the "wretched refuse" of somebody else's shore, dumped now on the shore of Lake Michigan. Most people we met in America wished we'd go back to where we came from, and that we'd take the rest of the Polacks with us.

As a result, if anyone had ever asked me when I was growing up, "Do you want to be a Polish-American writer or teacher or doctor?" I would have told him to take a hike, but not in words so gentle.

Polish-Americans, I felt, were losers. They worked in factories when they could get jobs. They were rag-and-bone men leading horse-drawn wagons through the alleys of Chicago. They went door to door selling bits of string and light bulbs. They didn't know how to drive cars or make phone calls or eat in restaurants. They stood on street corners with pieces of paper in their hands trying to get Americans to help them find the address printed on the paper, mumbling *"Proszę, Pana"* (please, sir) or *"Proszę, Pani"* (please, lady).

When I was a child, I thought that Polacks didn't know how to do anything while Americans knew how to do everything. Americans knew how to be happy. They could go to zoos, museums, planetariums, and movies. They could stroll freely through the great American, sunshiny-bright world like so many smiling Bing Crosbys, singing "Pennies from Heaven" as they strolled, believing every word of its chorus: *Every time it rains, it rains pennies from heaven.*

Americans could go to restaurants and order meals and not get into arguments with waiters about the price of a hamburger. They could go on picnics and not lose their children or their children's balloons. Americans could go to weddings and dance waltzes without ripping their pants, without falling down, without getting into fights.

Americans could laugh at the jokes Milton Berle told on TV and know what they meant. He could deadpan the punch line, "Sure, the lady was from Missouri," and Americans would roll in the aisles till they busted a gut. They could smile and mean it, show love, concern, happiness, sorrow, sadness. And all at the right time!

Polish-Americans, it seemed, were hobbled.

I actually believed there were places we couldn't go. When I was a boy growing up in Chicago, I never knew anyone who ever went to a professional ball game. This despite the fact I lived a short bus ride from Wrigley Field and Comiskey Park. It was as if there were written restrictions somewhere that no one had shown us, but we knew by heart anyway. Polacks could not go to ball games, or museums, or zoos. Ever! I'm sure now much of this was simply the result of growing up in a working-class neighborhood where the idea of even one night at a ballgame was an extravagance or if we simply believed it was against the laws of society. I realize now, that most of our neighbors and my family could simply not afford these things, but at that time I had the feeling that Poles simply by virtue of being Polacks just didn't do such things. Only Americans.

And nothing ever seemed to go right for us. Washing machines would break down for no reason. Repairmen were always crooks or incompetents. Shirts—even brand new ones—would be stained or missing a button. My father once spent what seemed like a year working on a drain pipe that wouldn't be mended, no matter how hard he struggled with his mismatched wrenches.

I remember one time when my mother went into a dime store and tried to bargain down the price of a Lincoln Log set. Of course, that didn't work either. Nothing worked. Our Polack fate was hard karma. And there was no one to tell you how to change that hard karma. Everyone was in the same boat and trying to find some way to keep afloat and survive. The Oleniechaks, the Popowchaks, the Budzas, the Czarneks, the Pitlaks, the Bronowickis, the Stupkas, the Milczareks, the Guzlowskis—all of us on Evergreen Street were drowning in the kind of hard karma that only the displaced persons, the dumb Polacks, knew.

I started running away from this hard karma, as soon as I could, and for most of my life I've been running. Not all the Polish kids I knew were like that, of course. I had a friend who held tight to his Polishness, and to hear us talk about our youth, you'd think we grew up in separate countries. He actually went to Polish School on Saturdays! Whereas I would sooner have worked a twenty-hour day at the kind of hard labor my parents knew in the Nazi camps. I didn't want anything to do with the Polack curse—I wanted to be an unmistakable and anonymous American.

Even though my first language was Polish and I spoke it exclusively until I went to kindergarten, I can barely speak a word of it now. I consciously fought to strip all of that away, and for the most part I succeeded. When I tried speaking Polish to my aged mother, she'd always say the same thing. "Johnny, please stop. You're hurting my ears."

So why am I now writing essays and poems about being a Polish-American?

I think a lot of it comes from who my parents were. If my parents had been Illinois farm people raising soy beans and corn, I don't think I would be writing about them. I would be like every other poet in America: writing about the weather or what it's like driving a big car west or east on I-80. But instead my parents were people who had been struck dumb and quivering by history.

My mom used to like to say, "*Slach traffi.*" I don't know if this is strictly a Polish idiom, but I believe it means "the truncheon or billy club will find you." Maybe it's something the Nazis used to say in the camps when they were beating the prisoners to get them to move faster when pushing cement-filled wheelbarrows. But whatever it means literally, here is what it means to me: shit happens, and not only does shit happen, it will find you no matter what you do, or where you run, and it will not just get in your way, it will cover you and smother you and kill you.

I grew up with people who had seen their families murdered, babies bayoneted, friends castrated and then shot to death. My mom saw her sister's legs ripped apart by broken glass as she struggled through a narrow window to escape from the Nazis.

And it seemed to them that no one cared.

Even if the world doesn't want to read what I write, I feel that I have to write about my parents' lives. My father never went to school and could barely write his name. My mother had two years of formal education. I feel that I have to tell the stories they would write themselves if they could. For the last thirty years I have been writing about their lives, and I sometimes think that I am not only writing about their lives, but also about the lives of all forgotten voiceless refugees, displaced persons, and survivors. All of history's Polacks.

Darrel Alejandro Holnes

HERITAGE STATEMENT:

I was born to Panamanian parents that immigrated to Houston, Texas, during the dictatorship of General Manuel Noriega.

AUTHOR BIO:

Darrel Alejandro Holnes is a writer and producer. He and his work have appeared in *Callaloo*, *The Caribbean Writer*, the *Best American Poetry* blog, *Poetry*, the Kennedy Center for the Arts College Theater Festival, *TIME* Magazine, and elsewhere. He is a Cave Canem and Bread Loaf Fellow with  degrees in creative writing from the University of Michigan and the University of Houston. He currently teaches at Rutgers University and resides in New York, New York. Follow him on Twitter @daholnes.

TO THE GENTRIFIED MAN WHO AVENGES: PANAMÁ 1999

for my father

I.
Dig, *Viejo*. Lay the foundation
beneath this land bridge, resurrected
seven times to heal a world
of shifting plates and allegiances.

Dig past the jaggedly
baked dirt and see your
shadow across the mud,
your reflection in the puddles.

See the foreign men in their new country
chisel and chow down journey cakes,
pull platinum dollars from silver cents.

See them all bridge
after-death, the buried
and dig up their lost journeys,
revive their dreams, mix them

with yours. Dig a canal: a *patria*
of gringos, white tails, and *panas*.
Now yours. Dig, dark one.
Like your forefathers, you dig

but on the first piece of white land
your family has ever owned.
Third son of Adam, first to become
a man, island boy, *jamaicano*.

Dig deep with your bare hands,
we lay the foundation tomorrow.

II.
Bury the broken. Raise the crane to lower the slabs today.
Cover old scabs, bad language, frowning family photos.

Bury the cheap wedding ring, the empty ceremony
with the diamond bride your mother said lacked earth,

wasn't coal no more, only shine, she said.
Yet you married and bore

two precious stones: half-mud,
half-treasure, you did.

Bury that witch woman who cursed your union
with onions and the ashes of a centipede.

Bury the sons, half-yours, half-gutter girls who loved you,
tired of sweeping the dust of dreams so old they wrinkled and shed.

Pour the concrete, give them all graves, and give birth
to this foundation—Build a better man.

Set in the anchor bolts for this new post-war home, coat it with
asphalt so death doesn't rise through when it rains.

Gather the builders. Say a prayer quick
enough for the wind to hear

and thread it through the needle.

TÚ

In the music video it looks like Shakira is dying.

I want to die for you
        though we've just met,

give you my bones to help you stand taller
and my feet for you to walk on when yours are worn.

        This is what she sings, love
worth dying for.

Seven years ago I loved her video

and now hear its song wailing in my head
as I struggle to hear what you're saying,

a good omen at Café Adobe,
        the setting of our first date.

Make love to me on this table for two.
I don't need my flesh if I have you.

So take my body as you need,
        breaking into the garden,

a wall to keep our home countries out on the other side,

your sins washed in my old
blood and complexion.

I can be your Shakira,
your personal Jesus Christ.

Listen to my swan song gospel,
the unusual yodel in my throat,

a ballad as I nail my limbs
to this restaurant table:

*Eres tu amor. Mis ganas de reír. El adiós que no sabre decir. Porque nunca podré
vivir sin ti.*

But for this feast to nourish your body we must first pray
or at least say we believe in something.

I don't believe in this nation

but can in your naked grace, come
make me a man   of faith.

And leave your body, too, if you'd like.

In my country I dreamed of leaving
my body all the time,

the scar below my right eye,
flesh broken by soldiers

trying to scare my mother
into telling them my father's whereabouts;

my sun kiss undertone torn open to reveal
an ancestor's sinless shame

mejorando la raza
brightening our brown.

But I don't want to be whiter, just free,

sweetly delivered into dark matter,
and its boundlessness.

Redemption in shedding
incarcerating flesh.

Redemption in being reborn
a forgotten song by a Shakira fallen

in love, risen
in translation.

Frank Izaguirre

HERITAGE STATEMENT:

Frank Izaguirre's parents are Cuban exiles who came to America in the late '60s to seek better opportunities and escape the deprivations and tyranny of the Castro regime.

AUTHOR BIO:

Frank Izaguirre is yet another travel writer eager to impress you by claiming he's been to all nine continents and more countries than any other travel writer ever. He recently overcame a battle with cancer and is now totally focused on getting as much of his writing out into the world as he can, because he should be dead. For more self deprecation, self aggrandizement, and possibly even a few good ideas about travel, follow him on Twitter @FrankMIzaguirre.

GROWTH IN THE GARDEN

Much of my childhood was spent searching for animals in my Cuban mother's garden. Any time of day I could find tiny brown anoles scurrying everywhere, and the green anoles that blended perfectly into the foliage. The geckos in the carport sometimes snuck into the house, and I would cup my hands around them and bring them back outside. Even black ring-necked snakes sometimes came out at dusk, slinking beneath my footsteps and further into the grass.

But the knight anoles were my favorite. They were the length of my forearm and bright green, with a thick yellow mustache stripe and another beneath their necks. I read about them in an Audubon guide my mother bought me. I learned they came from Cuba too. They were always high in the trees, but I remember easily picking out their slender profiles. My mother told me I had a special skill for finding them. When I was outside, I would often blurt out, "Knight anole!" and point up. Then I'd spend the next few minutes carefully explaining to whatever adult I was with which branch they were on and how they could see them.

I searched for them almost daily, and I named them. I could tell each individual apart from the subtle differences in the shapes of their bodies. The smallest one I named Spike, because I wanted a friend with a name like Spike. I saw him the most, usually stretched out on the boughs of the live oak. In truth, I didn't know Spike's gender, but I imagined he was a boy, like me.

Even when he saw me first and hid his body on the opposite side of the oak's limbs, I could still see the tips of his claws clinging over the edge of the branch. He would peek an eye over the edge to check if I was still there, and then hide again, maybe hoping I hadn't seen him.

But I would stay there watching him, proud that I was as good at spotting him as he was at spotting me.

In my elementary school, we could bring our pets on St. Francis Day. The Father would bless them by sprinkling each pet with holy water. Most kids brought their dogs and cats, and some brought rabbits and macaws. I brought a photograph of Spike my mother gave me. Some of the other children told me I should have caught him and brought him in a cage, if I really liked him so much.

I wondered if I should have caught Spike. After all, isn't that what young boys do with the small animals they admire? I thought I could catch the knight anoles if I wanted, but I never did. I enjoyed just watching them, knowing they were there, and searching for them amid the millions of leaves in the garden. The more the garden grew, the more challenging the game became.

One day, while walking through the garden looking for knight anoles, I saw Spike lying on the ground near the buttresses of the live oak. There was a wide hole in his neck with dried blood around it. He did not scurry away when I knelt down near him. I ran inside and told my mother. When she came out and saw him, her jaw clenched. She told me it had probably been the roofers who had been working near the oak that day. "They must have shot him with a nail gun," she explained.

I couldn't understand why someone would shoot Spike with a nail gun. I watched him until past dark through the cloudy eyes of a child, hoping that at any moment he'd climb up the oak and hide behind one of its branches, peeking back out at me. When I found him lying in the same spot the next day, I cradled his limp body in my small hands and buried him in the pot of one of my mother's plants. I didn't name any more knight anoles.

THE GUANÁBANA TREE

When I told my mother Guanábana had become my favorite fruit, she planted a tree in the garden of her Miami home. I later learned she disliked Guanábana as a child. In Cuba, my grandmother would often mix the sour pulp with water and sugar, the only food my mother remembers being consistently available.

Now, her Guanábana has difficulty growing because it's too tropical. When even a mild cold front passes through, she wraps a thick blanket around its base to keep it from freezing. One spring, knowing I was coming to visit, she took the tree's bark in both hands and wished that it would bear. It may have been a coincidence, she admits, but the tree flowered for the first time the week before I arrived. When the spiny green fruits ripened, she meticulously pulled out the large black seeds, sifting the gooey, white flesh through her fingers, and made milkshakes for my father, sister, and me. Our bellies were so full, we all sat around and talked about how much we loved Guanábana.

I know the name of the Guanábana in English, but I prefer to say it in Spanish.

Mohja Kahf

HERITAGE STATEMENT:

Poet and scholar Mohja Kahf was born in Damascus, Syria, in 1967. Her family moved to the United States in 1971, and Kahf grew up in the Midwest.

AUTHOR BIO:

Mohja Kahf earned a PhD in comparative literature from Rutgers University and is the author of the poetry collection *Emails from Scheherazad* (University Press of Florida, 2003) and the novel *The Girl in the Tangerine Scarf* (Public Affairs, 2006). Kahf co-writes a column on sexuality for the website *Muslim Wake Up*. Her nonfiction work includes *Western Representation of the Muslim Woman: From Termagant to Odalisque* (1999). Kahf is a professor of English at the University of Arkansas.

MY GRANDMOTHER WASHES HER FEET IN THE SINK OF THE BATHROOM AT SEARS

My grandmother puts her feet in the sink
of the bathroom at Sears
to wash them in the ritual washing for prayer,
wudu, because she has to pray in the store or miss
the mandatory prayer time for Muslims.
She does it with great poise, balancing
herself with one plump matronly arm
against the automated hot-air hand dryer,
after having removed her support knee-highs
and laid them aside, folded in thirds,
and given me her purse and her packages to hold
so she can accomplish this august ritual
and get back to the ritual of shopping for housewares.
Respectable Sears matrons shake their heads and frown
as they notice what my grandmother is doing,
an affront to American porcelain,
a contamination of American Standards
by something foreign and unhygienic
requiring civic action and possible use of disinfectant spray.
They fluster about and flutter their hands and I can see
a clash of civilizations brewing in the Sears bathroom.
My grandmother, though she speaks no English,
catches their meaning and her look in the mirror says,
I have washed my feet over Iznik tile in Istanbul
with water from the world's ancient irrigation systems,
I have washed my feet in the bathhouses of Damascus
over painted bowls imported from China
among the best families of Aleppo,
and if you Americans knew anything
about civilization and cleanliness,
you'd make wider wash bins. Anyway,

my grandmother knows one culture—the right one,
as do these matrons of the Middle West. For them,
my grandmother might as well have been squatting
in the mud over a rusty tin in vaguely tropical squalor,
Mexican or Middle Eastern, it doesn't matter which,
when she lifts her well-groomed foot and puts it over the edge.
"You can't do that," one of the women protests,
turning to me, "Tell her she can't do that."
"We wash our feet five times a day,"
my grandmother declares hotly in Arabic.
"My feet are cleaner than their sink.
Worried about their sink, are they? I
should worry about my feet!"
My grandmother nudges me, "Go on, tell them."

Standing between the door and the mirror, I can see
at multiple angles, my grandmother and the other shoppers,
all of them decent and good-hearted women, diligent
in cleanliness, grooming, and decorum.
Even now my grandmother, not to be rushed,
is delicately drying her pumps with tissues from her purse.
For my grandmother always wears well-turned pumps
that match her purse, I think in case someone
from one of the best families of Aleppo
should run into her—here, in front of the Kenmore display.
I smile at the Midwestern women
as if my grandmother has just said something lovely about them
and shrug at my grandmother as if they
had just apologized through me.
No one is fooled, but I
hold the door open for everyone

and we all emerge on the sales floor
and lose ourselves in the great common ground
of housewares on markdown.

Alan King

HERITAGE STATEMENT:

My parents grew up in the Chinapoo Village neighborhood of Morvant, Trinidad. My mom left to go live with her sister in Canada. My dad immigrated with my grandmother and his sisters to Washington, D.C. Both my parents left Trinidad for better opportunities. My dad is a self-employed electrician. My mom is an office manager for an orthopedic practice in D.C.

I was born in 1981 at Holy Cross Hospital in Silver Spring, Maryland. My parents raised me in Fort Washington, Maryland, where they currently live.

AUTHOR BIO:

Alan King is an author, poet, and journalist who lives in the D.C. metropolitan area.

He writes about art and domestic issues on his blog at www.alanwking.com. In addition to teaching at Duke Ellington School of the Arts, he's also the senior program director at the D.C. Creative Writing Workshop. King is a Cave Canem Fellow, an alumnus of the VONA Workshops sponsored by Voices of Our Nations Arts Foundation, and a graduate of the Stonecoast MFA Low-Residency Program at the University of Southern Maine. He's a two-time Pushcart Prize nominee and was also nominated twice for a Best of the Net selection. His first collection of poems, entitled *Drift,* was published in 2012 (Willow Books). His poems have appeared widely in such journals as *Boston Literary Magazine, Boxcar Poetry Review, Drunken Boat, Indiana Review, The Journal of Contemporary Literature, Little Patuxent Review, Naugatuck River Review, Rattle,* and *Umbrella.*

THE HOSTESS

She starts with oil. She simmers garlic
before adding curry. *Got to cook it real good,*
she says, *or else it'll mess up your stomach.*

Mom adds sugar to blacken the already dark
tint left on what pops and sizzles, what mixes
in the meat steaming in a bubbling bath of cumin,
turmeric and cayenne pepper.

Mom doesn't cook curry a lot, just on days
when my dad comes home tired, when each day's
an opponent that leaves him bruised
like the bags of fruit he brings her.

One time mom wrapped her arms around his neck,
and dad said, *You only love me for my mangoes.*
They both laughed when mom said,
You gotta bring mangoes home more often.

He'd tell mom about the days
when his drill burnt out, when his truck got a flat
in the rain or didn't start,
when days seemed to plot against him,
as if he was a fighter
past his prime, unwilling to lie
down and throw the match.

And there's mom's curry
lingering in every room opening the house
for his return. Dad enters her scent
that calls him to the kitchen, ready to put back
what the ring takes out of him.

THE LISTENER

for Marilyn King, "Mops" (1949–2009)

A woman in the next aisle,
laughs among the milk
and orange juice.

Laughter stops the words in her throat,
so no matter what, they won't finish the joke.
She laughs like my aunt "Mops,"

the one who was ready to drive
from D.C. to Baltimore to scorch my boss
with her fire-bottle words
when I told her what I made as a reporter
forced to work weekends.

She got her nickname, "Mops,"
from the Mopsy biscuits she loved
as a girl back in Trinidad.

Every Friday, I'd snatch a stack
of newspapers from my job and race down
to her house where the aromas
of pound cake and curry
fought each other like siblings.

I'd drop off a few copies at the salon.
She'd smile, *See how my nephew all ova'*
the front page, so! She'd keep a paper
to read my articles on city council corruption
and displaced east Baltimore residents
before she fell asleep.

If I was stressed from work, she'd always say,
Them can't play sailor and 'fraid powder.

When she died from cancer,
I thought I lost her forever.

But she's an aisle over,
laughing
behind the spice shelf.

THE WATCH

Like a magician's assistant
in a prop box, my watch
vanished from a gym locker.

Its Timex analog glowing hands
sliced at each other the way
dad and I crossed words,
when I started smelling my musk
and outgrew the lectures.

It kept kicking despite the gang
of years scuffing its silver band,
scratching its face.

The *tick, tick, tick* of seconds throbbing
the metronome of persistence
that woke my Trini parents, pushing them
to persevere despite coworkers' jokes
about foreigners, while providing
for their three kids.

It was dad's timepiece, a lesson
in patience the minute and hour taught me,
swinging their bright stems
like sabers in a lazy light battle.

It was the watch he sported
when he took mom to the movies.
His English Leather cologne,
splashed across it, a fragrant stain
that followed me when he passed it on

until that day after gym class
popping up years later, the absence
still worn under replacements.

BRINK

In an Eastern restaurant,
a server became a stone
when asked for a refill on Sprite.
Closing my eyes, my nose remembers

the seduction of turmeric and
mustard seed, my tongue tingles
of cayenne and rice flavored
with cumin and mint leaves.

In that restaurant where I won't return,
a server brought me half a glass of Sprite.
The sound of glass slammed on a table
made me think of gavels.

*Everyone knows black people
demand high but tip low*, a friend says.
The owner's expression dark as a judge's robe.
I closed my eyes and I thought

of a jury with everyone like him.
What my nose and mouth
once knew disappears. I could be
at my aunt's table in Trinidad,

devouring dumplings and lentil soup,
guzzling a cherry Kola Champagne—
far away from this place that reads
my dark skin like a police blotter.

Jenna Le

HERITAGE STATEMENT:

My parents immigrated from Vietnam to the U.S. shortly after the Fall of Saigon. They were among the hundreds of thousands of Vietnam War refugees who fled their native shores by boat in the ensuing chaos, for fear of being imprisoned in "reeducation camps" by the victorious North Vietnamese government. After brief stays in New Jersey and New Mexico, my parents eventually settled in the suburbs of Minneapolis, Minnesota, where my father started working as a college professor and where I was born and raised in the 1980s.

AUTHOR BIO:

Jenna Le's first book, *Six Rivers* (New York Quarterly Books, 2011), was a Small Press Distribution Poetry Bestseller. Her writing has appeared in *32 Poems*, *AGNI Online*, *Barrow Street*, *Bellevue Literary Review*, *The Massachusetts Review*, and *Post Road*. She has been a Pharos Poetry Competition winner, a *Minnetonka Review* Editor's Prize winner, a Pushcart Prize nominee, and a PEN Emerging Writers Award nominee.

TRICK

America, you're
the Halloween costume
my immigrant father
rented and never returned.

Dad clambered inside
your baggy interior
because he wanted his share
of the season's sweet treats.

With your reptilian tail,
Dad batted away
his rivals and scampered
on to his goal.

Dressed up in you,
my father seduced
my starry-eyed mother
behind a tall hedge.

But now the costume shop
is demanding you back.
He calls our house daily,
ringing the phone off its hook.

MOM'S COCKS

Mom grew up beside the Perfume River in Vietnam,
in a brick house overrun by chickens.
Those horny-footed fowl were always
rubbing their feather-padded genitals
against sofa legs and children's shoes
as if they were fit to burst. Mom laughs

as she tells me how they ground
their pelvises against her leather sandal,
stuporous with misdirected lust—
How strange that she
is talking to me about sex
in this casual way. She's returning to her roots

as a child who lived among
unmannered beasts. And I, through hearing her words,
am returning there with her: I
am the aggressive rooster; I'm the hens
cowering behind the outhouse; I'm the much-abused,
much-abraded, Size Four shoe.

INHERITANCE

the dead
who gave me life
give me this
—Lorine Niedecker

I have my ancestors to thank
for the skin between my stretch marks:
the yellow-tinged and paper-thin covering
that I wear on my gregarious cheeks and in
my secret armpits.

No other heirlooms have lasted.
Nothing else tangible, nothing else that mists
when, despite your awe, you breathe on its
semiprecious surface. Only my yellow body fits
the bill.

I have last century's war-mongers
to thank for this sorry fact:
politicians, children trained to kill,
and an ocean, stormy-yellow-black.

Li-Young Lee

HERITAGE STATEMENT:

Li-Young Lee was born in 1957 in Jakarta, Indonesia, to Chinese parents. His father had been a personal physician to Mao Zedong while in China, and relocated the family to Indonesia, where he helped found Gamaliel University. In 1959, the Lee family fled the country to escape anti-Chinese sentiment and after a five-year trek through Hong Kong, Macau, and Japan, they settled in the United States in 1964.

AUTHOR BIO:

Lee attended the Universities of Pitts-  burgh and Arizona, and SUNY–Brockport. He has taught at several universities, including Northwestern and the University of Iowa. He is the author of *The Winged Seed: A Remembrance* (Simon & Schuster, 1995); *Behind My Eyes* (W. W. Norton, 2008); *Book of My Nights* (BOA Editions, Ltd., 2001), which won the 2002 William Carlos Williams Award; *The City in Which I Love You* (BOA Editions, Ltd., 1990), which was the 1990 Lamont Poetry Selection; and *Rose* (BOA Editions, Ltd., 1986), which won the Delmore Schwartz Memorial Poetry Award. His other work includes *Breaking the Alabaster Jar: Conversations with Li-Young Lee* (edited by Earl G. Ingersoll, BOA Editions, Ltd., 2006), a collection of twelve interviews with Lee at various stages of his artistic development; and *The Winged Seed: A Remembrance* (Simon and Schuster, 1995), a memoir which received an American Book Award from the Before Columbus Foundation. He has been the recipient of a fellowship from the Academy of American Poets, a Lannan Literary Award, a Whiting Writer's Award, the PEN Oakland/Josephine Miles Award, the I. B. Lavan Award, three Pushcart Prizes, and grants from the Illinois Arts Council, the Commonwealth of Pennsylvania, the Pennsylvania Council on the Arts, and the National Endowment for the Arts, as well as a Guggenheim Foundation fellowship. In 1998, he received an honorary DHL from SUNY–Brockport.

ARISE, GO DOWN

It wasn't the bright hems of the Lord's skirts
that brushed my face and I opened my eyes
to see from a cleft in rock His backside;

it's a wasp perched on my left cheek. I keep
my eyes closed and stand perfectly still
in the garden till it leaves me alone,

not to contemplate how this century
ends and the next begins with no one
I know having seen God, but to wonder

why I get through most days unscathed, though I
live in a time when it might be otherwise,
and I grow more fatherless each day.

For years now I have come to conclusions
without my father's help, discovering
on my own what I know, what I don't know,

and seeing how one cancels the other.
I've become a scholar of cancellations.
Here, I stand among my father's roses

and see that what punctures outnumbers what
consoles, the cruel and the tender never
make peace, though one climbs, though one descends

petal by petal to the hidden ground
no one owns. I see that which is taken
away by violence or persuasion.

The rose announces on earth the kingdom
of gravity. A bird cancels it.
My eyelids cancel the bird. Anything

might cancel my eyes: distance, time, war.
My father said, *Never take your both eyes
off of the world*, before he rocked me.

All night we waited for the knock
that would have signaled, *All clear, come now*;
it would have meant escape; it never came.

I didn't make the world I leave you with,
he said, and then, being poor, he left me
only this world, in which there is always

a family waiting in terror
before they're rended, this world wherein a man
might arise, go down, and walk along a path

and pause and bow to roses, roses
his father raised, and admire them, for one moment
unable, thank God, to see in each and
every flower the world cancelling itself.

I ASK MY MOTHER TO SING

She begins, and my grandmother joins her.
Mother and daughter sing like young girls.
If my father were alive, he would play
his accordion and sway like a boat.

I've never been in Peking, or the Summer Palace,
nor stood on the great Stone Boat to watch
the rain begin on Kuen Ming Lake, the picnickers
running away in the grass.

But I love to hear it sung;
how the waterlilies fill with rain until
they overturn, spilling water into water,
then rock back, and fill with more.

Both women have begun to cry.
But neither stops her song.

Joseph O. Legaspi

HERITAGE STATEMENT:

I was born in Manila, Philippines, in 1971. My family and I immigrated to Los Angeles in 1984. It was a tumultuous time in the Philippines. The resistance against President Marcos's regime was cresting, fueled by the assassination of Benigno Aquino Jr., the exiled leader of the government opposition. Along with the political upheavals, employment was scarce. My father worked abroad in Saudi Arabia for a few years to save for our passage to the U.S. My parents decided to immigrate to create opportunities for their five children.

AUTHOR BIO:

Joseph O. Legaspi's debut poetry collec-  tion *Imago* was published by CavanKerry Press in 2007. His chapbook, *Subways*, was published by Thrush Press in 2013. His poems have appeared and/or are forthcoming in *American Life in Poetry*, *From the Fishhouse*, *Gay & Lesbian Review*, *jubilat*, *The Normal School*, *PEN International*, *Smartish Pace*, *Spoon River Poetry Review*, and the anthologies *Language for a New Century: Contemporary Poetry from the Middle East, Asia, and Beyond* (W. W. Norton, 2008) and *Tilting the Continent* (New Rivers Press, 2000), among others. Legaspi resides in New York City and holds degrees from Loyola Marymount University and the Graduate Creative Writing Program at New York University. A recipient of a New York Foundation for the Arts (NYFA) Poetry Fellowship, he is one of the co-founders of Kundiman, a non-profit organization dedicated to serving Asian American poets (www.kundiman.org).

ALASKA

That summer back in the desert,
I had grown too big for my family.
In that two-bedroom apartment
which squeezed seven adults
I was one more stone
thrown in a jar filled to the brim
with water. My college books spilled
out of closets, my pine cone collection piled
up between intersections of furniture,
and my clothes baked in their trunk.
Nights, I slept on the couch,
often dreaming of birds
and skeletons, skeletal
angels, as my brother turned
his heavy, comatose body
on an air mattress
below me. That summer
I spent hours cramped
in the bathroom, reading, just
me, Kierkegaard, Faulkner
and Gide. Life traveled
like a boat
in the middle of a lake.
My mother talked slowly,
my sisters dressed slowly,
the ceiling was too low,
too little room to visit.
And I was tired of the same
reel of scenes,
of the women gathered
around the table, cutting

bok choy and tripe,
my father asleep, to be
awakened and driven
to work at 10:30 p.m. and me,
slumped on the couch, watching
a documentary on Alaska,
the final frontier
of dog sleds, Eskimos,
and big chunks of ice
splitting away from glaciers,
crashing into the frigid ocean.

MY FATHER IN THE NIGHT

My father sleeps when the city rages
around him and rises to work the graveyard
shift in the linen department of a hospital.
Boxed in his heavy-curtained room,
the glass window shut,
we would think him dead if not for his
snoring, amplified by the thick, stagnant air
which holds the sound before it
dissipates and is absorbed by the walls.
Before he leaves for work,
my father sits at the table, eating
his meat and rice, his children
bewildered by the sight of him.
With boiled eggs and bread slices in a brown bag,
he steals away into the urban darkness
while his wife stumbles into bed, alone,
rearranging the disheveled sheets.
        And my father in the night
changes the sheets on hundreds
of hospital beds, the kind where he laid
when his skin was like potato-sack burlap
from dialysis and chemotherapy.
He removes the soiled pillow cases, replacing
them with starched ones. He puts on the white
sheet, unfolding it in the air like a woman's
skirt, settling it down onto the mattress.

THE IMMIGRANTS' SON

In my house, nuzzled in leafy suburbia,
ants nest on the chinaware and chip away
the designs; seafood remains frost-bitten
in the freezer; pubic hair thrives under the dampness
of mats and towels; and my grandmother's overripe
bitter squashes burst in the backyard,
dropping to the ground, uneaten.

I give you my mother,
mourning our adulthood
like any other deaths.
She holds nightly vigils
watching shows she doesn't care for.
Forget it. She has given up on prayers;
she doesn't read books. She worries
about her sons chasing white women,
about her daughters being chased
by white men, or worse, black men.
My mother misses the splintered Old World
house where my grandmother resided
upstairs with her unmarried children
and in the apartment rooms below lived
her married children and their children,
families sleeping side by side
on beds pushed together.

And I give you a memory
of that year when my aunt gave birth
to her first born: twin stillbirth boys,
grayish, mummified cupids.
They were placed in a pickled egg jar

and buried in the dark, musty earth
beneath our protruding house,
creaking heavily under too much weight.

Looking out at the backyard, leaning
against a weakened wall, a splinter
throbbing in the palm of my hand, I wonder
whether I would find the jar half-filled with
brittle baby bones
if I dug deep enough where
the next overripe bitter squash falls.

THE RED SWEATER

slides down into my body, soft
lambswool, what everybody
in school is wearing, and for me
to have it my mother worked twenty
hours at the fast-food joint.
The sweater fits like a lover,
sleeves snug, thin on the waist.
As I run my fingers through the knit,
I see my mother over the hot oil in the fryers
dipping a strainer full of stringed potatoes.
In a twenty-hour period my mother waits
on hundreds of customers: she pushes
each order under ninety seconds, slaps
the refried beans she mashed during prep time,
the lull before rush hours, onto steamed tortillas,
the room's pressing heat melting her make-up.
Every clean strand of weave becomes a question.
How many burritos can one make in a continuous day?
How many pounds of onions, lettuce and tomatoes
pass through the slicer? How do her wrists
sustain the scraping, lifting and flipping
of meat patties?   And twenty
hours are merely links
in the chain of days startlingly similar,
that begin in the blue morning with my mother
putting on her polyester uniform, which,
even when it's newly washed, smells
of mashed beans and cooked ground beef.

David Licata

HERITAGE STATEMENT:

My mother, Neva Crovatin, was born in 1925 in Trieste, Italy, a city with a complicated modern history. In the spring of 1945 the city was occupied by Allied troops, and it was sometime during that year that she met an American GI named Joseph Licata, a child of Sicilian immigrants who spoke Italian. On April 14, 1946, they married in Trieste and four months later Joseph Licata received an honorable discharge. The couple came to the U.S., moving in with his parents in Brooklyn, New York. In the late 1950s the couple relocated to the state across the Hudson River and early one August morning in 1961, David Licata was born in Margaret Hague Maternity Hospital, Jersey City, New Jersey.

AUTHOR BIO:

David Licata is a writer and a filmmaker. His fiction and nonfiction have appeared in *Boston Literary Magazine*, *Hitotoki*, *The Literary Review*, *Sole Literary Journal*, *Word Riot*, and others. His films have shown on PBS stations across the country and screened at festivals all over the world, including New Directors/New Films (curated by The Film Society of Lincoln Center and MoMA), the Tribeca Film Festival, and dozens of others. He lives in New York City.

THE WOLF IS IN THE KITCHEN

After we ate the cake, we played Twister in Steve's playroom, which is a basement with paneling, and that's when the teasing began. A group of boys that weren't invited to the sleepover were beside an open window and we couldn't see them but we knew who they were and who they were making fun of.

"When's the flood?" George Nardini said to Paul Francolino because Paul wore hand-me-downs and all his pants were too short. "It tastes better with salt, Walt," Patrick Jamison said to Walt Gillombardo because Walt chewed on the collar of his shirt a lot. We all lived within two blocks of 10th Street and Central Avenue, where Steve lived, and we all played stickball and football and skully in the street together and we teased each other like this all the time and it didn't mean anything and tomorrow Paul might say to Patrick, "Pick me a winner," because Patrick always has his finger up his nose and Walt might say to George, "Georgie Porgie pudding and pie, kissed the girls and made them cry" because his name happened to be George. It was all just silly and never meant anything ever.

My cousin Dom was with them. Dom is a year older than the rest of us and he and the others went to Thomas Edison public and me, Steve, Paul, and Walter were all in the same grade at Holy Rosary Academy and that's why we were inside and they were outside. It was a Holy Rosary sleepover, not a block sleepover.

Dom said to me in a high-pitched voice, "Dave, dhere iz a volf in dhe chicken." This was new and the others with him laughed loudly, then they mimicked him.

Dom's mother and my mother are sisters. They both came from Trieste, which is in northern Italy. Our mothers look alike and make the same food and both speak English poorly and with the same thick accent. They are sometimes mistaken for each other, but my mother is a little older and heavier.

Steve's mother went to the window and said, "That's enough. Now you boys shoo before I call your mothers," and closed the window and drew the small curtains, but they didn't stop.

"Just ignore them, David," Steve's mother said to me. Everyone else calls me Dave, only Steve's mother calls me David. Steve's mother smokes and she put the radio on and my favorite song was playing, "Crystal Blue Persuasion," but we could still hear them.

"Dhere iz a volf in dhe chicken." Dom was making fun of my mother, of her accent and how she would sometimes say chicken when she meant kitchen and kitchen when she meant chicken. *There is a wolf in the kitchen* didn't make much sense either, but it made a little more sense once you knew that. But what really didn't make any sense at all was how Dom could be making fun of my mother like that because he was also making fun of his mother, too.

I listened with all my might to the words of "Crystal Blue Persuasion" because I was trying not to hear Dom and the others, and though I had sung along with it many times before and knew all the words by heart and knew what the individual words meant, I didn't understand it; for the first time the song didn't make any sense.

Jane Lin

HERITAGE STATEMENT:

My father came from Taiwan to New York in 1966 for a job training as a doctor. My mother arrived a few months later with my brother and sister. They planned to return to Taiwan, but Nixon's visit to China, my brother's asthma, my birth, and a good job kept them here.

AUTHOR BIO:

Jane Lin is a poet and a software engineer for an environmental consulting company. She received her MFA from New York University's Creative Writing Program. Her honors include a Kundiman Fellowship and scholarships from Bread Loaf Writers' Conference and Taos Summer Writers' Conference. Jane lives in Northern New Mexico with her husband, daughter, and three cats. She was born and raised on Long Island, NY. Poems have recently appeared in *Duende*, *Nimrod*, *Spillway*, and *The Wide Shore*. Her first book, *Day of Clean Brightness*, is forthcoming from 3: A Taos Press.

ANCESTRY

1.
I remember my father's mother,
the skin stretched over
where her right eye once was.

She was as small as me, and her back curved
as my father's curves.

I did not cry when I heard she died, I said
I was sorry to my father.

2.
Dry snow eddies in the curve of a mountain road,
vanishes into January like Grandfather to rock face.

Steam cloud streams from factory like a derelict
train still urging. Dissolves in the rise, the passage of time.

Two coyotes break into yips in the lot below. One slips
into canyon scrub, the other stands for minutes under lamplight.

3.
I can count on one hand the times I saw my father's mother,
my mother's father. The distance of a continent and ocean

has shrunk little. My last trip, I went alone. Mitzi's daughter!
my aunt shouted in Grandfather's ear. We swept the ancestral home,

the family altar. In the photo he stands like a stranger
though my arm is around his shoulder.

4.
The countdown has begun for my daughter who remembers
Ah Mah. Remembers a trip to New York with cousins she loves,

an open casket, sitting for a long time while people spoke
in languages she did and did not know.

In a photo my father holds her before the weeping cherry
full of blooms, my mother touches her cheek.

HOUSE RULES

1.
Once there were neighbors my mother spoke to,
one with dead sons in uniform on the wall.
She liked to talk, housebound with her smoky shuffle.
I was my mother's timer, sent to retrieve her if kept too long.

I crossed the street after school once and found her alone.
Waiting for my mother, we folded socks into soft, lopsided balls
I carried as she leaned on my arm. "I was young and didn't
know better when I started smoking. Don't you go wrong."

2.
When you are told to set the table, you set the table. Call Father
to dinner. An ambulance sirens you to a window, and you watch
the flicker of lights, the gurney silvered then shadowed then departed.

The neighbor   (you know her name, *Gloria*)
                    lies in her hospital gown, her peace bed,
while you are in school, and the possibility of disobedience
will not occur to you for fifteen years, when what was improper
becomes proper, the impulse to press a hand, to speak, insist—

I will see you.

3.
And you, Grandfather.
                    Twenty-eight and still I did not insist
when my mother, your daughter, said *time*, said *money*, said *ocean*.
Said *shame* to Eldest Uncle if I attended while his eldest son did not,
the grandson who by tradition should return. She was
embarrassed for them.

In the photo, a public grieving hall that resembled a cafeteria—
tile floor, plastic chairs, cement walls. Rough cloth hats
tented the heads of your sons and daughters and their spouses.

Middle Uncle's only son—my cousin who greeted you each morning,
spooned sugar in your rice bowl—was angry more grandchildren
did not come. Of those in America, only one, Youngest Uncle's
youngest son, sat bowed in the white shirt, the rough, unbleached vest,
shaming me in my mother's house.

Timothy Liu

HERITAGE STATEMENT:

Timothy Liu (Liu Ti Mo) was born in 1965 in San Jose, California, to parents from the Chinese mainland.

AUTHOR BIO:

Timothy Liu studied at Brigham Young University, the University of Houston, and the University of Massachusetts–Amherst. He is the author of *For Dust Thou Art* (Southern Illinois University Press, 2005); *Of Thee I Sing* (University of Georgia Press, 2004), selected by *Publishers Weekly* as a 2004 Book of the Year; *Hard Evidence* (Talisman House, 2001); *Say Goodnight* (Copper Canyon Press, 1998); *Burnt Offerings* (Copper Canyon Press, 1995); and *Vox Angelica* (Alice  James Books, 1992), which won the Poetry Society of America's Norma Farber First Book Award. Liu has also edited *Word of Mouth: An Anthology of Gay American Poetry* (Talisman House, 2000). His poems have been included in many anthologies and have appeared in such magazines and journals as *American Letters & Commentary, BOMB, Grand Street, Kenyon Review, The Nation, New American Writing, The Paris Review, Ploughshares, Poetry,* and *Virginia Quarterly Review.* His journals and papers are archived in the Berg Collection at the New York Public Library. He is currently an Associate Professor at William Paterson University and on the Core Faculty at Bennington College's Writing Seminars. He lives in Manhattan.

THE REMAINS

Wuxi, China

Walking out of the new cemetery, my father
takes my hand, having just re-interred the remains
of his own father and his father's two wives—
his mother dead from TB by the time he was ten.

He takes my hand and says, *Now I can die in peace*
even if we didn't get the actual bones. Village thugs
hired by my uncle made sure the burial mounds
behind the house my father grew up in would not feel

a single shovel blade go in as they stood there
sentinel with arms crossed. My uncle's wife
had a dream that out of the grave's opened gash
demons rushed—ancestral ghosts not wanting to be

disturbed. *In less than a decade, bulldozers will come*
to take the Liu village down. My grandfather's
ashes, my grandmother's bones, my own father
walking away with two fistfuls of dirt and saying,

This will have to do. So many others have died
who've left nothing behind. I'll never come back
to this place again. My father kisses my hand,
I who've flown across twelve time zones to be here

at his side in a borrowed van, me looking out
the window at a countryside once overrun
with Japs marching West along the railroad tracks,
my father and his siblings hiding in an outhouse,

a dead horse found in the schoolyard soon after
the soldiers had gone. Your hands are so soft! I say
to my father. *So are yours*, he says. *Remember*
when it was we last held hands? I must have been

a kid, I say, maybe eight, or ten? *You were six*,
my father says. And I'm still your son, I say,
leaning into his shoulder, our hands the same size.
And I'll always be your father, my father says

before I have the chance to say another word,
my eighty-year-old father nodding off into sleep.

CLASSICAL MUSIC

On the day my mother died, I unplugged
the stereo at a time when record clubs
still sent out their selections of the month

unless you said otherwise. The mail piled up
on a table in the entry hall—an avalanche
of bills and condolences I knew I didn't

have to respond to. People would understand.
My cat stopped sitting on the amplifier,
found other sources of heat to get through

a winter punctured by the clang and hiss
of radiators built before my mother was born.
Feeding the cat, changing the litter—done

without music in the house. Months later,
I took myself to a live concert, something
by Mozart, something I remember first

having heard in the back of a '68 Rambler,
the radio on, my mother and father trying
to guess the name of the composer, the one

game I knew my mother would win. It comes
to that. One moment you're turning a dial
lit up on the dash, and the next, you're not—

Helen Losse

HERITAGE STATEMENT:

Born and raised in Joplin, Missouri, I am the daughter of an American father and an English mother. My parents met and married in England where my father (an American soldier) was stationed during WWII. My parents met through a couple, Mr. and Mrs. White, who attended the St. Augustine's Church in Swindon, the same church my mother's family attended. The Whites hosted and chaperoned socials for American soldiers and young women from their church. My parents first met at their home. Later, my father walked seven miles each way to see my mother at her home. In 1964 (when I was seventeen), my mother took my sister, brother, and me to England for six weeks to visit our grandmother, aunts, uncles, and cousins. We attended services at St. Augustine's Church and met Mr. White (his wife had already died). The trip confirmed what we always knew: we were *multi-cultural* long before that word came into vogue. Our values are American, but they are English, too.

AUTHOR BIO:

A former English teacher, Helen Losse is a Winston-Salem poet; the author of two full-length books: *Seriously Dangerous* (Main Street Rag, 2011) and *Better with Friends* (Rank Stranger Press, 2009); and three chapbooks: *Gathering the Broken Pieces* (Foothills, 2004), *Paper Snowflakes*, and *Mansion of Memory* (Rank Stranger Press, 2012). Helen's poems have been nominated twice for a Pushcart Prize and three times for a Best of the Net award, one of which was a finalist. Her book *Seriously Dangerous* was nominated  for a 2012 SIBA Book Award. Helen has a BSE from Missouri Southern State University and an MALS from Wake Forest University, where she studied creative writing and African American history and wrote her thesis, *Making All Things New: The Value of Redemptive Suffering in the Life and Works of Martin Luther King Jr.* She is the poetry editor for the online literary magazine *The Dead Mule School of Southern Literature*.

THE POWDER BOX

for Elsie R. Jones

As a child, I loved cleaning day, my mother
taking her special things from the top of her dresser
and placing them gently on the bed. She let Pam,
Michael, and me look at them, touch them.
We promised to be careful, while she worked her
soft dust cloth. Among the items
was the Powder Box that's in the bathroom now—

the one at the back of the house near the kitchen,
near the drawer where Grover Pinky slept,
when it was too cold to keep him in the hatch,
near the place where the low table held Jergens lotion
to keep our mother's soft hands soft. The box is not gold,
though it seems so to me. Perhaps, it's ivory—or stone.
I saw a matchbook inside, when last I lifted its lid.

After our parents married in Swindon,
Mummy's hometown in green and southern England,
Daddy, who was then a soldier, was sent to Belgium,
then shipped back home to Joplin. Mum followed,
taking the Queen Mary and a train ride from New York.
I digress here into the drama of an oral history,
(for I was not yet born). It seems

another American soldier, who was going home
before Daddy, offered him the box, which Daddy took,
thinking his young wife would like it. The box had
had a lid, but the soldier dropped it, when
full arms would hold no more. And still, he had
presence of mind to describe his walking route,

in the off-chance that his comrade might find
the lost piece like Daddy did, and pluck it—
retrieve it, from a foreign storm-gutter.

PRODUCT OF WAR

I am a product of war:
a product made large
largely from passion
grown strong in England
and America.

Long before egg and sperm united,
Elsie, who became my mother,
used her tiny arms
to move a capstan lathe
as part of *the war effort*.
In days of brown outs, long walks

when Earl, an American soldier
stationed in Europe—
came courting . . . They married in England,
and in America, worked long hours
to make home, (he back home,
she on this continent for the first time).

I was the growing child,
running in quiet evenings, chasing fireflies,
tasting raspberries, while they
let love make me the person I am.

Tara L. Masih

HERITAGE STATEMENT:

My father was born in Almora, Uttarakhand, which is found in northern India among the Himalayan Foothills. He came to the United States on a scholarship from the counseling and psychology department at Syracuse University, where he received his PhD. During a summer job at a Thousand Islands club along the St. Lawrence River, he met my mother, who is of European descent. They eloped and married in Syracuse, where I was born in 1963.

AUTHOR BIO:

Tara L. Masih has won multiple book awards as editor of *The Rose Metal Press Field Guide to Writing Flash Fiction* (Press 53, 2010) and *The Chalk Circle: Intercultural Prizewinning Essays*. Author of *Where the Dog Star Never Glows: Stories* (a National Best Books Award finalist), she has published fiction, poetry, and essays in numerous anthologies and literary magazines (including *The Caribbean Writer, Confrontation, Hayden's Ferry Review, The Los Angeles Review, Natural Bridge*, and *Night Train*). Several limited-edition illustrated chapbooks featuring her flash fiction have been published by The Feral Press, and awards for her work include *The Ledge Magazine*'s fiction award, finalist placing in the Reynolds Price Fiction Awards, and Pushcart Prize, *Best New American Voices*, and Best of the Web nominations. More about the author can be found at www.taramasih.com.

EXCERPTS FROM "VIGNETTES FROM A CERTAIN SOURCE"

Imagining a Hero

There is no one in the media that I can identify myself with, no star I can emulate. My hair does its own thing—curly and straight where it wishes; my skin looks wrong with Coty's rouge. One day I listen to Cher singing "Half-Breed" on my bedside radio. Through the summer and into ninth grade I wear hip-hugging bell bottoms, Indian beads, grow my hair long (though it never hangs straight). I stand in front of a mirror and wish for small breasts, boyish hips, and high cheek-bones. I take guitar lessons and try to learn her songs. I try to forget she's Native American. It doesn't matter—she understands, and I like the look of my braless right breast nestled in the instrument's curve, of the image I'm trying to be.

My parents are appalled.

My Brother Is Made from the Same

I know of only two other families on the whole of Long Island who share my heritage: My parents have friends in Stony Brook whose children are Indian and Swedish; in high school, my brother and I discover two sisters who are Indian and Japanese. But all of us look very different. The only similarity is in varying degrees of dark skin and hair. So my brother and I become tolerant of being mistaken for Italian, Greek, Jewish. At least he and I look alike, and do remember a few people in our lives who have guessed correctly. He remembers a woman he taught how to hit a better forehand; I remember my gentle art teacher, who knew I was Indian because of my eyes.

We have this romantic vision of us, my brother and I, as dark rebels. We plan how we're going to make our entrance. It's Thanksgiving and the dinner is to be held at the club this year. My grandmother's club is exclusive, white, and did I say exclusive? Not even Jews or Italians are allowed in. We picture old men with shiny white hair and plaid pants, leaning on wives with silver perms and brooches clasping silk scarves around their surgically smoothed throats. We picture me, dark eyes lined in black eyeliner, mimicking kohl, and my brother, long brown hair flowing over his suit jacket, looking like a civilized Tarzan. Tarzan in a suit, in my grandmother's club. What fun, we laugh.

It's always better to laugh at yourself first.

Two Men on Opposite Sides of the World

Dada, my father's father, was a minister and a doctor. I hear tales of his dedication, of being offered many women to be his wife, of traveling throughout India on horseback, trailed by tigers and mountain lions. He worked with lepers in a leprosarium, a gentle group of patients. He was afraid of cobras. My brother and I made friends with a leper once, a discharged patient Dada had worked with.

Granddaddy, my mother's father, worked for Singer Corporation and was very successful. He traveled all over the world by plane and by boat, meeting the natives of every country. He spoke with the Masai and ate and drank with Alaskan Eskimos. He was afraid of heights. We went fishing with Granddaddy, and I named a pet spider after him.

They both had snow-white hair and could never be still.

A Father's Confusion

My father tries to bridge the gap with his children. Respect is not something American kids grant their parents unconditionally, and respect is something my father needs. He will accept children less interested in schooling, and children who curse, fight with each other, and dress badly. But he will never accept a small child who talks back to him from below belt-level. We say, "When in Rome . . ." He says, though more eloquently, "Bullshit." "We are Americans," we say. He says, "Don't talk back to me. I'm your father. There are things that other countries do better." It takes years for him to gain our respect, the way it's done in America—conditionally, and hopefully before it's not too late.

Reality

The sun makes a brief appearance after a day of dark rain. The pale, watery light, not strong enough to warm us, slowly spreads itself to the porch where we sit. It is Dana, Mike, David, Joe, and Joe's girlfriend and I, eating sandwiches and chips and fruit and washing it all down with beer. It is Mike's house, his front porch on which we are sitting. I perch on the rail, saying I always wanted to perch myself on the rail of a proper Victorian house, watch the neighbors stroll by, just a few feet away. I have always wanted to be in an era other than my own, not realizing that I wouldn't exist as I am, as who I am, in any other time than this.

Komal Patel Mathew

HERITAGE STATEMENT:

I was born in the U.S. and raised in Rome, Georgia. My family has had quite a "diasporic" life with ties to Africa, India, and England. My work reflects on the deconstruction and construction of South Asian identities formed from being raised in a Hindu family but being called to the Christian faith as an adult. Although our roots trace back to India, all of my family, including my grandparents, live in America or England. My parents raised me in a moderate Hindu home that welcomed both Eastern and Western culture. We barbequed in the backyard during the summers, had samosas for my dad's birthday, and devoured snow cones in state parks when we visited our families in Florida. Diverse cuisine was not my only acculturation; I was able to attend friends' church functions without any hesitation or concern that it would replace Indian Hindu festivals like *Diwali*. Until, I encountered a different (to them, American) God.

AUTHOR BIO:

Komal Patel Mathew is co-founding editor of *Josephine Quarterly* and a lecturer of English at Kennesaw State University. She received an MFA from Sarah Lawrence College and a BS from Georgia Institute of Technology. Her work has appeared in *The Atlanta Review*, *The Comstock Review*, *The New Republic*, and *The Southern Review*. She has also been working on a full-length poetry collection, which has been a finalist for the National Poetry Series Open Competition and a semifinalist for the Alice James Books' Beatrice Hawley Award.

AN AMERICAN

Every Diwali, I explain
to my friends at school
why I am so tired—*garba*
it's like dancing—pujas? I guess
like praying—

I explain in fragments
because even we don't know
why we wash statues with milk,
why worshipping God takes
so many coats. I don't ask,

just sit beside my mother
when she sings. My sister and I
watch our father struggle
to cross his legs; his laughter
resting on his lifted knees.

He closes his eyes, pretending
to pray. We believe my mother
made this temple herself,
found pictures and tiny *murtis*, gold
coins with Shiva, rice and turmeric

stored in tiny steel jars. Only she knows
where everything goes and how to use it.
I have sat at that temple many times,
looking at Krishna's blue face
and pleasing smile framed inside

where life is easy—
My mother tells me he is blue
because he is so dark; *we would not be
able to see his face otherwise*, she says.
Every time I close my eyes to pray,

I see Jesus on that cross and taste
pennies. His blond face like the girl
in music class who told me not to
take the Lord's name *in vain*.
I feel guilty wanting to

have stew and tuna sandwiches
instead of *kichree*. So when my Ba
showed up at school this afternoon
in her maroon and gold sari, and called
my name, I didn't answer.

I walked past her to the car, slid
between my sister and her white friend.
I wanted to believe that I was still
American, hiding in the back seat
like a crumpled sari.

COVERING CANDLES AND OTHER FOLLIES

A year after I became a Christian and before I moved to New York for grad school, my family and I went to New Jersey for a wedding, the kind of affair that starts on a Wednesday and ends with fireworks spewing out of the top of centerpieces. On our way to the Newark airport, I pleaded for a visit to Ground Zero—"Just ten minutes," I promised. My father, afraid of missing our flight, sped up and illegally parked our blue rental car on a side street in the Financial District. They stayed in the car.

September 11 happened at the beginning of my sophomore year and at the end of my first real relationship. That semester, secretly, I spent days reading stories of the ones left behind, of all the mothers and fathers and daughters. At that time, their stories made my parents' disapproval seem minor, and so I was able to attend class and surprise birthday parties and wedding celebrations that required five outfit changes and a three-night hotel stay without feeling sorry for myself.

When we reached Canal Street, the rain started. I searched for an umbrella to protect my camera—although I couldn't decide if it was appropriate to take pictures of American destruction and chaos. But when I reached the site, I saw crosses constructed out of sheet metal and couldn't stop clicking. Maybe this is the reason why a homeless man plodded through the crowds to meet my eyes. I put my camera down, to hear him whisper, *Are you happy now?* Are *you* happy now? When I got back to the car, after running through every crosswalk, I didn't tell my parents what had happened at first. The raindrops on my cheek made this easy to do. I kept thinking about the metal crosses and the homeless man. I don't know if I did the right thing, not saying anything. Jesus would have felt compassion; He would have known the right thing to say. Not like me who is still searching for the right words, still listening for some kind of strategy to say who I really am to someone who doesn't trust who they see.

My cousin's engagement was announced months before mine. She is an orthodontist, and her groom-to-be is a doctor. They are both from the Indian state of Gujarat, both obey their parents' wishes, and both are from well-off families with the perfect amount of liberality.

(I heard her say this.) Although none of this is news to me, I am realizing how important all of this is to my father, despite how "liberal" my family considers themselves.

During the engagement reception, which was more elaborate than most weddings I have been to, I was cornered by my aunt and her sister who offered me broken pieces of information about a boy: a "good boy" ... "Stanford" ... "McKinsey" ... "his own business too." With some hesitation, I told them about my boyfriend Lance, to my father's disappointment.

Although Lance was raised in a South Indian Catholic family, at twenty-seven, he encountered God at a local Pentecostal Church, miles away from the traditions and culture of his Syro-Malabar Catholic family. After a year of conversations with my parents about our inevitable engagement, I was given one limitation by my father: don't talk about my conversion, about "what's happened to you." It's funny, after ten years, how some things don't change: my grandparents' furniture, the individual baby pictures of all ten grandchildren stuffed in one frame, the loud brown clock, and my father's inability to talk about pressing things. He has always been more interested in the paint than the builder and the architect.

I recently heard an interview from an indie band where the lead singer said that the music may be what they have, but the relationships (in the band) are why they keep playing. I've thought about how similar that is to my relationship with my family. Last year, in a surprising confession, my father told Lance that it is hard for him to see me as a Christian, that he has to see me as a Hindu to feel like everything is all right, to have a relationship with me. I've been noticing the way he looks at me now, not at all like the father in Luke 8 who will do anything to keep his daughter alive and close to him. His look is more like the look Jesus gave Peter after he denied Him; it is a well full of lost and hurting things. It's the look I wanted to give the homeless man in New York—disbelief mixed with wrath mixed with His unchanging desire to love me.

And still I heard myself, like Peter, blaming Jesus by saying, "We have left everything to follow you! What then will there be for us?" God has been telling me that I will be in exile, a foreigner in my family, that I will feel more at home somewhere else, even though it means leaving parents who have done so much for me. But, I am trying to remember that if we are following anything other than what our community approves, then all of us are foreigners—misunderstood and misaligned.

This weekend was my mother's sixtieth birthday celebration. My sister Jayna and I planned to take her to Asheville for a day trip. From the moment we got there, my mother could not stop smiling. My whole life I can't remember my mother laughing and not covering her mouth.

She does it out of pure reflex now—as if it isn't polite to laugh that barefaced. Jayna and I have never been that polite. But, this weekend, she laughed and boldly left her mouth completely exposed, her smile like rows of uncovered candles.

On the way up to North Carolina, my father had been on the phone counseling a close-acquaintance-turned-patient's mother. He kept telling her not to worry, but that her son was a danger to himself, so she needed to dial 911 to get him the help he needed. I don't know if she heeded that warning because as we were waiting to be seated for brunch at the Tupelo Honey Cafe, my father got a call that this son shot himself and died.

All day, as we celebrated my mother's birthday, I watched my father hide the news from her in kindness. Every once in a while, he would stare off with watery tears, but she didn't know it. I wish I knew what he was thinking, what weight he continues to keep to himself. This man shot himself, and somehow we were still ordering pimento cheese sandwiches and blueberry waffles. Everything and nothing changed. I wanted to tell my father that I loved him and that I am proud of him and what he does, that he was doing the best he could. I didn't though; like him, I silently held onto heavy things.

Margaret McMullan

HERITAGE STATEMENT:

My mother was born in Vienna, Austria, and after Hitler took the city, she was forced to leave with her mother and father in 1939. Her father left first, then about a week later, my mother and her mother followed. All of them crossed the border by train into Switzerland. From there they travelled through France, stayed with my grandmother's family—I say "stayed" when in fact they were hidden—then they went to England where they had to split up because they could not find a British family who would house all three of them. My grandparents lived in Cambridge while my grandfather taught at King's College, and my mother lived with a family in the South of England. Eventually, they reunited and left for America. I wrote about this in my novel *In My Mother's House* (Picador, 2005). I was born and raised in Newton, Mississippi.

AUTHOR BIO:

Margaret McMullan is a recipient of a 2010 NEA Fellowship in literature, a 2010 Fulbright at the University of Pécs in Pécs, Hungary, and the National Author Winner of the 2011 Eugene and Marilyn Glick Indiana Authors Award. She is the author of six award-winning novels, including *In My Mother's House* (Picador, 2007), a Pen/Faulkner nominee; *Cashay* (Houghton Mifflin Harcourt, 2009), a Chicago Public Library 2009 Teen Book Selection; and *When I Crossed No-Bob* (Houghton Mifflin Harcourt, 2007),
a 2008 Parents' Choice Silver Honor, a 2007 School Library Journal Best Book, an American Library Association Best Book for Young Adults, a Booklist 2009 Best Book For Young Adults, and a 2011 Mississippi Center for the Book selection at the National Book Festival in Washington, D.C. Both *When I Crossed No-Bob* and *How I Found the Strong* (Houghton Mifflin Harcourt, 2004) won the Indiana Best Young Adult Book in 2005 and 2008. Margaret's latest book, *Sources of Light* (Houghton Mifflin Harcourt, 2010), is an American Library

Association 2011 Best Book for Young Adults, a Best 2011 Book of Indiana, and a Chicago Public Library Teen Selection. She is Professor Emeritus at the University of Evansville in Evansville, Indiana.

WHAT'S IN A NAME?

My mother has the kind of maiden name I always wanted, a name I coveted, a name that was long, hard to pronounce, European, and decidedly "other." Many women learn very early that they will probably lose their names when they marry, so it goes without saying that if you know you will lose something, you don't get very attached to it. I can't help but wonder sometimes if my mother found tremendous relief when she married and forfeited her maiden name: Engel de Janosi.

It's a beautiful, terrible name. The *de* means *of,* and the word *Engel* means *angel* as in the angels of Janosi. Janosi is a house that no longer stands in a town that does not exist in Hungary which is barely still a country.

My mother was meant to inherit a palace with her name, but you can't smuggle that kind of property across borders and into a new country.

The angels of Janosi were aristocrats who also happened to be Jewish, a fact I had to find out for myself because my mother, who was and always has been Catholic, never spoke of the angels in her family. After my grandfather died, I read his memoir and his grandfather's memoir. My grandfather wrote about all the important people he knew such as Freud and Ibsen. He mentions my mother two times in his memoir. He never mentions my sister or my father or me. I think to him we did not exist, so why name us?

My grandfather's grandfather, Adolf Engel de Janosi, wrote that he was writing only for his descendents. He tells us about his love for his religion, his hard work during bad times, and his very successful parquet floor factory. He knew a lot about wood and how to get lumber from here to there. He wrote about his family (each of whom he names), his town, and his workers and how he built them a swimming pool and a temple.

They're mostly all gone now—most of the houses, the factories, the silver, the art, the pool, the people. Confiscated or blown up during two World Wars. Hitler played a big role in the destruction of the angels.

The Nazis were a lot like the crusaders, taking out people, buildings, towns, even graveyards. We know now that their goal was not only to erase a people but to erase their history, and to do that you've got to get rid of documents and names.

Maybe more than any other group, the Nazis taught us the power of fire and the documentation of names.

I first read about the Engel de Janosis the summer after I married, when my husband and I moved into a rented farmhouse in Darmstadt, Indiana, which was, and still is, a German settlement.

The house was small, but it had a big kitchen and it sat on top of a windy hill surrounded by pine trees and fields that alternated between corn, soybeans and winter wheat. It was the most beautiful place we could imagine living, and I tried not to care that we rented from a family named Goebel.

German family names appear on almost every mailbox on the side of the road and umlauts are engraved on practically every other gravestone in the cemeteries of Darmstadt, but still, it was a struggle to grow accustomed to living among the Schmidts, the Bucheles, the Kuhnes and the Hohmers. School children there learn and often speak German and not French, which is what I studied in school. My husband and I were temporary settlers in Darmstadt, and we laughed about our neighbors' odd habits of boarding up their windows in winter, losing the fantastic views and light, but saving on heat. Even though we were renters and we knew we would eventually move, I had trouble with the place, even resented knowing that most of these families immigrated to the area in the 1820s when there was a rising tide of emigration from Germany. Even the name, Darmstadt, which most people pronounce in the correct, German way, *Darmshtadt*, made my skin—what can I say?—crawl.

According to the literature I've read, Hesse-Darmstadt is an agricultural area in southwestern Germany dotted by villages, deep forests, medieval towns and castles. You've got the Rhine River to the west and the main river to the east, and between these rivers, in the Hesse Highlands, sits Darmstadt.

Darmstadt, Indiana is a landlocked village with two railroads and an abundance of corn, wheat, soybean, pumpkin and Christmas tree farms. Even though the current sign on the outskirts of Darmstadt says the town was formed in 1822, the land was purchased from the government as early as 1818. Darmstadt was probably named by an early settler and community leader named Michael Bauer to honor his wife, Barbara, who came from Hesse-Darmstadt, Germany. Darmstadt officially became an incorporated village on July 2, 1973, the year of the

United States energy crisis. In the summer of 1987, the Village Square shopping center was remodeled to look like a German village.

During our first years of marriage, living in Darmstadt, I was writing about one woman's first years of marriage and another woman who was trying to be something she was not—Jewish. It was odd and seemingly revolutionary to be researching and writing about the Sabbath, Rosh Hashanah, Sigmund Freud and Hannah Arendt, then glance out the window to see a young, shirtless Goebel riding a John Deere tractor through the soybean fields.

I would go back to my books, thinking surely in this twentieth-century village, on this road called New Harmony, Goebels can coexist with Engels.

While living in Darmstadt, I attempted to get over my inherent "issues" with Germans, but all around me there were hints of anti-Semitism or simply anti-other-than-German. We drove a Volvo then, and I recall somebody once asking me why I owned a Swedish car. While walking once in Evansville near the university where I work, I saw a swastika chalked on the sidewalk. Nearby sat a gorgeous brick house with intricate designs in the brickwork, and even though the owner trained ivy to grow over it, one of the designs was a swastika, and I knew, like everyone else in town, that the symbol was more Germanic than Nordic in meaning.

Still, our hilltop house and the village around it seemed to be isolated from all that was ugly in the world, even most economic and natural disasters. Neighbors told me that during the Depression, there was plenty of food and produce from the farms and no family went hungry. Darmstadt sits on higher ground, so, unlike Evansville, it missed the Flood of 1937.

Darmstadt was and still is so beautiful. There are hills there and they really do roll. Winters were straight out of a Currier and Ives painting. Even horses and buggies passed our house from a nearby Amish community. In the spring we could smell tortillas and taco shells cooking at the Azteca Milling Company and from where we sat perched high up on our hill, we could watch trains go by three or four times a day. All year round you can get a dozen fresh brown eggs for seventy-five cents. In the summer, big black and yellow butterflies fluttered all along the side of the road and while the oil-well moved up and down in the front yard, we could hear the machines drying the corn. In the fall, when we saw the sun coming up from our bedroom window, the plowed fields were so flat and vast, we thought for a moment we were near some wide, sandy beach. Even thunderstorms were beautiful. We sat on the porch, watching them come in from the distance.

I wish I could write a valentine to Darmstadt without any hesitations or discomfort.

In the course of our three years there, my husband and I finished a book and a movie between us. Now we live on a street named after Samuel Bayard, an Evansville banker whose father was French. Some years we go to the Volkfest where some of the people wear chicken hats or paper *lederhosen* because August in southern Indiana is too hot for leather. At Christmas concerts, I can even sing "Stille Nacht" and "O Tannenbaum" without flinching, mainly because they are beautiful songs, but still, I must confess to some degree of pleasure when I learned that the German newspaper, *The Democrat*, folded.

I know now that, like names, facts, information, families, towns, and countries can sometimes disappear, get ignored, or even buried over time. I know that 22 percent of adults think it might be possible that the Holocaust never happened.

I know that the farmers in Darmstadt use tons of fertilizers and it doesn't seem coincidental that Darmstadt has an unspoken but high rate of breast cancer. I know that buried beneath many fertile, rolling fields, lies a certain degree of danger.

When I was born my mother loaded me up with Christian, Anglo-Saxon names, and even though I was never confirmed, she went ahead and tacked on a confirmation name long before I was of age so that I would be "safe." She loved that I was her blonde, Catholic, American daughter. No one could get me. So of course, when my son was born, I stuck my mother's maiden name into his middle name. She is the last Engel de Janosi and I did not want the name to die with her.

I could not name a town, but I had a son. And behold, there he is, the last angel: James Raymond Engel de Janosi O'Connor running across the room in his Superman cape.

Nancy Anne Miller

HERITAGE STATEMENT:

I have been writing about the influences of two cultures for most of my writing life. Although I note myself as a Bermudian poet because I was born there into a longstanding Bermudian family, my father was American and registered me as a U.S. citizen at birth. We then moved to this country in my early teens.

AUTHOR BIO:

Nancy Anne Miller is a Bermudian poet. Her book *Somersault* is forthcoming from Guernica Editions (CA). Her poems have appeared in *The Caribbean Writer* (VI), *The Dalhousie Review* (CA), *Edinburgh Review* (U.K.), *The Fiddlehead* (CA), *Hampden-Sydney Poetry Review* (U.S.A.),  *The International Literary Quarterly* (U.K.), *Journal of Caribbean Literatures* (U.S.A.), *Journal of Postcolonial Writing* (U.K.), *Magma* (U.K.), *The Moth* (IE), *Mslexia* (U.K.), *A New Ulster* (IE), *Postcolonial Text* (CA), *Sargasso: Journal of Caribbean Literature* (PR), *Stand* (U.K.), *Theodate* (U.S.A.), *tongues of the ocean* (BS) with poems forthcoming in *Agenda* (U.K.). She has an MLitt in creative writing from University of Glasgow, is a MacDowell Fellow and teaches workshops in Bermuda.

CHRISTMAS TREES AT HOME
AND ABROAD

The first Christmas tree I see
this year is in front of St. John's,
in Washington, CT, with one string
of lights. It has the clumsy
innocence of a child's drawing.

The second one is at the liquor
store in Bantam, CT, over-decorated,
plump, cut off by the top and
bottom of the window,
a beer belly hangs out.

The third is on the porch of
the country store, Dorset, VT,
cards tied to each branch, like
young girls would wrap hair
in paper to curl at night.

The last one is a stately Palm
in Paget, BDA, waist held in
tightly by a corset of sparkle,
large fronds wave arms,
welcome all wayfarers home.

LOQUAT TIME

Leaves turn tawny yellow,
the colour of loquats ripening
in March on the island. We

ate them too soon, pulled
branches down to share
still in their winter uniforms. Spat

seeds out, enjoyed a show of
bad manners, the juice smeared
our chins, streaks of war paint.

Bright foliage outside like
my tongue after a feast,
sweet flavour promised days

to come. Here each leaf tells
of months drinking warmth in,
now orange liquid will spill.

The sun comes in close
as small fruit pulled to faces,
brings summer's chatter to ears.

Sahar Mustafah

HERITAGE STATEMENT:

My late father was born and raised in the town of al-Birah, bordering Ramallah, a Palestinian city in the central West Bank. My mother is originally from al-Khalil (Hebron) though her parents also lived in al-Birah in a house that faced the road to Jerusalem. In the mid-twentieth century, my paternal grandfather, Mustafa Museitif, came to the United States and made a living as a merchant on Chicago's Southside. My grandmother stayed behind in al-Birah to raise a family of nine children. My father and uncles eventually joined their father and took over his business. As my mother tells it, she spied my father when he was on a visit home driving around town in a white Cadillac convertible and proclaimed she would marry him and go to America. She created quite a scandal by marrying outside the Khalili clans—and to a *fellahi*, no less. After their wedding and visa processing, my father met her at O'Hare International Airport in 1970, bringing her to their Chicago apartment. My sister Hala was born months later. I was born in August 1973 and, along with my remaining four siblings, was raised in Chicago. In 1983, my parents fulfilled their dream of returning to Palestine where their children would be immersed in their native culture and religion. We lived there until 1988, a year after the First Intifada broke in the Occupied Territories.

AUTHOR BIO:

Sahar Mustafah's work has appeared in *The Bellevue Literary Review, Chicago Literati, Great Lakes Review, Story,* and *Word Riot.* She was named one of "25 Writers to Watch" by Chicago's Guild Literary Complex and is a member of "Voices of Protest," a collaboration co-sponsored by the MacArthur Foundation. Her short story "Shisha Love" won the 2012 Guild Literary Complex Fiction Prose Award and was nominated for a 2013 Pushcart Prize. She obtained her MFA in fiction at Columbia College Chicago. She's co-founder  and fiction editor of *Bird's Thumb.* You can visit her at www.saharmustafah.com.

THE ARABIANS

We weren't the only Arabs in the neighborhood.

Technically, we were the only Palestinians on our side of the block on Fairfield Street, but if you cut through the alley to Washtenaw, two other families like us could be found. Well, one of them was like us. The other was comprised of *nawar*, as my mother called them: trash. Their two-story house was like a clown car of never-ending big kids chasing each other out the front door, and younger ones spilling out of the first floor windows. We referred to that family as the Arabians—a designation respectably separating us from them, though the white people called us the same in our neighborhood. It was all in the tone.

Another family—Jordanians, but still Arabs—lived on the corner of Washtenaw and 54th Street. Those kids went to school with us and we had a pleasantly detached friendship whenever we saw them. My mother secretly disliked their mother and was only being polite at luncheons and shopping dates. The truth was, my mother was happy there was someone near who could appreciate the Arabic puns and reminisce about black-and-white Egyptian films with Mervat Amin and Ahmed Zaki. So, she disguised her disdain for her companion's heavily made-up face and perpetual nosiness about my father's profitable liquor store. My mother would tell my father later, "That's how Jordanians are—obnoxious." It was an unqualified conclusion she cloaked over anyone or anything she disapproved of:

"That's how these *amarkan* are—always a beer in their hand."

"That's how Khalil family is—generous with strangers and stingy towards their own blood."

"That's how small dogs are—more vicious than big ones."

Still, with the Jordanians, my mother felt she was in respectable company. However, the Arabians around the block were never to be associated with. They occasionally walked past our house when we were playing with other kids. My mother would be perched on the top stair of the porch, cradling our little brother Feras in her lap, and our baby sister Linda clinging to her side.

As soon as we caught sight of them turning the corner, my sister Abeer and I would pull each other's arms and call out, "The Arabians are coming! The Arabians are coming!" Our stunned friends followed us up the stairs near my mother's feet, unsure of the impending threat.

To us, those Arabians appeared swarthy with ebony pupils fierce against the whites of their eyes, sometimes jaundice-colored. The young girls had long and thick hair down to their waists, some of them fiddled with their unkempt braids, others skipped, their wild strands blowing behind them. The boys were rough tumbling, particularly the youngest ones, scrappy and nipping creatures. They would approach just close enough to sniff and bare teeth before moving on.

The women in this caravan would nod their heads in greeting to my mother who inadvertently rose above them from where she sat on our high porch, exuding superiority. My mother was a *mediniyah*—a city girl. These were peasant women—*fellaheen* like my father. She was polite, but refrained from inviting these women to stop and join her for coffee or tea. Though my mother would soften her haughty resolve over the years, she never relinquished her *medini* status. It was like a pail of scalding hot water she held over my father's head as a constant reminder of her worth.

One day, the Arabians, sans parents, rounded the corner. They looked like a small, disordered parade. The big kids clutched the littlest ones' hands as they trotted along, sometimes tumbling onto the sidewalk. The middle ones rode on Big Wheels or tricycles too small for them, so that their knees nearly reached their chests as they pedaled.

We froze for a moment, panicked. Should we flee and listen to their mocking laughter from the safety of our backyard? Though none of us said a word, we'd silently agreed to hold still and resume our hopscotch game, or at least pretend to be playing, concentrating hard on my sister Abeer whose turn it was to toss the stone. They drew closer and were finally upon us as Abeer twisted her body around to hop back to the starting line.

They stopped at the head of our chalk-drawn squares and Abeer did, too. She just stood poised on one leg with her arms slightly extended at her sides. None of us were sure what was about to happen.

The oldest girl with coffee-colored hair and thick eyelashes asked for a turn. Abeer was about to put her leg down, then must have realized it would be nobler to finish her turn before we turned it over to the interlopers.

The girl wiped the stone across her shirt and tossed it. She hopped from square to square, dropping both feet when required, and spinning back home. The toddler clapped her hands each time her sister twirled and blew her a kiss. When her turn was over, she handed the stone to me and then their procession continued down the block.

For the rest of the day, I wondered what their house was like—the Arabians— if they ate the same dishes we did, like *maklooba* and *adas*, if they had friends like Teresa on their side of the block, or weren't in need of any because there were so many of them. I wondered if my mother had ever actually had a conversation with the grown-ups among them. I asked her that evening as she supervised our stripping down in the laundry room before sprinting across the hallway to our awaiting baths.

"From the other side of the block?" she asked, pulling Linda's shirt over her head. It got stuck over her face and Linda began to cry from this temporary blindness. "*Istani*! Wait, wait! I've got it."

"Mommy? Did you ever talk to them?"

She held each of Linda's arms as my little sister crept out of her shorts that had gathered at her ankles. "They're *nawar*," she said. "Their kids are filthy. What would I have to say to them?"

I couldn't answer her at the time.

Jed Myers

HERITAGE STATEMENT:

I was born in Philadelphia in 1952 to parents of Eastern European Jewish heritage. For many years, a good share of the poems I wrote explored the infinitely complex matter of the multigenerational resonances of immigration, and while I am the grandchild and great-grandchild of my immigrant forebears, I am deeply aware of the ongoing shaping power of this history. My paternal grandmother was born in a *shtetl* somewhere near St. Petersburg, and came to this country when she was probably four years old. My paternal grandfather was born in Philadelphia in 1898 of recently arrived parents. My mother's parents were also born here of recently arrived immigrants. All who came were escaping the pogroms of Eastern Europe. I do not know what my last name might have been, nor what countries most of my people came from.

AUTHOR BIO:

Jed Myers is a Seattle psychiatrist who maintains a solo therapy practice and teaches at the University of Washington. He is author of *Watching the Perseids* (Sacramento Poetry Center Book Award) and two chapbooks. Honors received include Southern Indiana Review's Editors' Award, the Prime Number Magazine Award for Poetry, the Southeast Review's Gearhart Poetry Prize, and the McLellan Poetry Prize (U.K.). Recent poems can be found *Rattle, Poetry Northwest, The Greensboro Review, Valparaiso Poetry Review, Shining Rock Poetry Anthology, Canary,* and elsewhere. He is Poetry Editor for the journal *Bracken*.

THE DEAD'S TREMORS

Am I the one meant to remember
too much? It has to be someone.
By the time my brother came,
I was in another house, claimed
by my father's parents. I remember
the torch flares in their eyes,
the rage of unanswered prayers . . .
I, the grandson they'd need to wield
memory's sword in the New World—
would I? My mother remembers
she just couldn't hold me. She offered me
up to those immigrants she despised—
to their history. Then they'd leave her
alone, she hoped. They didn't.
But my brother became her protector.
Claims he can't even recall
my grandparents' house. I depict it
in words at the table—he squints
as if trying to see it, or not.
I speak of it further—he winces
as if someone's made an incision
in his abdomen—it's the literal pain
of being disbelonged. Seems
I've taken up a saber-like instrument,
contraband of the pogroms,
and drawn it across his middle, his being
my mother's bodyguard after all.
Well, I want someone to feel it—
the sear of urgency in the nurture
my refugee comforters had to offer.
How in my viscera twisted

the terrors stirred into the *borscht*
and *tsimis*, meant to breed a deliverer
who in victory, in their fantasy,
would at last commandeer the opiate
for the past. And my brother, he was not
spared—second lord, defender
to another sphere, our mother's
orphanhood in a mountain coal town,
all her care rattled for good.
Her stories are in my veins too.
I'm named for her lost father.
But she and I abandoned each other.
And there's no surgical blade
to cut through time, to excise
the buried man's tumor. Our nerves,
as they are, conduct the dead's
tremors through lifetimes. And brothers,
soldiers, serve different ghosts.

SAME FIRE

I lost my name half a century before
I was born. Across the Atlantic
a ship came, bearded man on the deck,
same fire in his chest as mine,
preparing himself to give up
whatever can be forsaken, shaved,
stripped, or hidden away nameless
in his nervous marrow, to save
that spinning flame (he doesn't know
it's there behind his awareness, the harbor
too bright with churn and wake, tugs
and heaving crowds, too loud
with horses, groaning docks, men
unlashing crates—too much crashing
at his senses, for him to sense
the roar under his breath, the engine
that drives him to this shore). He stands
and waits to answer the cold uniform
questions that will pour through the grating
in the clearinghouse down the ramp,
where he will further unknow himself,
his tongue will fail his grandfather
glaring at him through the East Wall,
his curls will splash out from under
the black wool hat, he'll forget
to mouth the familiar blessing
for this moment of his arrival
in the new wilderness. He's willing
to lay down the white silk of his ritual
fringes on the concrete, to walk over it
if this is his pathway to the street.

He's already sold his prayer book
at a dark shop in Leeds, he's told himself
as if in prayer, over and over,
he comes from nowhere, and practiced
the melodics of all the accents
flooding his ears. The blaring
clanging stomp-march of boots
and carts, hooves, horn-blasts, gears,
government stamps pounding the blotters,
the howls, cheers, and chatter
of the ten thousand tramps
awaiting official passage into chaos
and all its chances, *is* the music
to which he chants (devout
as the sons of Aaron who disappear
into fire) into the empty
basin of his processor's face,
his new name, by which he will go
where the fire takes him. Here I am
Great-Grandfather, one burning
branch of your profane devotion.

Paul E. Nelson

HERITAGE STATEMENT:

My dad was a lifelong railroad man and, at the low end of the seniority totem pole at the Milwaukee Road, had last choice for annual vacations. He ended up taking his in February and March, in Florida, to see baseball's spring training. A railroad employee's discount for a boat ride to Cuba got him to Havana where he met my mom and then married her in November 1957. He brought her back to Chicago where I was raised. My mom, Lesbia Matilde Pino Roque de Nelson, always assumed she would send her four kids to Cuba in the summers, but the U.S. economic blockade put an end to that idea and the only Spanish we picked up was when mom was angry, so you can just imagine the things I am capable of saying in her native tongue. My parents separated in 1972, so she was the main force shaping me and my younger siblings after that time. I was ten. The funny thing is, we were raised as Americans, but it was not until *years* later that I realized I was ever the subject of racial discrimination. It is clear I am Cuban in spirit and intensity, something that was validated when I visited Cuba in 2005, as the poem suggests.

AUTHOR BIO:

Paul E. Nelson is founder of The Spoken Word Lab (SPLAB) in Seattle and the Cascadia Poetry Festival. He wrote a collection of essays, *Organic Poetry*, and a serial poem re-enacting the history of Auburn, Washington—*A Time Before Slaughter* (Apprentice House, 2009)— which was shortlisted for a 2010 Genius Award by *The Stranger*. One of his main writing projects currently is the next chapter of the history-in-verse mode of the Slaughter poem entitled *Pig War & Other Songs of Cascadia*. He has interviewed Allen Ginsberg, Michael McClure, Wanda Coleman, Anne Waldman, Sam Hamill, Robin Blaser, Nate Mackey, Eileen Myles, George Bowering, Diane di Prima, Joanne Kyger, George Stanley, Brenda Hillman, Emily Kendal Frey and many Cascadia poets. He has presented his poetry and poetics in London; Brussels;

Vancouver; Qinghai and Beijing, China; Victoria; Nanaimo, British Columbia; Lake Forest, Illinois; and other places and writes an American Sentence every day. Learn more at www.PaulENelson.com.

GUANABO BEACH, 2005

It was a Wednesday, four destinations.

Nilda would feed us *ropa vieja*: better than
        Miami. Raphael puts on his helmet
        or cashes in

his chits for a Lada for a day, we would
        drive to Cemetario Colón.

How a Cuban does this.

Here is a stranger, but *familia también*
        on to the city of dead, having
        workshopped *en* Miramar
        and played

beisbol on the Varadero beach
        with a tennis ball, three bases, one

swig of rum crossing home
        with another run.

(ron)

Each shade of blue off the beach
        at Varadero, successive
        and deeper

hues to the sky

y Matanzas will I ever avoid
        Slaughter? Will the
        máscara

ancestrales ever adorn the spot
next to Joan's treat, will he ever

see the *brooks of the mountains*
        the spot where Rio Guanabo
        begins?

She'll tell stories of Mongilo
        Fe grills pork chops
        at 10:30 p.m. & *Buck*

& the Preacher is a lesson
        in U.S. history

till the power fails.

Homemade *miel*
        y jugo de mango too poor to put in
        Splenda© or corn syrup, Lidgia always
        w/ an angle to beat the bus line *Ultimo*

one'll say when we are waiting *Permiso*
when we want to get off in Habana Vieja. My father

what did he know when he came here
        except that he could. He did.

Got his
railroad man's discount (25% off)
            boat entertainment Larry "F-Troop"
            Storch & on the beach, he knew.

Like I knew seeing the Rio Guanabo
            I wanted to find its source
            as I found mine in Pinar del Río.

You just know. It's working enough
            to stain a shirt in tears (diphtheria)

a single parent.

Track it down. Fend off a Doberman
            named Lassie with a fist, go back
            to Esquina Caliente they'll remember

the gringo

(¿era él gringo?) who told them about *el Duque*
            y Contreras the *marzo* before they won it
            all on the South Side *por Medias*
            Blancas.

In Cuba we are poor she says
but we have a spiritual rhythm.
            Mascaras the shape of Norte America.
            Mascaras to honor *los antepasados.*
            Mascaras en blanco y negro, pushed
            by another calm breeze, obscured

by smoke flavored by the iron content
in dirt   earth acting
as fire.

Joey Nicoletti

HERITAGE STATEMENT:

I was born in Astoria, Queens, New York City. My mother and her parents immigrated to the U.S.A. from Orsogna, Italy, in the early 1950s. They departed because, in my mother's words, "Mussolini stole Italy from Italy," meaning that the fallout of Mussolini's domestic and foreign policies left the Italian national identity and economy in shambles. Consequently, employment opportunities were either scarce or scant, and some other family members had secured jobs in America, so they followed suit. For my family, to immigrate meant transforming from Italian to American: to live, to have a fighting chance for prosperity—emphasis on fighting—rather than to survive.

AUTHOR BIO:

Joey Nicoletti is the author of two full-length and four chapbook poetry collections, most recently *Reverse Graffiti* (Bordighera, 2015) and *Wide Asleep* (NightBallet, 2016). His work has been nominated for a Pushcart Prize and has appeared in various journals and anthologies, including *Valparaiso Poetry Review*, *Stymie Magazine*, and *Voices in Italian Americana*. He teaches at SUNY–Buffalo State and blogs at balldurham.tumblr.com.

ONION PIE

The wind, the rattling wall, dinner
baking in the oven, the dead of winter
a string of salt diamonds
alight in a street of slush and moonlit ice,
and the cat retires
to his feathery bed.

I'm the child who's read
every issue of *The Amazing Spider-Man*:
I spin webs of all shapes and sizes
in my sleep, on and off the page,
to capture the nebulous villains of memory and tradition
who would otherwise evade or defeat me.

I investigate my mother's stories
about her childhood in Orsogna, Italia.
The latest case: Lisa,
my mother's kid sister,
who went to school one day and didn't
return. Three army soldiers stormed
into her classroom.
Reeking of pipe smoke and wine,
they demanded everyone's jewelry,
including the teacher's
for the war effort. The class obeyed.
The soldiers sang
"Il Canto degli Italiani,"
then left, and set
the school ablaze.
The firefighters saved some
of the children.

Lisa wasn't one of them.
I've never seen a picture of her.

Thus, the character Almost Aunt Lisa has appeared
in my life like a phantom
in the mausoleum of my imagination.
My mother, Nonno
Giovanni, and Nonna Ida were in America;
Astoria, New York, eleven months later.

My mother's recollections of the journey were limited
to adjectives and events:
long, cramped, vile;
a cousin and an uncle dead.

The cause:
Malaria. Maybe scurvy.
Death had a clammy grip
on the forehead and the heart.

Since we've been partners,
my wife and I have tried
to find the answers together.
We have yet to fill in all of the blanks
of the blue exam books
of our respective cultural and familial histories.
Mastering recipes is the closest we've come
to a thoroughly successful search.

Tonight features a succulent trip
to the old country;

a buttery, spicy-sweet taste of Italia:
I pull the Onion Pie out of the oven,
my face kissed by steam.

RISOTTO ELEGY

The day crushed me
like a grape in its green pain as I read
a few words about my uncle Enzo
at his funeral mass. My voice cracked
as I tried to decipher my handwriting.
The windows rattled a stained-glass hymn
when an airplane flew above the church. I wondered
if its passengers were shuffling in their seats
as nervously as my relatives were in the pews.
Then we went to a bistro around the corner.
Our whistles wet with Chianti,
everyone told uncle Enzo stories, even my aunt
Zia, his widow, who usually said
yes as a long answer to a question.
No was her short one.
She talked about the time he tried
to build a campfire in their backyard
by rubbing my brother's Lincoln Logs together.
My mother's hapless sigh rose in steam
from her plate of risotto,
her attention divided
between aunt Zia and the crash
of broken plates; an off-key choir
scattered in the kitchen
like uncle Enzo's ashes in the East River,
telephone wires stitching the sky.

SYLVESTER STALLONE OVERDRIVE

was how my mother referred to her godfather, my Uncle Enzo; she called him that because of his passion for muscle cars and Sly Stallone movies—*da best talkies*, as Enzo once told me; *Da best*. Enzo was partial to John Rambo; his jet-black Belvedere GTX; its purple fuzzy dice, hanging from the rearview mirror like square grapes, like the fruit her father, my *nonno* Giovanni, picked for a living in Italia. He drove John Rambo mostly in the summer, during *pompadour nights, on streets of dungarees and wide-eyed streetlights*. The voices of stoops cracked in concrete tenors when he asked his wife, my Aunt Zia, out for their first date. Enzo hurled his popcorn and soda at the cinema screen when Apollo Creed won the split decision over Rocky Balboa. Perhaps above all else, Enzo was indefinitely awestruck; always taken with the slow burn of Aunt Zia's impossibly long red hair *in curly wind*; with the moon, burning a hole in his pocket: a token to enter the turnstile of night.

Naomi Shihab Nye

HERITAGE STATEMENT:

Naomi Shihab Nye was born on March 12, 1952, in St. Louis, Missouri, to a Palestinian father and an American mother. During her high school years, she lived in Ramallah in Palestine, the Old City in Jerusalem, and San Antonio, Texas, where she later received her BA in English and world religions from Trinity University.

AUTHOR BIO:

Nye is the author of numerous books of poems, including *You and Yours* (BOA Editions, Ltd., 2005), which received the Isabella Gardner Poetry Award; *19 Varieties of Gazelle: Poems of the Middle East* (Greenwillow Books, 2002), a collection of new and selected poems about the Middle  East; *Fuel* (BOA Editions, Ltd., 1998); *Red Suitcase* (BOA Editions, Ltd., 1994); and *Hugging the Jukebox* (Far Corner Books, 1982). She is also the author of several books of poetry and fiction for children, including *Habibi* (Simon Pulse, 1997), for which she received the Jane Addams Children's Book award in 1998. Nye gives voice to her experience as an Arab American through poems about heritage and peace that overflow with a humanitarian spirit. About her work, the poet William Stafford has said, "Her poems combine transcendent liveliness and sparkle along with warmth and human insight. She is a champion of the literature of encouragement and heart. Reading her work enhances life." Her poems and short stories have appeared in various journals and reviews throughout North America, Europe, and the Middle and Far East. She has traveled to the Middle East and Asia for the United States Information Agency three times, promoting international goodwill through the arts. Nye has received awards from the Texas Institute of Letters, the Charity Randall Prize, and the International Poetry Forum, as well as four Pushcart Prizes. She has been a Lannan Fellow, a Guggenheim Fellow, and a Witter Bynner Fellow. In 1988 she received

The Academy of American Poets' Lavan Award, selected by W. S. Merwin. She currently lives in San Antonio, Texas. She was elected a Chancellor of the Academy of American Poets in 2010.

TWO COUNTRIES

Skin remembers how long the years grow
when skin is not touched, a gray tunnel
of singleness, feather lost from the tail
of a bird, swirling onto a step,
swept away by someone who never saw
it was a feather. Skin ate, walked,
slept by itself, knew how to raise a
see-you-later hand. But skin felt
it was never seen, never known as
a land on the map, nose like a city,
hip like a city, gleaming dome of the mosque
and the hundred corridors of cinnamon and rope.

Skin had hope, that's what skin does.
Heals over the scarred place, makes a road.
Love means you breathe in two countries.
And skin remembers—silk, spiny grass,
deep in the pocket that is skin's secret own.
Even now, when skin is not alone,
it remembers being alone and thanks something larger
that there are travelers, that people go places
larger than themselves.

BLOOD

"A true Arab knows how to catch a fly in his hands,"
my father would say. And he'd prove it,
cupping the buzzer instantly
while the host with the swatter stared.

In the spring our palms peeled like snakes.
True Arabs believed watermelon could heal fifty ways.
I changed these to fit the occasion.

Years before, a girl knocked,
wanted to see the Arab.
I said we didn't have one.
After that, my father told me who he was,
"Shihab"—"shooting star"—
a good name, borrowed from the sky.
Once I said, "When we die, we give it back?"
He said that's what a true Arab would say.

Today the headlines clot in my blood.
A little Palestinian dangles a toy truck on the front page.
Homeless fig, this tragedy with a terrible root
is too big for us. What flag can we wave?
I wave the flag of stone and seed,
table mat stitched in blue.

I call my father, we talk around the news.
It is too much for him,
neither of his two languages can reach it.
I drive into the country to find sheep, cows,
to plead with the air:

Who calls anyone *civilized*?
Where can the crying heart graze?
What does a true Arab do now?

HALF-AND-HALF

You can't be, says a Palestinian Christian
on the first feast day after Ramadan.
So, half-and-half and half-and-half.
He sells glass. He knows about broken bits,
chips. If you love Jesus you can't love
anyone else. Says he.

At his stall of blue pitchers on the Via Dolorosa,
he's sweeping. The rubbed stones
feel holy. Dusting of powdered sugar
across faces of date-stuffed mamool.

This morning we lit the slim white candles
which bend over at the waist by noon.
For once the priests weren't fighting
in the church for the best spots to stand.
As a boy, my father listened to them fight.
This is partly why he prays in no language
but his own. Why I press my lips
to every exception.

A woman opens a window—here and here and here—
placing a vase of blue flowers
on an orange cloth. I follow her.
She is making a soup from what she had left
in the bowl, the shriveled garlic and bent bean.
She is leaving nothing out.

Oliver de la Paz

HERITAGE STATEMENT:

I was born in Marikina/Metro Manila in February 1972. On September 21, 1972, Ferdinand Marcos issued Proclamation No. 1081, which was a declaration of martial law under the pretext of an assassination attempt on the Defense Secretary and an alleged growing communist insurgency. People were being put on a black list. Among the people on the black list was my uncle (who subsequently got his name removed by someone, but that is another story). We left the country as soon as we could and found ourselves aboard a plane three weeks after Marcos's decree and three hours after my father got our passports stamped, approving our departure from the Philippines. All sorts of professionals were leaving the country and to this day the leading export from the Philippines is people with professional expertise. Like many immigrant doctors, my mother found a practice in a remote, rural area of the country with a large indigent population and a deficit in medical caregivers. So we ended up in Ontario, Oregon, a small town in Eastern Oregon. That's where I lived and grew up from kindergarten through high school.

AUTHOR BIO:

Oliver de la Paz has a BS in biology, a BA in English from Loyola Marymount University, and an MFA in creative writing from Arizona State University. He is the author of four collections of poetry, *Names Above Houses* (Southern Illinois University Press, 2001), *Furious Lullaby* (SIU Press 2001, 2007), *Requiem for the Orchard* (U. of Akron Press, 2010), winner of the Akron Prize for poetry chosen by Martín Espada, and *Post Subject: A Fable* (U. of Akron Press, 2014). He is the co-editor with Stacey Lynn Brown of *A Face to Meet the Faces: An Anthology of Contemporary Persona Poetry* (U. of Akron Press, 2012). He co-chairs the advisory board of Kundiman, a nonprofit organization dedicated to the promotion of Asian-American poetry, and serves on the Association of Writers and Writing Programs Board. A recipient of a NYFA Fellowship Award and a

GAP Grant from Artist Trust, his work has appeared in journals like *Chattahooch-ee Review*, *North American Review*, *Tin House*, *Virginia Quarterly Review*, and in anthologies such as *Asian American Poetry: The Next Generation*. He teaches at the College of the Holy Cross and in the low-residency MFA program at Pacific Lutheran University.

MEDITATION WITH SMOKE AND FLOWERS

It is Monday and I am not thinking of myself. My son, asleep
in his stroller, the dark conifers holding nothing but their scent.

I'm walking him to the place where loggers have cleared thirty acres,
leaving only ash and stripped tree limbs. The light now comes

to the places once dark—and now wildflowers where once
the moss grew thick and complete. The flame of something around the corner

and I'm thinking of the wild tiger lilies that line this gravel road below my house,
how they clump together, their stems bent down from the weight

of their flowers. How mouth-like they are, and how
their speechlessness makes the road quieter. Each flower is a surprise,

like the flaming tip of cigarettes in the dark. I think that the road
cannot contain all these mouths, though there are mythologies held

in check by the tongue. Like the story my father told me
about his father in war time, and how his own father forced him, with the threat

of a beating, to go under the house for a cigarette from a Japanese foot soldier
bunkered down. I can see my father's small trembling hand,

outstretched to this man whose face is mud-caked, smelling
slightly of fire and lubricant for his rifle. The smoke from the soldier's own

cigarette takes the shape of the underside of the house and I imagine
my father can hear his own father above him pacing.

But this road now, is free of smoke. The logging trucks have taken off
for the night and the tree remnants have smoldered into nothing

but charcoal. The wreck of everything is a vacuum, so too the wreck of a village
after war or the floorboards above a son's head in fear of his own father.

Here, though, there is nothing to fear. The wheels of the stroller on gravel
is the only sound and the idleness of the excavation trucks harkens to

someone asleep in the uneasy dark. No, I am not thinking of myself. I'm thinking
of an agreement my father must have made with himself years ago

when the houses were burning into bright bouquets in the nighttime. How, perhaps
he swore he would not beat his own son while somewhere in the afterlife his own
father

smokes and paces. Perhaps there are no flowers in that place. Perhaps
the lone soldier through with hiding, crawled out after the guns had stopped

and dusted himself off, the sun striking his face with its unreasonable light.
I'm thinking of my son, asleep, and of the wild tiger lilies. How frail they are

in the new light. Why they come. Why they spring up, unannounced
as suddenly as the promises we make with ourselves when we are young.

IN DEFENSE OF SMALL TOWNS

When I look at it, it's simple, really. I hated life there. September,
once filled with animal deaths and toughened hay. And the smells

of fall were boiled down beets and potatoes
or the farmhands' breeches smeared with oil and diesel

as they rode into town, dusty and pissed. The radio station
split time between metal and Tejano, and the only action

happened on Friday nights where the high school football team
gave everyone a chance at forgiveness. The town left no room

for novelty or change. The sheriff knew everyone's son and despite that,
we'd cruise up and down the avenues, switching between

brake and gearshift. We'd fight and spit chew into Big Gulp cups
and have our hearts broken nightly. In that town I learned

to fire a shotgun at nine and wring a chicken's neck
with one hand by twirling the bird and whipping it straight like a towel.

But I loved the place once. Everything was blonde and cracked
and the irrigation ditches stretched to the end of the earth. You could

ride on a bicycle and see clearly, the outline of every leaf
or catch on the streets, each word of a neighbor's argument.

Nothing could happen there and if I willed it, the place would have me
slipping over its rocks into the river with the sugar plant's steam

or signing papers at a storefront army desk, buttoned up
with medallions and a crew cut, eyeing the next recruits.

If I've learned anything, it's that I could be anywhere,
staring at a hunk of asphalt or listening to the clap of billiard balls

against each other in a bar and hear my name. Indifference now?
Some. I shook loose, but that isn't the whole story. The fact is

I'm still in love. And when I wake up, I watch my son yawn
and my mind turns his upswept hair into cornstalks

at the edge of a field. Stillness is an acre, and his body
idles, deep like heavy machinery. I want to take him back there,

to the small town of my youth and hold the book of wildflowers
open for him, and look. I want him to know the colors of horses,

to run with a cattail in his hand and watch as its seeds
fly weightless as though nothing mattered, as though

the little things we tell ourselves about our pasts stay there,
rising slightly and just out of reach.

Michelle Peñaloza

HERITAGE STATEMENT:

My parents both immigrated from the Philippines, separately. My mother came from Malolos, Bulacan, and my father from San Pablo City, Laguna; both on the island of Luzon. They met in Detroit while both working at a dental manufacturing factory. My father worked on the factory floor. My mother was a chemist, running labs on the products being manufactured. I was born in Detroit.

AUTHOR BIO:

Michelle Peñaloza is the author of two chapbooks: *landscape/heartbreak* (Two Sylvias Press, 2015) and *Last Night I Dreamt of Volcanoes* (Organic Weapon Arts, 2015). Her poetry and essays can be found in places like *New England Review, THIS Magazine, TriQuarterly, Pleiades*, and *The Collagist*. She is the recipient of fellowships and awards from the University of Oregon, Kundiman, 4Culture, Artist Trust, and Hugo House, as well as scholarships from VONA/Voices, Vermont Studio Center, and the Bread Loaf Writers' Conference, among others. Michelle lives in rural Northern California.

LETTER FROM MOTHER

Dear Bunso: Fall settled in the backyard today.
I finally turned on the heat inside the house—
it gets so drafty—maybe I should get someone
to seal the windows? Maybe Clay can do it
next time you visit? The green herons have stopped
visiting my pond and the cattails you broke apart
this summer are gone. The maples, though, they
look like they're on fire. I was single the first time
I saw fall, you know. Single and newly arrived.
So many leaves, so many new colors of leaves.
Did I tell you? Wowie's planning a fall wedding.
She's picked the bridesmaids' dresses (I hope you like
orange). Be nice. Don't complain to your cousin.
Maybe you and Clay should start some planning.
Fall is a fine time. Did I ever tell you the time
Daddy took me on a hayride? He picked the fallen oak
and maple leaves from my hair. I think we carved
pumpkins that day. I know we drank warm cider
under a cold sun. Anak, that day, like a postcard.
I went to Meijer today. They had pumpkins for sale
and a deal on apple cider—2 gallons for $4.
I bought some mulling spices for you. *Kumain ka ba?*
Have you been eating? What did you make Clay for dinner?
Remember: be patient and kind. Even though you aren't
married, love is all kindness and patience (Daddy—
always that way). Have you bought any pumpkins?
Maybe I'll buy one for myself this year. I haven't
carved a pumpkin since you were a little girl.
Lately I've thought: A decade is a long and not long time.
I'm getting old. I feel it when I climb the stairs before bed.
But, don't worry. I go on walks. I did some Tai Chi yesterday.

Maybe show me how to yoga when you come home
for Christmas. You still have a lot to learn from me;
what I know fills books. That's what they say, right?
You could write about me, about things that happen to me.
I'll send you poem ideas. The other day a bird with a
snake in its mouth crashed into the Blazer's windshield!
Talk about symbolism. You should write a poem about that.
Or your cousin Andrew, who's too stubborn to speak,
or Lola and Daddy—you should write poems about them.
Oh, I know what you'll say—They're dead, Ma,
let them be dead. But you're more like me than you'd like.
I'll be glad for you to come home, Bunso.
For now, I'll watch *Dancing with the Stars*
with your Tita Nora. Watch for the birds that are left.

MY FATHER, ON THE LINE

He never went to the bar with Ernie, Pete and Dave
after they'd been given notice.
Once, years before,
he brought me to the factory floor—
a vast and harnessed frenzy—beginning with the body bank,
where operators assigned VIN stamps and specs,
then the line that dressed and plumbed the engines.
Men and machines were partners in an endless dance—
welding fenders, assembling brake lines and rear axles.
I ambled, my gaze following my father's:
a finished motor guided to the chassis line;
a subframe mounted onto a carrier truck, waiting
for its front suspension, steering and link.
My father waved to his buddies on the line—
he pointed to the plant's robotic limbs,
grinned at each arm securing each part into its place.
He explained—*uniting cluster and wiring, brake booster,*
rear bumper and guards—his specific labor, his line.
My father's work—didn't matter which shift—made him
happy with purpose; the rush of assembling, constant;
the outcome of completion, assured. I don't know
what he'd say about my Japanese-made car.
He did not live to see the plant close.
Now, there is only the assemblage of stories we tell.
I watched the almost-cars—subframes, rear springs
and shocks bolted up—reach the final line; chassis after chassis,
molded to body after body. My father stood beside one,
pointing with pursed lips, nudging my arm:
See, what it takes?

THREAD RITE

I pluck silver and white hairs from Lola's head,
each one for a penny,
as she sits at her Singer.
Bridesmaids' dresses and wedding gowns
drape from the ceiling,
down from hooks meant for hanging plants.

Sundays, beneath Santo Niño and Santa Maria,
beneath the flaming, thorned heart of Christ,
Lola and I and her altars and her trilling Singer.
She pieces together lined panels of gowns
while I pull triplets of silver and white from thick black.

Triplets of silver and white, easy to find in the altar light.
Her hair smells like simmering sinigang.
She and Ma whisper fierce, below Santo Niño's painted eyes,
words I do not know.
I will buy a jawbreaker with the pennies Lola will pay me.

I don't remember their words, only their cross faces.
Their mouths move quick, twisting in ire;
these faces, someday, my mother and I will make.
We will twist our mouths, angry lines stifled—
saying and not saying what we mean.

Lola hums.
White and silver hairs gather upon satin—
ruby, coral, cerulean—
leftover from finished gowns.
My fingertips massage her crown.
Lola hums a song from her throat to her skull to my fingers.

Each errant hair I pluck: a line in a sketch in a dream
where we divine patterns upon red shantung.
The song she will sing. The room where she will die.
Ma will ask everything aloud. Lola will not answer.
We wait for thread and needle, for the Singer, for satin
and sinigang, for shears.

We watch her confusion during dialysis.
Ma and I whisper fierce in the midst of her begging.
Lola asks me to pluck her weak bones, her kidneys.
She will pay me with pennies taken from mason jars.
I sit with her—each time she is sewn, pieced together,
needles going in and out,
as Santo Niño and unfinished wedding dresses watched.

Each hair a line we divined in a sketch in a dream—
a path leading, a cord binding, a rope to pull,
a sheet to cover, a handkerchief to wipe blood and tears.
Ma's triplets of silver and white multiply each time I see her.
I pluck her silver and white hairs, each one for a penny.

Shin Yu Pai

HERITAGE STATEMENT:

I was born in the Midwest and grew up in the Inland Empire of Southern California. My parents are first-generation immigrants from Taiwan. My father moved to the United States to pursue graduate-level studies at a small Midwestern university. My mother joined him a year later and they married. We spoke Taiwanese and English at home and though I very briefly attended Chinese language classes on Saturday mornings as a kid, I chose to drop out of Mandarin classes after being bullied by other students and the Chinese-born teacher. I spent my formative years in predominantly black and Latino communities, where my family was one of a handful of Asian families. I'm fluent in Spanish, with zero proficiency in Mandarin. Since 1998, I have traveled to Taiwan on four separate occasions to conduct research and spend time with my father's extended family. In 2006, I served as an artist-in-residence at the Taipei Artist Village.

AUTHOR BIO:

Shin Yu Pai is a 2014 Stranger Genius Award nominee, and the author of eight books of poetry. Her work has appeared in publications throughout the U.S., Japan, China, Taiwan, the U.K., and Canada. Her poems have been commissioned by the Dallas Museum of Art and her work is also featured in the Poetry-in-Motion Program. She has been a featured presenter at national and international literary festivals including the Geraldine Dodge Poetry Festival and the Montreal Zen Poetry Festival. In 2010, she  became a member of the Macondo Workshop for Writers. Her essays and nonfiction writing have appeared in *Ballard News-Tribune, City Arts, International Examiner, Medium, ParentMap, The Rumpus, Seattle Globalist, The Stranger, Thought Catalog, Tricycle,* and *YES! Magazine.* She is founding editor of Lawrence & Crane publications. Shin Yu's visual work has been exhibited at The American Jazz Museum, Center for Book and Paper Arts at Columbia College

Chicago, The International Print Center, The McKinney Avenue Contemporary, The Paterson Museum, and The Three Arts Club of Chicago. She is a member of the MotherLoad collective. Shin Yu has served as a poet-in-residence for the Seattle Art Museum and produced literary programming for the Crow Collection of Asian Art, the Women's Museum of Dallas, and the Rubin Museum of Art. She is former assistant curator for the Wittliff Collections. Shin Yu received her MFA from the School of the Art Institute of Chicago and an MA in museology from the University of Washington, where she specialized in oral history.

A MIDWINTER'S DAY

On Beigan Island in the Matsu archipelago of Taiwan, my seventy-one-year-old father insists on walking everywhere, as he did during his military assignment nearly fifty years ago. We retrace the path from Tangqi to Houao Village, a trek that he made almost daily in 1964. The two villages were once connected solely by Baisha Beach, a long sandbar, where crossing was made at low tide. But now, a paved road and bridge connects the two centers. As we enter Houao, my father gapes in disbelief at the two-story houses lining the main road. At the time he left, villagers lived in primitive structures with straw roofs, dirt floors, and no electricity.

At the eastern edge of town, we stumble upon the "ghost house" where my father was stationed as an officer. "I set a bad example for other soldiers by rolling up my shirtsleeves and refusing to wear my cap, so I was transferred to the barracks up the mountain." The house has survived time—never razed nor rebuilt due to the villagers' fear of the ghosts that have haunted the property for over a century. We enter the structure through a portal where there was once a door, fighting wild grass and brush to get to the back room where my father once made his bed on a wooden board. The villagers congregate outside, curious to know more about the foreigners. "Do you remember me?" an old woman asks my father. My father has vivid memories of the family that lived next door to his haunted house. The young daughter of the family would haul crabs in from the sea and share her bounty with my father. "What happened to the young girl who lived next door?" The old woman shakes her head. It isn't her. "She grew up to be a teacher and moved to Taipei. She's retired now." Another villager explains the government's subsidization of housing, which has allowed the town to modernize. "I always wanted to show your mother this place," my father says.

I've come to Taiwan with my father for a reunion of the living—to visit his remaining siblings. My father is the only family member to have relocated to America. One after another, my cousins drive the aunts and uncles home to Ching Shui, a small town on the central coast. At his fourth brother's house, my father receives his relatives over cups of oolong tea harvested from Alishan, while I thumb through tourist guidebooks and Skype my husband back in Seattle. The conversations between my father and relatives span health ailments, wayward children, bad sons-in-law, financial troubles, and the differences between life in Taiwan and abroad. A television broadcasts news in the background of the Newtown shootings in Connecticut, while relatives speculate on the circumstances that resulted in the shootings. "He came from a broken home—his parents were divorced. His mother told him Doom's Day was coming," an auntie declares with absolute authority.

A little over a year ago, our Taiwanese family embarked on a grave reorganizing project, bringing the remains of our ancestors together into one central burial site. Hired men dug up five plots in cemeteries scattered across the township, only to find that the bones at three of the graves had been pillaged. The bones of the missing include our relative from China that crossed the ocean to first establish my family in Taiwan. The ancestor is reputed to have been so filial that the only possession he crossed with were the bones of his parents strapped to his back.

Now, the rain hasn't stopped falling and delays us from visiting my grandparents' muddied graves on the hillside behind my uncle's house. So we head for what we hope will be better weather.

Back on the Matsu archipelago, we scale a small mountain to climb past barracks, abandoned cannons, and artillery training stations, to arrive at the island's military museum. My father chats with visitor services staff and learns that the young soldier manning the desk attended college for engineering. But like all of the other young men on the island, he's now putting in his obligatory time in the service. "This kid's got it easy," my father mutters, while pointing out a glass case that displays the kind of Howitzer shell that rained down over Houao during his assignment to the village. "I brought one of those shells back as a souvenir for Grandma, but it kept getting rusty."

We take a taxi southwest to the Wusha Beihai Tunnel, a decommissioned military area that was carved out of solid granite by soldiers using pickaxes, shovels, iron rakes, baskets, and other tools. The building of the tunnel took three years, and the lives of over 100 soldiers were lost to careless blasting. My cousin Sue-Juen's last words, before we got on a plane to Matsu, echo throughout my mind: "There were so many men that never came back." As the tide rises, we hurry out of the cave, water lapping our ankles.

We leave Beigan to fly to Taipei, where my father and I spend a few days touring heritage sites. On the northern coast, we make our way to Yehlio, where I beg my father to pose for a picture in front of Queen's Head Rock. Recalling a black-and-white photo of my father from the 1960s, I want to recreate the moment. Overheated and uncomfortable, my father complains about all the Chinese tourists cutting the line. Around us, security officers outfitted with whistles sound their alarms any time anyone gets too close to a rock formation or past the line of safety. After twenty minutes, my father has not stopped being sour. I finally take a picture.

We spend the last leg of our trip on Ludao (Green Island). Neither my father nor I have ever travelled to the notorious island. Under Martial Law, twenty thousand political prisoners from Taiwan were shipped off to "Oasis Villa." Our relatives and friends can't relate to my curiosity—"What's to see there? It's the dead of winter—you won't even be able to go snorkeling."

The tourist bureau transformed the site of the former prison into the Green Island Human Rights Cultural Park, the first human rights memorial in Asia. A verse written by poet Bo Yang is inscribed outside the prison walls on stone: "In that era, mothers cried night after night over their children imprisoned on this island." As my father and I tour the ruined buildings, we catch sight of workers sweeping the grounds. Inside the part of the prison that's been transformed into a museum, I enter a panopticon to walk down unending hallways of empty cells. At the end of one wing, I discover two padded cells without windows. My father translates the exhibition in the main hall—explaining the journal excerpts and drawings of those that were tortured and imprisoned. He grows somber, remembering the father of a classmate who was incarcerated for years on Green Island during the White Terror.

A friend connects me to a Green Island local who takes us on a tour of the major sights. When Mr. Tsun asks me what we want to see, I ask, "Can you take us where the bodies are buried?" He agrees to drive my father and me to the cemetery outside of Swallows Cave. We drive the car off a paved road and hike into a seaside area surrounded by wind-fallen trees. As we turn a corner into the graveyard, wild goats grazing in the cemetery scatter across the hills. My camera jams just as Mr. Tsun points into the distance and casually reveals, "That cave is where they burned the bodies."

I discover later while reading a local guidebook that locals promote this myth, though it's untrue. But I sense my father's reluctance to disturb the spirits by walking too close to Swallows Cave. One can't be too careful. I think about the gust of wind that blew my father off his electric bike when we arrived, the fragility of human life, my recent miscarriage.

On Dongzhi, a midwinter's day, the rain ceases and my body stops bleeding. Upon our return to Ching Shui, my father and I hike up a hillside near sunset to pay our respects at the gravesite of his parents. My uncle leads us to the grave by memory, through wild grasses as high as our shoulders, full of bramble and thorns. The mosquitoes swarm. We make an offering of fruit and chocolate and return back home to dumplings, balls of dough eaten all over Taiwan on this day—in common households, and in prisons, marking the passage of time and one more year.

Catherine Rankovic

HERITAGE STATEMENT:

My father Dragomir Rankovic arrived in the U.S. at Ellis Island in 1950, brought by the U.S. Displaced Persons program to work in the Bell City Foundry in Racine, Wisconsin. He was born in 1919 in a village twenty miles outside of Belgrade and in boyhood was apprenticed to a blacksmith. He joined the Royal Yugoslav Army in 1940 and was a prisoner of war in Germany from 1941 to 1945. He became a U.S. citizen in 1955 and was a member of the United Auto Workers and a founding member of the St. George Serbian Orthodox Church.

AUTHOR BIO:

Catherine Rankovic's books include *Fierce Consent and Other Poems* (WingSpan, 2005) *Guilty Pleasures: Indulgences, Addictions, and Obsessions* (Andrews McMeel Universal, 2003), *Island Universe: Essays and Entertainments* (WingSpan, 2007), and *Meet Me: Writers in St. Louis* (Penultimate Press Inc., 2010). She received her MFA from Washington University in St. Louis, where she taught from 1989 to 2010; she now teaches poetry and creative nonfiction writing in the online MFA program at Lindenwood University. Her  essays and poems have appeared in *Boulevard, Garbanzo, Gulf Coast, The Iowa Review, The Missouri Review, Natural Bridge, The Progressive, River Styx, The St. Louis Post-Dispatch, Umbrella*, and other journals, and the anthology *Are We Feeling Better Yet? Women Speak About Health Care in America* (Penultimate Press Inc., 2008). Her awards include the Missouri Biennial Award for essay writing, first place in the Midwest Writing Center's annual Mississippi Valley poetry competition, and an Academy of American Poets award. She is a professional book editor and her website is www.BookEval.com.

YOU BUY NICE—YOU GOT NICE

My father came to the U.S. from Eastern Europe on a steamship in 1950. He learned English, but he spoke it like a telegram, so he couldn't really lecture his four American-born kids, or talk things over with us, and the words of wisdom we got from him were few. When his children began dating he warned us, "You marry ugly, you get ugly children!" We still quote him, laughing, before we take to the road: "Don't drive like-a nuts!" And one more bit of advice crossed our language barrier, a tip on the nature of material things:

"You buy nice—you got nice. You buy junk—you got junk."

That's my father, Dragomir; I hear his voice whenever I am thinking about saving a few cents by purchasing something cheap instead of a higher-priced item that will last twice as long. I use his advice for everything from light bulbs to lawnmowers.

In his way, my father was saying, "You get what you pay for," and the maxim has guided me when major purchases loomed—a one-year-old Buick versus a snazzy four-year-old Mustang with 73,000 miles; a VCR that cost $100 more than the standard model but after thirteen years refused to die. It helped me choose a larger, brighter wedding diamond over a smaller, yellowish one I was tempted to choose just to save some money. I mean, save it for what? If you're buying a diamond, you should buy nice!

I couldn't always follow my father's advice, but always regretted ignoring it. Once I furnished a bedroom and chose to economize on the mattress. It soon developed a deep lengthwise crease, in which I lay like a hotdog in a bun. Trying to sleep, I pictured my father—short, compact, olive-skinned—in the doorway, wagging a hairy finger and saying, "You bought junk—you got junk."

Although he relished cheap novelties—he was a big fan of those wooden "drinking bird" toys that bowed perpetually to a brimming shot glass—and souvenirs such as the plastic zoo animals vacuum-formed in a vending machine. "For memory," he said, sliding coins into our hands. Mom wailed whenever he spent a buck or two on rubbish. Yet he paid cash for a new family-sized Chrysler every seven years while the all-American father next door worked a second job to buy his family five matching snowmobiles. And whenever Dad knew better, he bought better. He knew of only one place to buy his wife and kids boxed Valentine chocolates, and that was the grocery store—but at least he bought them.

Having a foreign-born father gave us a dual cultural perspective we didn't always appreciate. Americans thought backyards were for swing sets and patios; he and his Old Country friends thought backyards were for vegetable gardening. When I pleaded for an allowance because my friends all had one, I explained that it was an American custom for parents, each week, to owe their children free money. He was miffed, not by my calculating approach but at the implication that he did not provide everything his kids could want. Instead of giving us allowances, he bought the things we pestered him and my mother for, but only after he made sure that they were good. In my guitar phase I received a nice guitar. Promptly I changed my career plans to photography and wanted a camera I couldn't pay for. Dad might have then told me, as he sometimes did, "Go jump in the lake," or "You don't got two cents in you brain." But maybe because he'd been granted the chance to start over and do better, he granted me the same. We went to a camera shop, where he spent two weeks of his pay on a camera and equipment.

I hope I told my father, "Thank you," because I remember hesitating to say it then and there. I felt overwhelmed, sensing that this gift, to be well-used, would demand character and discipline that he was only betting I had. The gift was the only way he could say this in a way that I could possibly understand. He was also betting that I would someday know enough to understand, because at the time I was seventeen, radiantly ignorant, spoke only English, and was trying to hide my feelings by fussing with the camera that I would use for the next twenty years.

You buy nice—you got nice.

Yelizaveta P. Renfro

HERITAGE STATEMENT:

I was born 1975 in the former Soviet Union to a Russian mother and American father but moved to the U.S. at the age of three and grew up in Riverside, California.

AUTHOR BIO:

Yelizaveta P. Renfro is the author of a collection of short stories, *A Catalogue of Everything in the World* (Black Lawrence Press, 2010), winner of the St. Lawrence Book Award. Her creative nonfiction book, *Xylotheque: Essays*, was published by the University of New Mexico Press in the spring of 2014. Her fiction and nonfiction have appeared in *Adanna, Alaska Quarterly Review, Bayou Magazine, Blue Mesa Review, Colorado Review, Fourth River, Glimmer Train Stories, North American Review, Parcel, Reader's Digest,*

So to Speak, South Dakota Review, Untamed Ink, Witness, and the anthologies *A Stranger Among Us: Stories of Cross Cultural Collision and Connection* (OV Books, 2008) and *Commutability: Stories about the Journey from Here to There* (Main Street Rag, 2010). She holds an MFA from George Mason University and a PhD from the University of Nebraska. Born in the former Soviet Union, she has lived in California, Virginia, Nebraska, and Connecticut. Her virtual home is at www.chasingsamaras.blogspot.com.

BUTELA

Riverside, California, 1979

I watch you as you stand with a metal basin in your hands near that spindly tree at the edge of a dust-choked field, and your pause is long, deliberate before you finally tilt the basin and pour the water into the dry earth bowl around the birch. You have come not with a hose or a watering can, not with a proper vessel for the job, but with an old-fashioned basin for the washing of hands, and as the thin stream hits the dirt and sends up a small eruption of dust, I can already see that you will fail. As the water disappears into the earth, you continue to stand in your house-dress, looking at the withered tree, which is hardly taller than you and no wider than your forearm, and I understand that there is meaning in your standing. You are a tragic heroine, troubled and doomed in a dark Dostoevskian way, though no Dostoevsky character was ever in your particular circumstances—uprooted from your native Russia, and deposited in the parched, ramshackle opulence of citrus country in Southern California.

Of course, since I am only four, I comprehend only the rough outlines of these larger themes, but you are already teaching me what it means to be Russian, what it means to live through symbols, and I recognize that your tragic pose carries a meaning far beyond your simple act of watering a thirsty tree. You've invested your future happiness in this pale, thwarted ghost tree from Russia that doesn't belong here, just as you, my ghost mother from Russia, don't belong here. Do you create this living picture solely for me? Or is it for my American father? His American family? Have you been reduced to speaking through imagery? You, who wrote a PhD dissertation on French literature and taught at a university, now struggle to say and comprehend the simplest things. You will never, in thirty years, hear the difference between *sheet* and *shit*.

We stand like this: you in the sun with your basin and tree, in the very center of everything, and I hanging back in the shade of other trees, not quite hidden, not quite revealed. You are turned away from me, but you know I am there, don't you? You speak to me, don't you? Because I am the spectator, the child you brought from Russia, and I am the one who has already begun to betray you, speaking more English than Russian, keenly hearing the difference between *peace* and *piss, height* and *hate*. Your standing is a langue that I am sure to understand despite my shifting linguistic allegiance, despite my responses to you in English, each word a fresh slap in the face. In your stoic standing you are telling me, sans words, that trees are to be loved and protected, that in them we invest our identities, that they carry within them the places we are from, and that even when they are doomed—or maybe especially when they are doomed—they are important beyond reckoning. My father bought this doomed tree and put it in the ground, so you would have Russia just outside the door. Perhaps you know already that the birch is dying. Perhaps you knew from the beginning that California would kill it. And this, too, is part of your message—that we do that which we know will end in heartache, that we relish poignancy, that we seek symbolism in misfortune.

Years later, I will read that birches are a pioneer species that spreads after ice ages, fires, or other ravages, colonizing the land. They live at the extreme northern limits of where trees go, but you are standing with your basin far from any northern limits in the Mediterranean climate of Riverside, California. Birches will not colonize this temperate land. Years later, I will learn that in Russian bathhouses—*banyas*—bathers flagellated themselves with birch branches, and you are flagellating us both, aren't you, in your pathetic stand to insinuate, among California flora, your native vegetation. Years later, I will hear that some of the earliest Slavic writing is preserved on birch bark. Your birch, I will finally see, is your writing on this alien landscape, a ghostly northern specter that for a season is writ against California sunsets glowing tangerine and plum.

And finally, the picture ends like this: simply, I tire of watching you, so I turn and run away from you into the other trees, both native and nonnative, that thrive here—palm, navel orange, eucalyptus, mulberry, pepper, floss silk, jacaranda, peach, apricot. I leave you standing with your dying tree, and I don't look back. That is my image for you: a daughter turning her back on her mother, a daughter turning American.

But even now, each time I see the silhouettes of palms against California sky, I am jolted again by the alien inscription they make, spelling out the exotic, the tropical and temperate, the not-me. Even though I spent only three years in my native Russia and the two decades that followed in California, I have yearned for other trees, other places. I live now in a northern clime where birches are native, where snow falls in winter, where the landscape, finally, feels like home. In this land of birches I nurture my own birch, which I planted just outside my front door, and it flourishes, spectral and graceful, but it is a weaker symbol, an echo of you and your birch, an echo of that other time, that other place. And still this is not Russia, and I do not write these words in Russian. I turn away from you, I disappoint. And though a transplant myself, unlike you I am fluent in the language of my country. Unlike you, I do not need the birch to speak for me.

Susanna Rich

HERITAGE STATEMENT:

My mother, Susanna Szilágyi, and my father, Nicholas Lippóczy, met at the Hungarian Ministry of Defense in Budapest, where they were working in 1945. When the Russians invaded Hungary, they fled to Bad Wörishofen, Germany, where they married in 1946. With my mother's help, my father founded *Hungaria*, the first refugee newspaper. Because of its political and editorial nature, the regime in Hungary threatened them with death. My parents fled to the United States in 1950. My mother's mother soon followed with her husband and two sons. I was born and raised in Passaic, New Jersey. Since my parents divorced soon after my birth, my grandmother was my primary caretaker. I did not start speaking English until I entered kindergarten, at the age of five.

AUTHOR BIO:

Susanna Rich is a 2009 Mid-America EMMY Nominee for her poetry in Craig Lindvahl's *Cobb Field: A Day at the Ballpark*; author of two Finishing Line Press poetry collections, *The Drive Home* (Finishing Ling Press, 2009) and *Television Daddy* (Finishing Ling Press, 2008); the recipient of the first joint Fulbright and Collegium Budapest Fellowship in Creative Writing; and a Pushcart Prize nominee. She won both the Twentieth-Century America and Twenty-First-Century America Poetry contests of *Sensations Magazine*. Susanna is Professor of English and recipient of the Presidential Excellence Award for Distinguished Teaching at Kean University in New Jersey. Susanna is also founder of *Wild Nights Poetry Productions*, through which she tours unique staged, one-woman, audience-interactive poetry readings.

DIRTY DANCING, JÁNOS, WITH YOU

If we were continents—I nearer fifty,
you, one hundred—an Atlantic of time
would slosh between us: your tsunamis of wars,
depressions; my billows of New Age,

strip malls, Facebook. So who knows what
started *this* in our fruit-smelling church hall,
Wednesday night social—for all to see:
some line dance—"New York, New York,"

maybe; some sock hop flashback.
You bob a hip at me. I flick one at you.
And you're the dapper grandfather I never met,
a heel-clicking Austro-Hungarian morphed

into a soft waltz. I am my own grandmother—
a girl again, with a Danube of star-swept nights
before me. You catch my hand in yours—
my father leaps a brook, sees me as he never has:

a young woman testing herself on first love.
You spin me around and you are Tom Kulick—
my unrequited high school crush. You're Elvis-
pelvising at me—and I, Isadora-ing you—

the brook between us becomes our moist mingling
breath. We're swiveling our belly-dancing bums,
the muck of age and gender spun away—
animated, mirroring twins whirling

in our private Istanbul harem—our days,
like coins, jangling—we two gyrating because . . .
just because. Others circle around us,
holding hands, bumping shoulders and chests;

whooping, whistling, *yee-hah*-ing us on;
stamping and thundering out the dance
master, who stands on the shore
pounding his staff by the parting sea.

PENTECOST SUNDAY:
MÁTYÁS CHURCH, BUDAPEST

Coming late (almost not) into this medieval dusk,
I sit in the way-back of the church,
on stone steps leading down from the old

barricaded entrance—where other tourists
with single camera eyes, Christophers
with noisy toddlers, and the unaffiliated flock.

Haydn's *Kyrie* has pinioned the priest
to a sanctuary chair—he in his sure red chasuble,
I in my red voile dress—facing each other

from far ends of the nave.
The "Nelson Mass for Times of Distress"
is all trumpets, tympani, organ, and voices.

How can I deserve their piercing fullness?
I'm tempted to flip open the Motorola to call
my sleeping husband—*come hear*—

as if his being lofted into this soprano's reach
would make me worthy to hear it, myself.
This fiftieth day after Easter that closes corner ABCs,

frees fathers to pocket playgrounds,
slows trams and the underground.
My father died a year ago today

back in my America—while his friends
prayed at Hungarian Mass.
Kyrie, Kyrie . . . so I have come this morning.

A baby burbles with the strains of music,
an ancient whacks his walker along the floor.
How can I find my father's Jesus in me?

The Blessed Mother rises above the altar
in a frankly vaginal frame. This vault, this
overturned ship is hers, but they call it

"Mátyás's Church" for the warrior, wealthy donor,
twice-married here, namesake of Matthew
who replaced Judas. My twice-married father

disavowed me as not Hungarian woman
enough—I who betrays him now by playing
at belief in the church he loved.

Tammy Robacker

HERITAGE STATEMENT:

My father was U.S.-born and met my mother in West Germany while he served as an MP in the U.S. Army. They married and lived in Germany where I was born. In late 1969 we came to the United States to live as a family after my father was discharged from the military. I grew up as a child experiencing the duality of having a Western father and an immigrant mother speaking with a native German tongue and never feeling like America was her home. I lived with a foot rooted in both countries.

AUTHOR BIO:

Tammy Robacker was Poet Laureate of Tacoma, Washington, from 2010–2011 and is a 2011 Hedgebrook Writer in Residence award winner. Her manuscript, *R*, was the recipient of the 2016 Keystone Poetry Chapbook Prize and her newest poetry collection is *Villain Songs* (ELJ Publications, 2016). In 2009, Ms. Robacker published her first collection of poetry, *The Vicissitudes* (Pearle Publications), and also co-edited a poetry anthology, *In Tahoma's Shadow: Poems from the City of Destiny*. Her poetry has appeared in *The Allegheny Review*, *Columbia Magazine*, *Floating Bridge Review: Pontoon*, *Up the Staircase Quarterly*, and *Wild Goose Poetry Review*. Her poetry manuscript, *We Ate Our Mothers, Girls*, was selected as a finalist in the 2009 Floating Bridge Press chapbook contest. She earned her MFA in creative writing from the Rainier Writing Workshop at Pacific Lutheran University.

KUCHEN AND CANCER

for my Mother

On the very bad days,
you baked cake. Made things better
with butter, zucker, and eggs. Now
creamed white and sacked thin; folded
sheet-tight to the hospital corners,
my mother batters and stirs in and out
of opiate-laced sleep. *Have you ever
tasted a cloud, my Angel? Ach
Gott, is it sweet!* My heritage
has been beaten and sifted through
you. Passed over memories become
final mementos. Of dirty bed pans. Of
jaundice eyes watered down and reading
me last rites from the old, piss
yellow pages of your cookbooks. I am
a recipe. Woman, following directions well,
I rise dependably as any Deutsche daughter.
Rise like yeasty cake
to serve you. To tend to the affairs
as you heave up from bad dreams,
pillow-bloated and malignant.
I spoon mouthfuls of your bile
out. Measure more morphine.
Hold you like a loaf, born
fresh out of the oven. Loved. Pressing
the whole, thick, warm middle
of you, Mother, close to me.

SAUERKRAUT

Meine Mutter Tote Mutter
how many years
will you be pickling
before that sour face
can dissipate for good
in rotted steam wafts
above the black crock
where we buried you
where I have eaten
my fill of your bitterness
but still I taste the sharp
tang teeth that bite
through memory or dreams
of that old orange kitchen
you controlled and cleaned
throat thick with Ich Hasse
simmering pissed in that heavy
stink of early cabbage
and fermented weeds
turning time salty with brine
kept alive in wild yeast slime
eat eat eat girl I still eat
what's grown bad and buried
barrel-deep in the dank tomb
of that family heirloom
sealed shut by one stony
weight of the darkest slate
shaped like West Germany
Mutti Gitti Kriegi
what a Nazi I've become
I'm continually skimming off

clotted mold and runny scum
even though you're done
time after time you fester
you bubble up
you rise
avenged as Easter
and climb the sides.

Mary Lou Sanelli

HERITAGE STATEMENT:

As a first-generation American and daughter of Italian immigrants—Maria Antoinette Sinsigalli and Luigi Gabrielle Sanelli, coming to this country, like so many, after the Second World War, my father from Umbria, my mother from Puglia—I longed to break free of Old World constraints of religion and culture both emotionally and physically. Upon arrival from the East Coast (New York, Hartford, Boston) to the seemingly liberal West Coast, I felt at ease, connected to the land and mind-set with the wide-eyed glee of a newcomer, though this sense of place lessened with the years. I tried to imitate the laid-back dress and manners of my new Seattle friends, lowering my voice when I spoke, waving my hands around less. In a sense, I tried to leave my passionate way of communicating behind, though, in spite of my efforts to conform, I hauled my upbringing around with me. As the years passed, the more I tried to leave my truest self behind, the more it snuck up to embrace me.

AUTHOR BIO:

Mary Lou Sanelli is the author of seven poetry collections, and three works of nonfiction, including *Falling Awake* and *Among Friends: A Memoir*. She is a regular columnist for *City Living Magazine*, as well as for *Art Access Magazine* and *The Peninsula Daily News*. Her work has appeared in *The Seattle Times* and in *The Seattle Post-Intelligencer*, as well as *Seattle Metropolitan Magazine*. She is a regular feature on KONP AM, KSER FM, and her commentaries have been aired on NPR's *Weekend Edition*. She presents her staged reading of her book, *The Immigrant's Table*, throughout the country.

SLICED MEAT AND BREAD

I take a stand against Vietnam but nothing I say
sways my father. Secretly I know
I know nothing of war, but my temper is flung against his.
He loosens his belt. Counts to ten. I'm sobbing
by the time he says *cinque*.

From another room,
my mother pleads with the whole of my name
plus the one tacked on at Confirmation,
our Catholic coming of age: *Maria Louisa Gabriella*,
for the love of God, let us eat in peace,
before she repeats the words,
whispering her plea into two folded hands
as if it were prayer.

Now, the table is spread.
My mother throwing herself into it, bosom heaving.
Cheese is cut a tire-sized wheel, bread from loaves
long as my arm, meat sliced thin as cellophane.
Suddenly, as if on tiptoe, my fit shrivels, is gone.

We finish with fruit, rinds carved free, a family
of knives working rhythmically as the second
hand on a watch.

My father stands, grins
like an MC, walks to the den where he will read
from a book that opens his memories of war
like a scalpel. The war: Hitler's. Mussolini's.
He will remember the men who made camp on his family farm.
He will tell me stories that will permeate my childhood

thick as his cigar smoke: *Everything to eat, the army ate.*
Everything of value, stolen. Furniture, clothes, books,
burned to keep soldiers warm.

I can see it: My father trudging the land
for berries and squirrels to skin, his cache
bedded in straw. My grandmother so thin, so scared.
My aunt sleeping on floorboards in a corner of the goat barn,
her breath steaming, rising
to be part of the air.

PANE DI PASQUA ALL'UOVO
(EASTER EGG BREAD)

Vigorously, my mother kneads the dough,
punching with one fist, then both fists.
Flour dusts her feet. White tracts
by the sink, refrigerator, phone.

A damp cloth covers three milk-white balls.
When doubled, swollen like bellies,
she rolls each into equal lengths to braid,
her new friend saying she can't believe
how much preparation *Eye-talian* holidays take.
We flinch because there is no good way
to deny or correct this misuse of sound
light years from appropriate.

In a snowed-in cul-de-sac,
Protestant, Methodist, and atheist women
walk knee-deep in snowdrifts to our home
to be buoyed by homespun wreaths
of warm bread, peppermint-sweet,
dotted with six shades of eggs.

Before they come, I watch my mother stand
on a chair to remove the crucifix from our kitchen wall.

Our neighbors sit around the table, admiring.
Since moving from Italy to the suburbs of New England,
this is what my mother craves, to be unique
and not provincial in her new neighbors' minds.

Frances Saunders

HERITAGE STATEMENT:

My mother was the last of three daughters at home when pogroms raged in Odessa, Russia, on the eve of WWI. Her two older sisters left for Marseilles earlier. A third sister had chosen to settle in the United States. She married soon after. Her husband sponsored my mother, who landed on Ellis Island at age eighteen or so and went to live with the couple in the vicinity of Convent Avenue in Manhattan. Luba, my mother—renamed Lena passing through Ellis Island—was employed in a factory sewing linings inside winter coats. Two years later her sister grew concerned that her prospects for marriage hadn't materialized and she would have an old maid on her hands. So, she had a friend introduce my mother to my father, who was born in the U.S.

AUTHOR BIO:

Frances Saunders has been published in several anthologies, *Steeped in the World of Tea* (Interlink Books, 2004) and *When Last on the Mountain* (Holy Cow! Press, 2011), as well as the journals *Marco Polo Arts Magazine*, *Passager*, and others.

PICTURE THIS

"Is that so? Champagne taste, beer pocketbook and you're not even eleven."

"A cat can look at the queen."

My mother and I were window-shopping in front of Blum's Department Store. A watercolor of a ballet dancer in a blue tutu caught my fancy.

"In my day, if I wanted anything bad enough, I earned it. Made myself useful around the house. Saved my pennies."

I didn't get the ballerina. What I got instead set in motion a tug of war between my irrepressible fear and my mother's unreasonable obstinacy. We had just moved from Harlem to the East Bronx. Sitting on the edge of my bed in my newly acquired privacy, my eyes roamed the naked white walls. On the far side of the room, I saw a familiar mahogany frame. Could it be the same photograph I had unearthed from its hiding place? The one that raised goosebumps on my arms and sent shivers down my back? I had been rummaging for secrets in our old apartment. The kind my mother withheld from me. The secrets she shared with a sigh and whispers among her friends. Should I happen to be within earshot, her eyes would roll in my direction, stifling the gossip. Curiosity drove me to rummaging. I started in my mother's dresser, then in her closet, her nightstand. Having exhausted the obvious places, I looked under my parents' bed. Here, I came face to face with a corrugated box. Without wasting a moment, I slid the bulky carton from under the bed with the heart palpitations of a participant in a scavenger hunt and all the while, listening for the key in our front door and the rustling of shopping bags. Given a choice, I coveted the contents of antique trunks, tear-stained letters, diaries confessing illicit romances and, with a little bit of luck, ancestors with a past too shameful to speak aloud. Nothing up until now ever happened to me or my friends the way they played out in the library books we devoured. Later, I understood what I pined for came from my own heightened imagination. Kneeling and squinting, I saw a corrugated box labeled "photographs." I remember dragging the treasure out from under the bed, studying the arrangement of framed pictures to avoid detection, and unwrapping the one on top. I drew in my breath. My grandfather, dead in Odessa, long before I was born looked directly at me. He wore a black brimmed hat and a beard flecked with silver. His moist, staring eyes were disturbing, accusing. Did his mouth move? Or was my mother calling?

"Linda, come help with the groceries." In haste, I shoved the box under the bed, forgetting to fold down the cardboard extensions. When the carton resisted, I wasted another moment pushing it out of sight.

"Linda, where are you?"

Tripping on a throw rug, I came close to losing a few teeth. In the kitchen, I busied myself unloading groceries, managing to avert my guilty face from my mother's all-knowing suspicious one. Surprising encounters were nothing new in our household. Around the time I discovered the picture, another event kept me on high alert. My mother had finished scrubbing my back when a rat jumped through a hole in our bathroom ceiling; it vaulted the tub and squeezed through an opening under the sink. After that heart-stopping event, I insisted, long after the painter had plastered the openings, that she remain in the bathroom until I finished bathing. Then I took to worrying about the dark spaces under the footed tub where bugs might nest and spiders spun their webs, where silent creatures hid and shadows crawled on the walls. When my dread of imminent danger persisted, my mother consulted the family doctor. He dispensed a tonic and as he escorted us out of his office, I overheard him assure my mother. "Childhood fears are not unusual. My mother and I compromised. If I bathed alone, I could have a night light in my room."

Now, in my own room, I fought to distract my attention from my grandfather's gaze. I flipped the pages of my arithmetic book, and sharpened my pencil to a nub as if those gestures took the place of actually completing my homework. No matter how hard I tried to concentrate, an overpowering pull drew my attention toward the picture. Could it be the old man on the wall, in his ancient wisdom, read my mind and dallied with my intimate thoughts? My eyes followed the dust particles on the pale rays of sunlight that streamed through the window and bounced off the picture glass, distorting his face. A bitter taste rose in my throat, like car sickness on family outings. I shielded my eyes and squinted between splayed fingers, testing my courage, looking directly at the picture. All at once, the old man's face advanced and receded. His eyes glowed in their sockets. Shrieking, I ran down the hall smack into my mother's arms. She clutched me to her chest until I grew calmer. "What is it? Tell me." She touched my forehead to check for fever, ran her eyes over my face, and clicked her tongue. "You scared me half to death. I was sure you were getting killed." "His eyes light up," I said. "Whose?" she asked. I dragged her into my bedroom. The sun had set and the picture hung in the afterglow. "Him." I pointed. My grandfather gazed straight ahead out of an old man's dull eyes. Mom locked the window and lowered the blind. "You probably saw the sun's rays flickering on the picture. When you doze, sometimes you dream." She scrutinized my face as though she had overlooked something important. "That sweet man, may he rest in peace, wouldn't harm a soul. I hung his picture in your room to protect you from harm. Without his bravery, my whole family would have perished." She patted my head. "After a day or so, you won't even notice the picture. Go. Finish your homework and stop this nonsense."

I failed to make sense of my mother's thinking. If I'm frightened now, what makes her think anything will change as long as the picture hung in my room? I considered asking Pop to remove it, knowing he would be a willing ally, but that would arouse old resentments, and I disliked when my parents fought. The man in the picture was Mom's father, after all, and no matter what I did, it couldn't be undone without hurting her feelings. So until I came up with a foolproof idea I had to tolerate the picture. I slammed the door so hard, the frame shook.

Winter arrived, and with it, early nightfall. I came home immediately after school, I folded laundry, entertained my brother and felt resentful at having denied myself candy treats to save for the ballerina. At lights out, I burrowed under the quilt and turned my back to the picture. Out of sight, out of mind, as the saying goes. Dead men don't walk.

One sleepy weekend, with no good reason to leave the house, I amused myself with an experiment I had seen my friend Agnes try on her dog. We had been studying hypnosis in science and Agnes asked me over to review for a science test. Needing a break from quizzing each other, she hit on a crazy notion.

"Let's try the experiment in our science book on my dog." Our teacher had cautioned the class that no one other than a trained professional was qualified to perform hypnosis. The results might be catastrophic. I reminded Agnes what the teacher had said.

"A Mastiff is an animal, not a person. Bitsy *sit*." Holding him by his collar, Agnes looked steadily into the dog's eyes. He shook his head to free himself, growled deep in his throat, flattened his ears, and bared his teeth. Breaking free, he raised himself to his full height and lunged at Agnes. The screeching alerted her mother. She came running, upended a wooden chair, smashed it on Bitsy's head and coaxed him into the kitchen.

Some time later, desperate to overcome my irrational terror of a dead man's picture, I tried hypnosis. I stood on a chair, stretched my neck, and cautiously made eye contact for the length of time it took to hold my breath. The old man's piercing orbs woke in their sunken sockets. I gulped chunks of air, jumped to the floor and stealthily edged toward the door. Positive his eyes were tracking me, I dared a glance over my shoulder. My parents' bedroom door was closed. My brother slept in an alcove where Mom could hear him. Pop was on the late shift so there wasn't the rush for dinner. We had an unbroken rule that when Mom napped, under no condition should she be disturbed unless a fire broke out in the building. I jiggled her feet. She sat up bewildered, her face imprinted with chenille squiggles, her long, blonde hair disheveled.

"What's the matter?"

"If you loved me," I wailed, "you would hang your father's picture in your own room."

She brushed my hair away from my forehead, and said nothing for a while. "It's because I love you, I want you to have the little I saved from the old country. Your grandfather painted those nesting dolls you brought to school to show the class and the wooden pencil box with my name *Luba* written in Cyrillic letters. I hope one day when you're older, you'll understand what it means to lose a family."

She turned toward the kitchen, leaving me hopelessly confused, guilty as if I were a wretched traitor to the memory of her father, an ingrate for all she had done for me. Then again, I thought, I'm old enough to decorate my room any way I like. If she chooses to call Dr. Sorkin and have me committed to a loony bin like he did to the woman down the street who mumbled to herself and went to the butcher shop in her pink bedroom slippers, I'm beyond caring. When I confided to Agnes that my Mom was unreasonable, she said maybe it means she needed to arrange an appointment with Dr. Sorkin for what ails her.

My mother hadn't ever been mean to me before. She's respected by her neighbors, famous for reading tea leaves and capable of shaping a believable doll in a second out of a scrap of cloth and some string to soothe a cranky child. She taught me many useful tasks like how to knit, sew seams, and boil an egg. But, in this head to head, no matter the consequences, I was determined to come out on the winning side.

On a blustery morning, I walked to school with Agnes. We warmed our hands inside lobbies where we knew the radiators steamed. Along a small stretch of shops, we stopped to look in the window of a new store. A painting caught my attention. It stood among bibles, beads and crosses with instructions on a printed card; "Look at Christ's eyes. Walk slowly away without taking your eyes from his." "Let's try it Agnes. You first, then me."

"Holy Moses," she said. "His eyes followed me."

"See what I mean. That's what I've been telling you about my grandfather's picture."

She screwed up her face as though I had asked her to explain Isaac Newton's theory on gravity. "He's different," she said finally, which I found puzzling.

At recess I asked Sarah, a classmate, if Miss Rubin would think I was cuckoo if I confided about the strange goings on in my bedroom.

"What happened to the advice I gave you weeks ago? I told you to stand on a chair, cut the cord, and let the picture fall." She gave me a shove. "Go ahead. Try Miss Rubin. She can't grade you for asking."

Miss Rubin leaned against the chain-link fence, a red wool scarf wrapped around the lower half of her face. Seeing me approach, she freed her mouth, and flashed an encouraging smile, motioning me to come closer. I knew she admired my compositions. Always gave me an "A" and wrote things like *Good story*, *Imaginative*, and *Watch your spelling*. I poured out my fears quickly, too quickly, like duck pins colliding in a direct hit.

"Slow down. Start over." My second telling sounded even more bizarre. To my surprise she didn't laugh. I felt encouraged when she took time to give my curious tale serious consideration. Perhaps she was rooting around for a suitable answer to fit this special problem.

"Let's see if this helps. Last summer I vacationed in Paris, a city I hope you'll visit one day. My first stop was the Louvre, a museum ten times the size of our Metropolitan Museum of Art. I waited hours in line to see the *Mona Lisa*. Would you believe that woman's eyes followed me the same way you just described? She had been a mystery for centuries, from the expression around her mouth to her tricky eyes. No one has figured out for sure what Leonardo da Vinci had in mind." She lifted my chin with her gloved hand. The gold flecks in her brown eyes reminded me of walnut-studded chocolate cookies.

"Think of it this way. Maybe the photographer who took your grandfather's picture had a few tricks up his sleeve. Maybe he counted on someone with imagination like you would recognize his talent and play along." She stooped so our faces almost touched. "Try to understand your mother. She depends on you to pass on her fondest memories and to keep them alive when she no longer can."

Confounded, I drifted through the empty playground back to class. I spent the afternoon wrapped around Miss Rubin's complicated answer. I visualized a photographer with his head stuck under a black cloth, his hand squeezing a rubber bulb. In the end, as much as I adored Miss Rubin, she had it all wrong. What I didn't want was a dead man on my bedroom wall. I wanted him covered in the box under my parents' bed.

At bedtime I needed my mother to walk me into my room.

"Aren't you ashamed? A big girl like you can't go to sleep without her mother. Are you asking me to tell my father in my prayers his granddaughter is afraid of him? Try to imagine a pogrom. Then you would have a good reason to be afraid."

"Maybe," I said, "If he had smiled for the picture, he would look friendlier."

"Smile? There wasn't much to smile about in those days. Pictures were for remembering, not for entertainment. Take a look at Abraham Lincoln in your school auditorium. Is he smiling?" Abruptly, the overhead light clicked off.

The time had come for action. I would remove the picture on a night when Pop was home and my mother not likely to return once she kissed me goodnight. Why not now? I listened for the intermittent sounds of my parents' voices between sips of tea. Before I lost my nerve, I dragged a chair close to the wall and climbed up. I stretched my arms, stood on tiptoe and clung to the shelf of a tall bookcase for balance. Suddenly, the hall floorboard creaked. My heart beat double time. I heard the storage closet open. The light clicked off and the footsteps retreated. Up close, the old man's face ballooned and his eyes were enormous. I managed to swat the frame with my free hand. The picture swung to and fro like a pendulum. I jumped and caught the frame, tried to lift it from its moorings. I missed and it crashed with a thunderous roar. Shattered glass shot like comets every which way. A kitchen cupboard slammed shut. I hopped barefoot across the glass-strewn room and scrunched down in bed. My parents stood in the doorway.

"Well, well." My father surveyed the mess. "I never cared much for that old geezer's picture myself. All you had to do was ask, and I would have taken it down." He picked up the frame, a smile teasing the corners of his mouth. Mom gasped, as if she had witnessed a beheading. If only she would yell, beat me, put an end to her icy glare. A glass splinter dug into the sole of my foot. It stung and so did the tears behind my eyelids.

After what seemed an eternity, Mom heaved a sorrowful sigh.

"From now on, guilt will press on your heart. It won't give you a minute's peace until you mend your ways." I mended my ways as well as most teens, saw more clearly what Miss Rubin meant and why my mother and I were torn apart. Where I felt threatened, my mother saw hardship, bravery and loss. With the passing of time, I overcame my childish fears, only to replace them with weightier ones; such is the price of growing up.

Melita Schaum

HERITAGE STATEMENT:

My mother, father and grandmother fled postwar Germany in 1952 to settle first in Canada then in America. Refugees from Nazi Germany, they left it all behind—the suffering and guilt, the cooking smells and accents and rituals, their own conflicted loyalties—to cast off on the immigrants' journey from poverty to upward mobility. My sister and I were raised by my Oma, who spoke no English, so our only language was German until we were sent to kindergarten, where our difference from others was thrown back at us like a shock. I think that sense of otherness has followed me all my life, from my drive to become a writer—to claim and make beautiful my second, inherited language of English—to my life-long restlessness as a wanderer and artist.

AUTHOR BIO:

Melita Schaum is the author of two books on Wallace Stevens and two books on women's issues, including *Stalked: Breaking the Silence on the Crime of Stalking in America* (Simon & Schuster, 1995). Her fifth book, *A Sinner of Memory* (Michigan State University Press, 2004), a collection of her memoir essays, was named runner-up for Great Lakes Colleges Association New Writer Award for 2004, and finalist for *Foreword Magazine*'s Memoir Book of the Year. Her poetry, fiction and literary essays have appeared in such journals as *Briar Cliff Review, The Colorado Review, The Denver Quarterly, The Literary Review, Mississippi Review, New Letters Magazine, The Notre Dame Review*, and *PRISM International*. Among other honors, she was awarded the Dorothy Cappon Churchill Award in Creative Nonfiction, the Orlando Prize in Nonfiction, and the New Millennium Writings Prize. Three of her essays have been nominated for the Pushcart Prize. Schaum received her MFA from Stanford in 1980 and taught creative writing and modern literature at the University of Michigan–Dearborn from 1984–2014. She currently lives in Berkeley, California, where she has taught writing seminars for the University of California, Berkeley and The Writing Salon in San Francisco.

EXCHANGES

My mother's greatest fear was the telephone.

It perched in the kitchen of our small New Jersey subdivision home—black, fat as a roach, clinging to the wall above the breakfast table like the motionless carapace of some horrific beetle. It was an old rotary, with a bulbous earpiece and a Ferris wheel of startling white numbers, and it made a ratchety, clicking sound whenever anybody stuck their index finger into the holes and dialed. Forget the polite, melodic bleating of today's smartphones. That phone's ring was a screech, a yowl, a squall of angry ravens exploding from a tree. That phone's ring went up your ganglia shrill as a fire alarm, a black fist smashing open with its violent summons the safe and secret immigrant life of home.

When it rang, the family would fall into a panicked hush, a small tribe closing ranks. We were a household of helpless women at the sound of an intruder, huddled behind the hall door with raised candlesticks. My father, as usual, was away at the office. My grandmother, who'd immigrated along with my parents, spoke only German. My sister and I were just toddlers. It fell to my mother, whose English was precarious, to pick up the perilous, shrieking receiver, listen into it, and speak.

Allo? Her accent would quaver, inflected and doubtful. Everyone leaned forward on tiptoe, as if my mother were holding a ticking bomb.

Allo? Her ear covered, she'd turn to stare at us imploringly, frozen in a posture of anxious anticipation. One hand white-knuckled the black handset. The other coiled the cord until it looked like evidence of strangulation at a crime scene. Long, dreadful moments passed.

Ja? Even when she recognized the caller, still her eyes never lost the round, white-edged look of an animal in car lights. Sometimes I stood close enough to hear, at the receiver's far end, a small, tinny mimicry of human sound. No wonder my mother looked spellbound by fear. To me it sounded like the noises that praying mantises would make, or my sister's horrible glass-eyed dolls if they could speak.

It was that phone that fractured the calm on weekday mornings, to announce our neighbor Mrs. Akiama, stopping by to sit over coffee with my mother, two refugees from different shores. Mrs. Akiama was a little, round woman with a creaseless, shiny face; my mother a slim brunette, her mouth Valentined with lipstick that left stains on her cup like fallen red flower petals.

This bad, bad country, Mrs. Akiama would croon, staring into her saucer as if she could see there some different future. Soon she would begin to cry.

Outside our windows, the newly seeded lawns stretched out, a green grid curbing chaos, but not very well. There were wild, high fields behind our houses that led down to the lake where Nelson, her boy, had drowned the winter before, his red parka found floating under the ice like a bloodstain.

It was through that phone we learned that the Cronins were divorcing, that Mr. Cronin had gone to his office one day and never come back. *Rang off?* My mother repeated weakly, not understanding. The Cronins' house—an incongruous Victorian painted colors with names like *salmon* and *celery*—was always spotless, fanatically clean. Mrs. Cronin was an obsessive polisher, a frenzied scrubber of tabletops and silverware and mailbox flags. It was a sickness, my grandmother told us children, moving her finger in a circle near her temple, like she was dialing her own head.

One Halloween my sister and I saw inside the Cronin home; it looked a little like a funeral parlor. The white Berber carpet was as stainless as if it had just come from the factory. The pillows had been plumped and positioned on the couch in a perfect row, regular as false teeth. Every surface gleamed. We waited at the door—two spies from another land disguised as Minnie Mouse and Tinker Bell—while Mrs. Cronin went into the kitchen for a bowl of candy. We could hear a cabinet open and shut, then water running. My scalp itched under my vinyl Mouseketeers cap. My sister pulled at the crotch of her pink fairy tights.

"It smells sad in there," she whispered. "Let's go."

Everything paraded through our telephone. Births, catastrophes, gossip, wrong numbers, invitations. Everything heralded by that spine-jangling ring, that startling portent.

It was under that phone that my mother lifted me onto her lap one day, her new black crepe smelling like carnations and wrinkling against the backs of my legs like tissue paper. My patent leather Sunday shoes dangled against her shins, shiny as two bugs, and it amazed me that my mother and I were both wearing black.

When I looked up to tell her, her eyes looked rubbed and red, and she was staring across the room at something nobody else could see. "I've lost my mama," she said, nuzzling softly into my neck, lifting my hand to her cheek. "Who will be my mama now?" She began to rock gently, using me for balance. I could feel the buttons on her collar pressing into me hard enough to hurt, and I tried to wriggle from her arms, half-heartedly at first and then harder and harder until it seemed that she and I were locked in some desperate, drowning embrace.

One day I climbed up onto the chair myself and lifted the silent black receiver from its cradle. It was heavier than I'd expected and had holes in the earpiece like a cheese grater.

I clenched both hands around it and, summoning my courage, pressed the side of my head against the cold plastic.

I don't know what I thought I'd hear—words maybe, alien sounds. The mystery of my mother's grip. Enigma of a culture that never seemed to fit our family's awkward angles and edges. The puzzle of coffee cups and polished living rooms and tears.

What I heard was vacant noise—not silence, but a hollow, staticky sound. It was the sound that black made, a color like space, immense and empty, out of which voices called to my mother, messages of grief and loss and exile, the same voices that would someday speak to me. I knelt there, cocking my ear down that long, dark pipeline, listening for things I knew I couldn't understand but had already learned to fear.

PROVISIONS

It was the summer of wild cherry jam the summer we picked and picked in the new-found trees by the lake where sculls sliced the water into silver sheaves and at noon the old black men from Prospect Avenue fished for catfish along the riverbank

my mother's war so far away in that kitchen on Grover Street the want the disorder the lentils she detested as a child the thunder of air raids gauntlet of bodies on rubbled streets the soldier dying in their parlor (they crossed themselves and emptied his pockets) the tallow they used for lipstick the girls who slept with GIs for nylons and Baby Ruths

the war in my mother stood over the kitchen sink and scrubbed between the tines of forks, ran the vacuum loud around the pretty installment-plan furniture, it cooked up the fruit we'd hauled home in coffee cans, boiled the fresh berries into a steaming red mass and poured it in jars though we protested sealed each with a rime of paraffin like closing a coffin preserving making provision out of our windfall lives

then forcing us to eat it all *waste not, want not* or whatever its German equivalent heavy words followed by the threat of a heavier hand the misery of breakfast every day the red too runny too sweet mess dripping from brown sides of toast food thrust into our mouths as salve for her own childhood's lack the badness the mess that she too had to eat and was still swallowing

the war in my mother raged over the kitchen table with its sticky shiny cheerful vinyl its skin of normalcy its yellow light its birthday parties its radio and smells of coffee the clock on the wall ticking the timer chiming the kettle screaming *America America* the checkered aprons paper napkins watermelons in July iced tea orange cheese sugared cereals each bite each tick and pop and whistle and click of a can opener taking my mother further she thought from her hunger but it wasn't so. Each provision was something new to lose in the end she was no closer to the peace that must have smelled like honey those green distant shores of in-

different plenty where they spoke a foreign tongue of radio tunes and red melon
that she would never understand the war in my mother had no truce all it could
do was flow across new borders—and there in the spotlight of memory my sister
and I sit kicking the table legs refusing the jam that looks like congealing blood

that tastes of my mother's bitter handiwork that feels like all her battles boiled
down into this pulp that used to be our afternoon's wild joy of picking and now
was a lesson in a jar that we didn't, didn't, didn't want to learn.

Michael Schmeltzer

HERITAGE STATEMENT:

I was born in Yokosuka, Japan, in 1978, my mother in Okinawa in 1949. My Minnesota-born and -raised father met and married my mother (they have been married for over forty years now) while he was stationed in Okinawa. Our entire family moved to the United States in the summer of 1988, and I didn't realize until now our relocation was a thing we inherited together, a simultaneous and mutual estrangement. We moved to Elk River, Minnesota, where "city and country flow together" (at least, according to the town sign). Since my birth I think I've been caught in limbo, between island and inland, city and country. I am foreign and domestic, import and export. In my best moments, I like to think I am large, and contain multitudes. At my worst I think I am Legion, for we are many.

AUTHOR BIO:

Michael Schmeltzer is the author of *Elegy/Elk River* (Floating Bridge Press, 2015,) winner of the Floating Bridge Press Chapbook Award, and *Blood Song* (Two Sylvias Press, 2016) his debut full-length collection. He earned an MFA from the Rainier Writing Workshop at Pacific Lutheran University. His debut nonfiction book, *A Single Throat Opens*, written in collaboration with Meghan McClure, is forthcoming from Black Lawrence Press. His honors include numerous Pushcart Prize and Best of the Net nominations, the Gulf Stream Award for Poetry, and the *Blue Earth Review*'s Flash Fiction Prize. He has been a finalist for the Four Way Books Intro and Levis Prizes, the Zone 3 Press First Book Prize, John Ciardi Prize for Poetry from BkMk Press, as well as the OSU Press/*The Journal* Award in Poetry. He recently accepted an editorial position at Floating Bridge Press. He has been published in *Black Warrior Review*, *PANK*, *Rattle*, *Brevity's Blog*, *The Journal*, *Natural Bridge*, *Mid-American Review*, *Water~Stone Review*, and *New York Quarterly*, among others.

AN ACCENT LIKE GRIEF

From early on I've learned to hear accents like auditory Braille, bumps in language forming landscapes. Whenever my mother speaks in English it's apparent she is anything but. One linguistic turn of the tongue is enough to identify some of us as other.

For example, say the phrase *in a little while* or *take a right at the lights*. Say the word *water*. What sounds are swept away in mispronunciation, which letters like pits lodged in the throat?

Answer, and I'll tell you about cartography, where on the map you lie. I'll tell you if you're a native speaker.

I'll tell you if you're one of us.

Grief deranges the key on every single map.

This is why during times of profound loss we lose ourselves. The stars misalign. We can't find any treasure. We wander. We scrounge through mud and ash, shovel aside piles of bone.

Every X on the map turns out to be a hoax.

Two times in life I've been knocked dumb by grief. I stood in front of the bathroom mirror and repeated, "you are here, you are here." Despite the obvious acknowledgement, I was still off course.

The only way through grief is to create a map from scratch, to pencil and shade every landmark in sight. The goal is not to arrive where you started, but to study your new surroundings so well there is comfort in the cracks, ecstasy in the accents.

Listen carefully to the way my mother speaks English, or the way I speak Japanese with a sluggish tongue.

Better yet, listen carefully to the way my mother doesn't speak English, the way she hides her thick accent behind her native language.

Our accents, like grief, emphasize all the wrong moments.

My father retired from the Navy after twenty-one years of service. When I think back to the map of my childhood, his absence is a desert, a harsh and scorched nothing.

Say *parch*. Say *char*. Months without him burn away.

Then one day a letter, a keychain, a coin from a country I couldn't pronounce. These were the things I hid underneath to protect myself from the heat.

I was nine when we moved to America.

僕は日本人です。(Translation: I am Japanese.)

Sometimes this is the easiest way to self-identify. Other times I proclaim mixed-race, bi-racial, half or hybrid. A friend of mine uses the term "blended." When I was younger I had to X the box next to the designation "other." Now more often than not, I feel "other" suits me well.

On the other hand, there are moments we're defined by the things we're not: *He's no athlete. She's no beauty queen. They're not from around here.*

No matter what language I use, however, I'm reading a map without a key.

When I speak in my mother's tongue it's as if I'm writing with the wrong hand.

My oldest daughter, only four, already has a better accent than me. Though she's never set foot in Japan, linguistically speaking she is more at home there than I am. Culturally speaking, she will probably feel more at home in America than I do.

There is something to be said about inheritance. There is something to be said about being exiled, being unable to pronounce the words that can summon the child we once were.

The immigrant's story is inherently a tragic one, e.g., my mother left behind everyone and everything she ever knew: her family, her friends, even her very geography.

If I have to explain further, if you are one who says things like "land of opportunity" and "better off," then I'm afraid you are like an ignorant child who looks at a directory and does not know to panic. Unless you've paid attention to the steps you've taken, a map is useless. It will not tell you what's forgotten, what can never be recovered. It will not speak of your history.

YOU ARE HERE, it states in block letters, as if the journey didn't matter.

Repeat this to yourself like a charm against grief: Nothing is ever lost.

When I was young I'd shut my eyes. I'd do this everywhere my mother brought me: crowded malls, fieldtrips, the produce section of a grocery store. I *wanted* to be lost. The possibility of going off the map thrilled me. I'd stop moving and close my eyes; my mother walked forward.

Every second I waited in self-imposed blindness was like a whisk to the pit of my stomach. After half a minute I couldn't bear it; I'd peek. In those brief moments I couldn't find her, the world was foreign and familiar. Although I never took a step I was no longer where I was.

Then I'd spot a figure removing a white blouse from a clothing rack or inspecting a cluster of grapes. The world again would grow warm like cake.

How indiscernibly things shift from safety to instability and back again. How quickly the language we dreamt in becomes the language we no longer use.

We navigate society through maps, knowledge and ignorance like latitude and longitude. When I was a child I wondered how the directory knew where I was, how it so confidently and accurately declared every time, "You are here."

Remarkable what children don't know and all the things they do.

Remarkable how quickly we lose the accents that define us.

You are here—a simple way of stating the most complicated thing: You exist.

I am bilingual for the time being, and forgetting more of the child I was.

Every detail we chronicle in our small and ordinary lives . . .

We are here, we are here, we are here.

Then someday, all of us, irrevocably not. All of us crossed out, a black X on a map we hope someone knows how to read.

Willa Elizabeth Schmidt

HERITAGE STATEMENT:

My parents were immigrants from Germany and Austria. They met in Chicago, where I was born. I grew up with their German friends and their language all around me, though I only became fluent in it myself when I studied it in high school and college. My parents, wanting to be American, spoke English, only reverting to their native language when there was something I shouldn't understand. "Speak English!" I remember commanding, with indignation. Not that it helped.

AUTHOR BIO:

Willa Elizabeth Schmidt's work has appeared in *Amoskeag, Bellevue Literary Review, CALYX, The Mac-Guffin, Potomac Review,* and *Rosebud*. Ms. Schmidt was the winner of *Kalliope Journal*'s 2007 Short Fiction Competition and The Writers' Workshop of Asheville, North Carolina's 12th Annual Memoir Competition, and took second place in *Wisconsin Academy Review*'s 2004 Short Story Contest. A former academic reference librarian, Ms. Schmidt lives in Madison. She has recently served as Associate Editor of *Timber Creek Review*. She is also on the board of the Northwoods Land Trust in Eagle River.

SECOND LIFE

In the spring of 1944, my parents bought a white frame house on the edge of Chicago, where empty lots, remnants of the conquered prairie, were rapidly filling. My mother, an Austrian immigrant, was forty-two then, my father slightly younger, their only child going on three.

The backyard sold her, that March day they answered the ad; a forgotten, weedy patch between house and garage with room for all the planting she needed to catch up on. April mornings found her digging, raking, fingering the rich earth, harvesting radishes, starting peppers and beans. She had worked as a cook and as a governess: after years tending strange kitchens, guiding other people's children, here at last was *her* place, her own plot of ground. A new beginning; a better life. She had been in this country fifteen years.

On a day in June when sun and young green swelled the soft air she would have been outside as usual, weeding, staking tomato vines, clipping early blooms. Watching her fat-cheeked daughter rearrange clumps of dirt with a tiny shovel and pitch them importantly into her small wheelbarrow, a toy replica of the one at her mother's side. At that moment I imagine my mother's world seemed perfect, unerringly safe and complete; and maybe that is why the sound she suddenly heard or first only sensed but soon could not ignore, a sound so wrong in the midst of her world's smooth joy—maybe that's why it stayed with her, why she kept remembering, bringing it up days afterward until my father, tired, said no more, there's no point, Franzi! but later told me too, because he himself simply couldn't forget.

An animal's whine, low and singing at the outset but rising, growing quickly louder, from somewhere not so close, a quarter mile away, across our small street, past the large empty lot on the corner, over the busy thoroughfare that rimmed it, Forest Preserve Drive, where stray cats my mother took in and fattened made death runs during nighttime prowls.

Perhaps it seemed just that at first, some animal wounded in the road, slapped by a speeding car not hard enough to die outright. A moan that kept on and on, building from steady keen to harsh wail, now halting abruptly, now starting again, ragged at first, then bolder, finally harsh as a blaring siren but so full of heart-searing grief and hopelessness that she knew it for a human voice, a woman's: wailing, announcing itself with so much pain that everyone in the surrounding streets must have heard and marveled. How could a woman weep so long and loud that so many could hear so plainly, from so far away?

Neighbors, women younger than my mother but new here too, eager for talk and friends, stood outside with wondering eyes and whispered over fences, toddlers tumbling in the grass at their feet. *What can it be?* They asked each other. *Who is she? What has happened?* Shading eyes with hands they would have peered across streets and lawns to the small house almost hidden by thick yews, the cottage with chipped gray wood siding built long before their own sturdy homes. None of them knew her, the woman who lived there, the woman whose cries went on and on, withering their summer gardens, tearing at my mother's heart.

By the time my father got home that evening, the grapevine, like neighborhood grapevines everywhere, had done its work. By then everyone knew that the wailing woman, who lived alone—widowed, divorced, deserted?—had lost her son, her only child, in the Normandy landing. The mailman had brought a letter that day.

All evening, cooking dinner, sitting at the table, cleaning up afterwards, my mother was silent. It was my father who washed my face, read to me, and tucked me into bed. Alone in their bedroom, my mother wept.

She was no stranger to tears. Stray cats, sparrows, garter snakes: she wept at all their deaths. She cried when the second garden she planted on empty land across our alley was bulldozed for another new house. Yet in anger she was fiercely stubborn, rarely forgiving those who displeased her. Sometimes she seemed tired, unable to cope with a child's energy and fuss. When I was sick she was always there, full of comfort and love, never impatient or scolding.

She died in the cold winter of 1951. And one day, long after her death, years after my father told me about the woman whose lament had reached so many ears, I learned something new.

The purpose of a birth certificate, I suppose, is not only to record the coming-into-existence of a given individual but also to provide sufficient information to identify that individual as unique, not interchangeable with others of the same name or date or place of birth. I had no need to see mine until, grown up and away at college, I needed a copy for a scholarship application and so sent a check to the Clerk of Cook County, State of Illinois.

Birth certificates posed curious questions in 1941 to establish uniqueness, I again assume, otherwise why a question like No. 8: LEGITIMATE? On the photocopied document before me, and a big, reassuring check in the box next to "Yes." Or No. 21(a): INCLUDING THIS CHILD, NUMBER OF CHILDREN BORN ALIVE TO THIS MOTHER? And 21(b): INCLUDING THIS CHILD, HOW MANY OF THESE CHILDREN ARE NOW LIVING? Next to each of these in black ink a clear, unmistakable "2."

An error, a bureaucratic slip? For I was most certainly an only child, a cherished late-in-life, longed-for, unrivalled, object of undivided, unconditional love.

Wasn't I?

Soon afterwards my father came for a visit, and I presented him with my discovery in the off-hand, by-the-way manner it seemed to deserve. I expected surprise, or indignation. When he looked away and said nothing at all, my heart froze. I too kept quiet, waiting.

It was all history now anyway, he went on, because they were gone, all of them: my mother, her grandmother (I was only five but I remembered the light blue airmail letter, my mother's reddened eyes), even Bernhard, fallen in Russia, 1942, twenty years old. So it didn't much matter anymore.

Several years later, after graduation, I went to Austria. My German was decent; the relatives were discreet. We spoke endlessly of my mother, but no one mentioned Bernhard. When I finally mustered the courage to say his name, Poldi Tante, my mother's sister, seemed relieved and brought out pictures. She told me how he loved school, skiing, photography, hated being a soldier. That my mother had wanted him to come over, that he had thought about it, but Austrians are not like Germans, most don't like going so far away, for good. He *was* thinking about America, that much they knew, until the war came and it was too late. She gave me a small leather-bound book found on him when he died; among lists of addresses and birthdays, penned in a careful hand, I found my name.

The photographs: a dark-haired, dark-eyed teenager, gangly, pale, scaling a cliff in *Lederhosen*; on a snowy slope, posed jauntily next to skis and poles; clean-cut in uniform, with the slightest hint of a smile, marching off to his *Heldentod*.

Fresh face, face of a boy almost a man. His resemblance to my mother striking: eyes, cheekbones, hair. Her love child and my half-brother.

I revisit her on that June day in 1944, as she listens to a strange woman mourning her shattered son, weeping loudly, inconsolably for hours on end, wild and oblivious in her grief, and I know now that my mother heard herself in those cries. For she too had once received a notice, no United States Government reminder of glory in sacrifice but a simple announcement, an errand of mercy delivered by the International Red Cross. Because her son, lost child of her youth, was the enemy, soldier of a land with which communication must not take place. In a new country, where could she go with her grief?

She kept it inside, in her heart, within her own four walls. And by that time there was the new baby, child of her middle age, a new beginning, a second life. The little girl with blue eyes like her dad's, and wisps of reddish hair. Bernhard, Bernhard, she must have thought, sighed, wept so often silently, for herself, while I grew up secure and well-fed in a new world, certain her joys, her love, her silences were mine and mine alone.

Prageeta Sharma

HERITAGE STATEMENT:

Prageeta Sharma was born in Framingham, Massachusetts, in 1972, shortly after her parents emigrated from India in 1969.

AUTHOR BIO:

Sharma attended Bard College at Simon's Rock for her undergraduate studies and received an MFA in poetry from Brown University in 1995 and an MA in media studies from The New School in 2002. She is the author of three collections of poetry, *Infamous Landscapes* (Fence Books, 2007); *The Opening Question* (Fence Books, 2004), winner of the 2004 Fence Modern Poets Prize; and *Bliss to Fill* (Subpress Collective, 2000). She received a 2010 Howard Foundation Grant and has taught in the creative writing program at The New School in New York and in the Individualized BA program at Goddard College in Vermont. Sharma is currently an Associate Professor and Director of the Creative Writing Program at the University of Montana in Missoula.

A SITUATION FOR MRS. BISWAS

When I received the call I was in a store in Missoula, Montana.

A store stocked with sparkling ephemera: glass fauna, tiny belfry bulbs,

winter white birch and stump-lamps brandishing light cones,

little shelves and branches hung with drops of ice and round silver baubles.

I loved the store: it was cavernous, dark with wood and burlap,

a ruddy brick loft with lithographs and monographs on birds or bracelets.

The store owner, Fran, was away that day otherwise
I would have stayed in there a little longer.

She was a comforting friend—
she had impeccable taste, manifested in her put-together garments,
she also had a warming patient smile.

I didn't stay long, I didn't linger;
though linger is absolutely the wrong word,
more like I didn't stumble around there for hours.

(I would stumble around in that store for a full year.)

If she had been behind the counter I would have turned to her in bewilderment.

You see I had picked up my ringing cell phone while browsing
(I usually keep it off in stores),

and my father said, *There's something I have to tell you.*
I don't want you to find out any other way. I am leaving my job.
They want me to resign.

Fran had met my father the week before—
he wanted to see downtown, the campus, get to know Montana—
he had done research on the education opportunities.

He was interested in outreach.

People all over met him and found him to be a kindhearted man.

I had set up meetings, he was here to meet educators, mathematicians—
more spirited people—I told him—than Bostonians.

I told him the West was a magical place. He agreed.

Later he would tell me that this was his last best day, a strange pun on the *Last*
Best Place.

Little did we know we would have to fight a very public battle.

And apparently from the rumors and from the strange
treatment he received prior to his termination,
there was a plot in place.

We, as a family, felt the public ridicule.

And as an Asian family, we felt the acute Asian shame. It was a dark,
disastrous cloud *hanging, hanging, hanging.*

My father would be publicly shamed
and we were shocked at the racist narratives—
allegations—a greedy brown man—

mismanaging, mismanaging, mismanaging

One public interest story to release venom—
to tease out *real* feelings from strangers.

Blog comments were aggressive: the Indian was a con,
a snake-oil man.

You just have to give them a scenario
in which they can invest—in which to place those hard-to-place feelings.
White people bury their resentments beneath their liberalism.

We *knew* he hadn't done anything wrong—we *knew* this was bogus.

Like I said, I was getting ready for the holidays,
I played hooky that Tuesday excited to wrap gifts;
I wanted to decorate the house.

This was my first house.
My husband was out looking at Christmas trees.
Albeit I am a Hindu, trees are an awful lot of fun.

And this planning was quickly thwarted with the difficult—
my family was falling apart—
the droop in my life felt permanent.

I was more than 2,000 miles from my father, but the way he spoke
at the moment of the call becalmed me—

I felt anchored to his side—
I will stay there for as long as it takes.

Before this moment I was in a terrific mood.

I wanted to don the table
with the kind of candles that beckoned, pulling you into an aesthetic presence
fully-fabricated and lit, and yet looked like it came from snow.

I had been in Missoula for many months,
I had come from Brooklyn, where I had lived for twelve years.
Now I was ready to escape.

Having been born and raised outside of Boston,
without the opportunities say someone like Robert Lowell had.

I knew I was not of that ilk nor was my father—we now realize.

Boston was indeed for the rich—with its stodgy colonial identity,
with its ridiculous Brahmans—
its oddly cultureless stance
even with Harvard as its mirror.
(Even with Cal as front & center literati.)

Even so, I was pleased, I was unhurried in my new life, *I was, I was.*
I could feel how I stood, I could feel the rising happiness—of the belly, not the
gut.

I was consumed with the bliss of poetry,
so much poetry around me, everything with poetry.

I said and understood, the workshop will be my ideology,
my intentional community, front and center—with bells.

My family was overjoyed with the way our lives
were working together—

my father was comfortable, my mother pleased,
a professorship and presidential position
at a college, he was the first South Asian president.

He had come to America with very little and now had something.

As you can see, there is an immigrant narrative here.

When he first arrived, he made very little money as a visiting professor so he
worked
security at night at the Museum of Fine Arts. He kept thinking his colleague,
Bruce, was calling him bastard, when he was calling him buster.

It took him months to realize this. He first had to confront Bruce.

The sequence of his first major purchases and acquisitions, which took several
months:

a suitcase and a rug, then he found a dentist's chair for the living room.

He bought the Bob Dylan album that had "Blowing in the Wind," because it
really
sounded Hindu—it sounded like it came from the Rig Veda.

For many years I would say he was a model minority—he aspired to being
rewarded for his good work by white people.

We agreed, all was well—I had made my way to where I had wanted to be,
living a poet's life and it felt extraordinary—
all of the birch-stump lamps lighting up inside, this was a kind of bliss.

I had arrived where I loved in absolute terms.

Where I could love the poetics of if, then & thou. The luminous . . .

And yet poetry haunts with its suggestion that terrible things are true and stick,
as Rilke says:

I am much too small in this world, yet not small enough / to be to you just object
and thing / dark and smart.

The sun was hidden behind the darkest cloud.

I said what is happening to my father?

In response, my husband's back gave out,
he could not walk without whimpering, there was whimpering in the night

and I wasn't sure which one of us it was.

What was happening to my ableness?

We had failure, heaps of failure in our hands.

The world had recast itself in such a way that I had to address the power
behind it.

I kept saying strange things to people like *no one is exempt from suffering.*
I felt like a tiny bird with sinking feet.

There are assertions about difference
That I had not wanted to make in the past, but now did.

Where was I? Who was I?

My father was told he had to watch his back
and then they took everything away from him.

To take away his dignity with so many untruths. Do I have to watch my back
too?

What did I think I could have? I wasn't even sure if I had it here.
People hadn't seen me as me, I started to feel it. Those glass birds

and the birch lamps were a kind of privilege
only others could have—not "others" in the sense in which I was other.

I started to see how money worked the room: when we had it, when we didn't.

Imagine, we were so close
to the soaring sky, and imagine how we fell.
How we knew falling wouldn't end us,

fall right here, fall right there, cry out, oh blustering self,
it can't be as bad as you think.

I said let's remember how to do it so it won't hurt
this time or the next.

But I had to say the branches extended their arms,
there was a house attached to them—

we found ourselves languishing, then needing
to rebuild.

It was the turning of the year and then another one.

And the showy, extravagant people capped themselves
on the tops of mountain ash—

we came out to clear them away.

Laura Shovan

HERITAGE STATEMENT:

My mother, born in Nottingham, England, at the close of WWII, found herself at the 1964 World's Fair (New York), representing England as a Johnson's Wax Girl. My father, a business professor who grew up in the Bronx, dated several of Johnson's Wax's "countries" before settling on my mother. They wrote each other letters across the Atlantic, married twice (once in England, a second Jewish ceremony in the U.S.), and lived in Thailand for one year (1966–1967) before settling in New Jersey to raise a family. Much of my poetry deals with wrestling for my own space between my parents' two disparate cultures, personalities, and experiences.

AUTHOR BIO:

Laura Shovan is former editor for *Little Patuxent Review*. Her chapbook, *Mountain, Log, Salt, and Stone* (Citylit Press, 2010), won the inaugural Harriss Poetry Prize. Laura edited Maryland Writers' Association's anthology *Life in Me Like Grass on Fire: Love Poems* (MWA Books, 2011) and co-edited *Voices Fly: An Anthology of Exercises and Poems from the Maryland State Arts Council Artists-in-Residence Program*, for which she teaches. Laura is a Rita Dove Poetry Award finalist and *Gettysburg Review* Conference for Writers scholarship winner. *The Last Fifth Grade of Emerson Elementary* (Wendy Lamb Books/ Random House, 2016), her novel-in-verse for children, was published in 2016.

THE SWIMMER

The day was lovely, and that he lived in a world so generously
supplied with water seemed like a clemency, a beneficence.
—John Cheever, "The Swimmer"

The day is hot.
My mother's bathing suit

sticks to her shirt
and khaki shorts—

too short? why not
with legs like hers?

She walks
to the backyard.

Women talking
by the pool

take her in from the corners
of their eyes,

the sisterhood
of Temple Beth Rishon.

No one speaks.
My mother pulls off clothes,

dives in, crawls
one blue length.

The women believe
the water has been tainted.

They don't know
about my mother's

second wedding,
also to my father.

I imagine she wore
a knee-length dress.

I was there
and not there,

a presence kicking
under white cotton.

The rabbi laughed
at her fullness, said,

now that she was Jewish,
the first wedding

would not count
for more than photos.

Erase my mother
in white lace, a dress

with train trailing
up the cobbled hill.

Erase her village church
in another country,

people she had known
her whole life, parents.

Wash from her skin
Anglican vows,

and every hymn
she ever sang on Sunday.

Douse her in a mikvah.
Gather the women

to scrub her skin
so her children will be Jews.

And—this is finally clear—
it will not be enough.

She rises from the pool
without speaking,

pulls on shorts,
T-shirt, drives home

where the quiet
is a kind of companion,

where she has time to rub
her skin until it's dry.

PASTORAL WITH HEDGEHOG

I could imagine meeting
a prickly laundress on a walk
or picnic in the high grass,
my English grandmother with her
basket of fizzy lemonade and pork rolls
and cloth serviettes. My brothers and I
searching for clay pigeons broken
on the hill where our uncles
practiced shooting and every rabbit
ducking into its hole was Alice's,
every hedgehog might be
Mrs. Tiggy-Winkle who was
like my grandmother with her
cups of tea and foxgloves.
Her curled hair in a kerchief,
I could believe almost anything
we were so removed
from our other ordinary life.

SJ Sindu

HERITAGE STATEMENT:

I was born in Sri Lanka, and came to the U.S. at the age of seven with my parents, who immigrated to pursue graduate degrees at the University of Massachusetts. My parents liked to wander, and I never grew up in one place I can call home. My brother and I were carted from city to city, state to state, cementing a strong family bond but also cultivating in us a desire for permanency.

AUTHOR BIO:

SJ Sindu holds an MA in English with an emphasis in creative writing from the University of Nebraska–Lincoln. She is a PhD student at Florida State University, and has published in *Brevity*, *Harpur Palate*, *The MacGuffin*, *Sinister Wisdom*, *Water~Stone Review*, and elsewhere. Find out more at www.sjsindu.com.

TEST GROUP 4:
WOMANHOOD AND OTHER FAILURES

My love affair with women started when I learned about the female suicide bombers in Sri Lanka. I was five. It blew my mind that women—the make-upped, dark-eyed beauty queens of the Indian Bollywood movies—could be dangerous enough to strap on explosives beneath the folds of their sarees.

My lover's scar is crocheted across his chest with baby-pink yarn by someone who was just learning. The scar runs through like a tiny mountain range, stretching from armpit to armpit along the line of his pectoral muscles but never syncing with the contours of his body. When the surgeon scooped out the breast tissue, he left my lover's chest flat.

The scar is pink like his nipples, soft and spongy where it bubbled up from the stitches and healed around them. Sometimes he's afraid he'll catch his nipples on something and rip them off. He has nightmares about being nipple-less.

There is a dark spot where his nipples used to be, a sunset gradation of color into the scar. Dark hairs sprout, tall and curly, around the scar line. They weren't there before the testosterone. They grow a forest over his chest and down his stomach.

The outer edges of his scar bulge out in dog-ears, a side effect of having had large breasts.

His lovers, the ones before me, wouldn't look at his chest. They would turn away, mumble into their coffee, tuck their hair behind their ears. They wouldn't touch him there, their fingers cringing from the ridges of the scar, their bodies shivering at the absence. He can't feel his chest anymore. Numbness reaches up from his scar, a vacancy of nerves, hollow when he pushes on the skin. His lungs underneath can discern the pressure, but the message of touch is lost between the skin and his insides.

My mother keeps a leather-bound album of my baby pictures tucked away in the recesses of her closet. These pictures are few, and it took years—decades—to collect them in one volume. Most were lost to late-night flights from our family home in Sri Lanka, where we always kept bags packed. The bags had to be light enough to carry for days, spare enough to unpack and repack at the Army check-points. Photo albums were treasured but bulky, and my baby pictures won out over my parents' wedding album. We were ready to leave as soon as we heard that the battle line was nearing our town.

Now the pictures sleep peacefully in my mother's closet. I've stolen a few photos of my own. I need to remember.

It's tempting to retell my childhood veiled in virginity, a chaste Hindu girl's strict upbringing. But it's a little boy who stands in these pictures, one who was given too much freedom and adored to the point of exhaustion by extended family before they remembered that he would bleed every month.

I had short curly hair and wore boy's clothes. In beach pictures I wear only my panties. I mourn the loss of that flat chest that allowed me to be rambunctious. Wild.

At six years of age my best friend and I pretended to be Americans on vacation at a beach. We walked around in our panties inside locked rooms, windows shut for modesty. We played at being American women—smoking, drinking, kissing—unconstrained by sarees and rules.

To Emily Dickinson: I once met you—but you were dead—
To the middle-aged white lady who pretended to be Emily Dickinson at the library, whom I believed and loved until I told my friends and they made fun of me for not knowing that Emily Dickinson was dead and this lady was a fake: You were too pretty to play the part of a lonely writer. I should've known. Even the Americans like their smart women ugly.

The dusty, blue linoleum feels warm even though it snows outside. The tip of my nose is cold from the air. I lie against the warm floor, and the heat seeps in through the frilly cotton pajamas my mother made for me. My little brother laughs in the living room; his toddler voice hiccups around the walls as my dad plays with him. My mother types her thesis at the computer.

I am drawing. Today I'm practicing lips, diligently consulting a three-ring binder of tutorials I have printed out from the Internet. I fill my papers with lips like the ones the tutorials demonstrate, the round curves of women's lips that bite down on secrets and the flat plains of men's lips that don't smile.

I am in love with a man who doesn't believe in God but believes that English majors and hippies are the fussy frou-frou in an otherwise functioning society. He teaches me how to catch and throw a softball, and he buys me fountain pens and leather-bound journals. He tries to train our cat, and when he can't, he maintains that our cat over-generalizes. He lets me run my hands and lips along his chest scar, asks me to give him testosterone shots. I take pictures of the hairs that explode slowly on his jaw. Together we celebrate the dissolving curves of his body, my insides squirming at the woman slowly dying.

To my lover: Do you know, *kanna*, I learned about life from the female soldiers that patrolled my hometown. And about love, too. Those women had things figured out, their wisdoms wrapped away in the tight braids of their hair.

I see my best friend when I visit Sri Lanka after high school. We have seen eighteen from two different oceans. I wear makeup and short skirts in the Sri Lankan heat. She has hair braided down her back and makes tea for everyone. I wonder why she won't look me in the eye. I wonder if she remembers the pretend cigarettes and booze.

She doesn't talk. I talk too much.

When I bled for the first time on New Year's Day of 1999, my parents threw a party. We drove from Boston to Canada and rented a reception hall that specialized in Hindu celebrations. *Manjal neerattu vizha* loses its poetry when it spells "puberty ceremony" in English.

My parents hired a makeup lady who pulled and tugged my unruly hair into a bun, added extensions so that my flowered braid hung down to my butt. My chubby body wrestled into a saree. The blouse was tight and I could barely breathe. The makeup lady pinned jewelry to my head and brushed powder on my face, and when she was done, someone pretty looked back at me from the mirror. As a last touch she pressed a jeweled, fake nose ring into my septum. It dangled in front of my mouth. All day long I suppressed violent urges to sneeze.

I watch my mother kill mice. I kneel on an office chair, pumped up to its full height so I can see the frigid steel of the lab table from my fourth-grade height. The mice are a white that matches my mother's lab coat. She pulls them one by one out of their cage labeled "Test Group Four." They have to die, she says, because they are sick.

She presses a black sharpie to their necks, and they are dead, just like that, *tuk*.

SR-9

It stings the back of your throat, something sweet on the top of your mouth, the underbelly of your tongue. Squint through the thick gray air, the yellow haze of safety glasses. This is gunpowder, invading your lungs, combusting starchy smoke.

This was not your idea.

Even through the pillow mufflers over your ears, the bangs ring in your sinuses like a metal cup clanged on bar-like bones of your ribcage. Dusty stone walls hold in the shooting range and play catch with the bullet sounds. Casings clamor on the floor, glinting gold and spent.

You want to crouch, hold your arms above your head. You want to leave. But his hand lies heavy on your shoulder. A squeeze. A *you'll be fine*. An *I love you*.

What really bothers you is the newness of it all. This should be old news to you, who fancied yourself born into war. You should know the taste of gunpowder as it hits the back of your tongue. Unfamiliar, a challenge to the memories you thought were real. Maybe you made them up after all. Maybe you're not the war survivor you thought you were.

You were just a kid. Maybe—you were wrong.

The blue plastic tote weighs down your hands. You set it on the counter of Lane 2. The Ruger is black with a silver barrel. Metal warmer than you expected, heavier than you expected.

Small and smooth, the gold bullets quiver in their Styrofoam holder. He shows you how to load them in the magazine. Your breath is shallow. He says, "Breathe."

A bullet like this killed your uncle. You picture his blood glinting in the sunlight, staining his mother's cement porch.

You hook a large, beige target on the line with clothespins. You send the target backward into the hazy lane. Twenty-five yards. It dances on the line, bounces on the breeze from the vents.

Now you doubt yourself. You remember—

You're at a birthday get-together watching *Turtles Can Fly*, a documentary about Iraqi war children. Children and field mines are never a good combination, you know this—result in acres of small limbs strewn in intricate patterns. You sit through the movie thinking you don't need this shit you don't need this shit you want to go home you don't fucking need this shit. If you can say it enough times then maybe you can convince yourself to leave. But it's your friend's birthday, and you're already buzzed from beer so you stay.

After the film you lock yourself in the bathroom and throw up. The room is cramped, barely large enough for the toilet and sink. Open containers of make-up—half-used and half-rotten—spill over the faucets and crawl towards the drain. In your agitation you get foundation all over your arms, ten shades lighter than your skin.

You are shivering, but the heat in the house is on full blast. Your armpits are sweating but what do they know, right? They're just armpits. They're just doing their job. The chill is coming from inside, choking your veins as it works itself out, your teeth clattering and your body shaking.

—But maybe you were just sensitive. Maybe this didn't happen, after all. Maybe you overreact.

You hold the Ruger in your hands. Slide your palm into the curve under the barrel. Wrap your fingers around the grip, hang your finger on the bottom of the trigger. Breathe in, out, hold. Pull.

The sound is louder than you expect. It vibrates in your eardrums, shakes the dust from the ceiling of your memories.

Fire. Breathe. Fire. Breathe. Fire.

He is there, behind you, watching with his arms crossed, smiling at the way the other men in the room stare at your small frame, back stiff with pride, shoulders knotted.

From this end of the gun, you feel different.

From this end of things, you can do more than survive.

A month later you are able to watch *Saving Private Ryan*. Even when he looks away squeamishly, you squint through the virtual smoke, watch the blood, determined, as bodies explode in geysers, red pixels pooling into sand. The shots no longer remind you of your uncle, or of the soldiers who marched through your town. You think instead of the sweet burn on your throat, glittering casings that tinkle as you push them aside with your foot, construction paper targets, metal warm and heavy in your hands.

Zhanna Slor

HERITAGE STATEMENT:

I was born in Chernovtsy, Ukraine (though it was still the Soviet Union then), in 1986. My parents, along with me, my sister, and grandparents, moved to Wisconsin in January 1991—this was for many reasons, but primarily because of religious persecution. They did not treat Jews well in the Soviet Union, so we were given refugee status. In fact, we were a few days away from moving to Israel when our visas came through.

AUTHOR BIO:

Zhanna Slor was born in the former Soviet Union and moved to Wisconsin in the early 1990s. Currently, she lives with her husband in Chicago, where she is finishing up a young adult novel about Ukrainian-born twins with unusual superpowers. She has been published in numerous literary magazines, including *Bellevue Literary Review*, *storySouth*, *Sonora Review*, *Tusculum Review*, and *Michigan Quarterly Review*, which published a group of essays that later received a notable mention in *Best American Essays 2014*.

AN ECHO

"Spaceeba," says an old woman in a long, ivy-green dress and peacoat, as I hold open the glass vestibule door. She puts away her keys and shuffles ahead, past a mailman filling a long row of empty mailboxes, past the garage-sale impressionist paintings of flowers hanging on the walls, past an old man struggling with his cane, with wrinkles like rivers crashing into an ocean. Next to him, an equally wrinkled woman wearing an '80s-style flower dress stares at me, her hands folded behind her back. Her eyes are small and diminished. *"Zdrastvootie,"* she says, when she notices I've noticed, and turns her attention back to the man, her husband, presumably. I greet her back and walk past the elevator and party room and down the hallway of closed doors, where someone has clearly been smoking longer than I've even been alive, the smell clinging to every surface—the old, maroon carpet, covered in thick representations of roses; the dull, off-white walls with an olive-green trim; the plain brown doors.

A dog is yelping, probably my grandma's little terrier she named, of all things to name a dog when you don't speak English, "Jackie." I reach her door and knock.

Jackie rushes out into the hall, unable to decide between jumping up towards my knees or circling me, and trying to do both. My maternal grandma, Valentina, ushers me inside and squeezes me with all her might. *"Privet,"* I say, and pull out of her hug.

It's hot and smells like old laundry and cheap soap. On the television, the Russian news is blasting. She takes the remote and fidgets with it until she finds the mute button. I sit on a couch that hasn't moved in twenty years, taking Jackie into my lap while we relay the same conversation we always have:

"Kak dela?"

"Harasho."

"Have you heard from your sister lately?"

"No."

"That's a shame. You only have one sister, you know." She frowns.

I try to explain how Dina's residency in Philadelphia apparently precludes her from using a cell phone, and plus, we've never been close—but, as usual, it just becomes a mixture of pantomiming and guess work, by the end of which I just give up and tell her to ask my parents.

My grandma sighs. *"Bozhe moi"*—My god—"Your Russian is just awful."

"I know," I sigh back, sadly. And it only seems to get worse.

Jackie has finally calmed down and curled up on the opposite end of the frayed, gray couch. I look around at the walls covered in various displays of success: my sister's diploma from medical school, various oil paintings I made years ago when I was still an art major. My grandma asks me for the fifth time if I want something to eat, and I decline once again.

We move next door to see her sister, my great-aunt Anya, and great-uncle Lova, who used to be an amateur photographer and is responsible for our giant box of hand-developed black-and-white photographs from the '40s through the '70s. They are easily good enough to be in any exhibition. Soldiers in army uniforms, men in furry hats playing accordions, crowds gathered under Russian banners or pictures of Stalin, my dad on a cobblestone street, smoking a cigarette and holding onto a carriage of the baby version of me. My mom and grandma behind a pile of luggage, outside of our old apartment building on Kobylanska Street, pipes rusting and boarded-up windows behind them. I've practically stolen most of these pictures, slowly, over the years, trying to read the story behind them, the story of a place I'll never know.

Lova limps over to us from the tiny kitchen, the smell of fresh-baked bread coming along with him. He seems to have aged twenty years since recovering from prostate cancer; I can't remember the last time he smiled. His head is so shiny it looks ironed, his lips thin and pressed. Anya is lying on the couch again, and takes her time getting up. She doesn't have her dentures in, and her face seems crumpled. They ask me if I've painted anything new, and I tell them again that I haven't painted in years.

"Why not?" they ask me, and I shrug. "I don't want to," I say. Even if I could explain it, it definitely wouldn't be in Russian. In the last five, ten years, our conversations have become more and more limited, as my first language continues its retreat farther and farther away, where all that's left of it is an echo, like a song that sounds familiar but you can't remember the words.

I watch the TV screen, also on the Russian channel, trying to read the headlines, but it's moving too fast. Lova hands me a twenty and winks. "*Spaceeba!*" I say.

"Have you seen Khaya and Nikolai yet?" they ask.

"No, I'm going there next," I say, and my grandma smiles, secretly glad I saw her first. Putting a bunch of old people with nothing to do in the same building for twenty years may seem like a good idea, but only if the concept of human drama has completely slipped your mind. Many month-long battles have occurred on just the mere topic of who sees which side of the family first and who says what to whom.

Upstairs, it smells like potato pancakes and something burned to a crisp. The TV behind my dad's parents' apartment is booming, with those fast Russian words, tinkling like music, like the feeling of home, of a bed halfway around the world, neatly made and waiting for your return.

My grandpa Kolya pulls open the door, confusion melting into a beaming smile on his face. "*Zhankaley!*" he says. Then he looks behind him and yells, "Khaya, Zhanna's here!" He can barely contain his excitement. He tells me to sit down—"*seedee, seedee*"—pointing at the couch, while he fumbles around with the TV, also on the Russian channel news. But for the last twenty years—and in twenty years I still don't understand why—this couch has always been covered entirely by various old, itchy rugs, so instead I choose a chair by the small dining room table and look around.

The walls are cluttered with the identical displays from below. Some of my paintings, my sister's diploma from medical school, my undergraduate diploma from UW–Milwaukee. My grandpa points to a large empty space and asks me when he can expect to add my graduate degree up there. "In a month," I say. Then he asks me when my latest story publication is coming out. "It's already out on the computer!" I say, not sure how to explain that it's a digital copy of the magazine to someone who still doesn't know how to use a VCR. Understanding Russian is doable, but stringing together a grammatically correct, or at least sensible, response is like trying to solve a puzzle when you've lost most of the pieces.

My grandpa says, "Well, when I get a computer I'll be sure to look at it!" and then laughs at his own joke—a family trait.

My grandma finally waddles out from their bedroom wearing a large paisley robe. She sits down on the rug-covered couch and immediately asks me when I'm going to get married. "I want grandchildren!" she says, melodramatically. "You already have grandchildren," I say, pointing to myself—and then I also remind her that my sister is getting married in September so she shouldn't be so greedy.

"But I'm *old*! I'm going to *die* soon!" she says. Then she asks me, again, what exactly a graduate degree in writing will get me, and I explain to her that I already *have* a job, as an editor, which she doesn't understand from my explanation in Russian, so she asks me to tell her in English, and then she still doesn't understand, until my grandfather, who knows no English at all, explains it to her. "She reads books and fixes the mistakes! What don't you understand?" he screams.

My grandma has always been difficult to deal with, but lately, it's been getting out of control. She confuses her upbringing with my father's and mine, she thinks I used to speak Yiddish, like her, she can't remember the things I told her the last times I was here. Currently, she thinks someone is trying to sell her plot at the graveyard off Highway 94 and keeps accusingly calling members of my family and swearing at them. My grandpa, on the other hand, is sharp as a tack. He doesn't care what we do, as long as we're happy.

My grandpa disappears into their bedroom and comes back with a wad of fifties that he hands to my grandma to give to me. She looks at the stack, confused, and starts counting it.

"What are you doing?" he says.

"Why are you giving this to me?" she asks, still counting.

"It's for her!" he yells.

"Well then why don't you just give it to her?"

I walk up to my grandma and take the bills. My dad is always joking I'll never make more an hour than a visit to my grandparents. It must be that time of year when my grandpa receives his quarterly payment from the German government for being in a concentration camp.

"*Spaceeba!*" I say, and hug them both.

"Where's your boyfriend?" my grandma asks, after I've sat back down. "Working," I say, without explanation. Somehow they've gotten into their heads that he's in college, and has some other vague job that isn't playing the saxophone in a jazz band that moves from city to city all year long. "Is he Jewish? That last one—I never liked him, that *goy*," she spits. I roll my eyes. "Who *cares*?" I say, even though I know now she'll start her rant about how everyone hates Jews.

"You should *only* marry a Russian Jew," she states.

"Leave her alone!" my grandpa says again.

"Did we move to America just to marry Russian Jews?" I ask, my Russian getting better and better as it approaches a subject that it is so familiar with. "Why didn't we just stay where we were, then?" My grandpa laughs. My grandma continues to mumble that everyone hates the Jews.

"Everyone! They all want us dead. Believe me, I know."

"This is America," I say.

"It's all the same everywhere," my grandma continues, shaking her head. She's eighty-four (or possibly eighty-seven) years old and there's really no changing her mind about this one. My grandpa even argues with her. "Who cares if he's Jewish? None of that matters anymore," he says, with a wave of his hand.

My grandma continues her speech, so I decide not to remind her that yes, my boyfriend is Jewish, he's actually from Israel he's so Jewish.

My grandma places her thick, wrinkled hands on her lap. "Oh, to be young," she croons, onto another one of her favorite topics. "In Russia, I was *so* happy. I had my whole life ahead of me. Now I just sit around waiting for *death*."

The way she emphasizes the word death—*smerta*—makes me start laughing, I don't know why. But once I start I can't stop, until tears are streaming down my face.

"Oh, she's laughing at me now!" she says, staring straight ahead. "Ha-ha-ha. Ha-ha-ha. I'm funny to her."

"What a funny *shootka*, *baba*," I say, finally regaining control of my off-the-rails laughter.

"I'm a joke now?" she asks, slowly, looking at my grandpa.

"No, *babooshka*, I said you *made* a joke. It was funny."

"I'm a joke, she says."

"That's not what I said."

My grandpa claps his hands on his knees. "Khaya, come on. Let her go, it's getting late."

My grandma doesn't appear to have heard him and continues on. "Yes... I was happy in Russia. Even with Stalin, and the war, and all the lines," she says, swaying forwards and backwards, almost as if the last conversation hasn't even happened. With a wave of her hand, she adds, "*You* wouldn't know. *You* weren't there."

"No, I wasn't."

"*You* never had to wait in line for bread," she says.

"Why can't you be happy here?" I ask. "You don't have to work and you can sit around all day doing nothing."

"*Phoo*. You're young, so you don't understand. When I was your age I didn't believe the old people either . . ." she says, although I have a hard time believing she ever knew someone that made it past sixty in the Soviet Union.

My grandpa leans forward, claps his hands even harder on his knees, and says, "Enough, Hayoosa."

"Why, Kolya? What did I say?" she asks, looking more confused than ever.

"Do you want something to eat? Orange? Chocolate? What can I give you?" my grandpa asks.

"Nothing, Grandpa. I just ate," I say, standing up. "I better go. I'm only here for the day and I haven't even seen my parents yet."

They both stand up too and hug me again. "Come back soon," they say on my way out the door. "Don't forget about us old people."

As I walk down the hall, I hear their television back on, making the floors buzz. From a different room, I hear an Alla Pugacheva song from the '70s, an old voice singing along; slow, enunciated, so I can actually follow along:

"*Take me back, I wanna be there once again . . . Take me back to all the places I knew then . . . There's got to be a thousand ways to get back to my childhood days.*"

She's really on to something there.

Angela Sorby

HERITAGE STATEMENT:

My father and his family moved to Seattle, Washington, from Norway in 1957. WWII had devastated Norway's economy and my grandfather, Aage, found better prospects painting houses in the Ballard area of Seattle, which was populated largely by other Scandinavian immigrants.

AUTHOR BIO:

Angela Sorby was born in 1965 and raised in Seattle. She is the author of two poetry collections, *Bird Skin Coat* (Wisconsin, 2009) and *Distance Learning* (New Issues, 1998), and a literary history, *Schoolroom Poets* (UPNE, 2005). She teaches at Marquette University.

THE BORING SIDE OF THE FAMILY

Their dramas were too minor
even for the local paper,
Arbeiderbladet. No "family lore" either—
no drunks, no runaway brides.

Climate's half to blame,
though the dull nail in the dull
coffin was Christianity,
a faith that carried them mildly

on its back, like Mary and Joseph's
donkey. It walked. It never spooked.
Lady Luck? *Good fortune*?
No: they were Lutheran,

and what they had was Norway,
though its fjords and peaks
allowed only partial visibility.
They carried it across the ocean

and unpacked it in Seattle:
Norway. My grandmother
taught piano, playing with perfect
posture the music of composers

more tortured than herself,
while my grandfather carved
Mickey Mouses (Mice?)
from scrap lumber.

His Mickeys were clever
contraptions: gravity forced
their hinged legs down a slope,
Hop! Click! Hop!

But then Disney lawyers
sent him a threatening letter,
so he boxed up his mice
in the basement, which was a "finished"

second house under the first:
same wall-to-wall carpet,
same muted pinkish furniture.
                          Later, my grandfather

told us that in 1940s Norway,
during the German Occupation,
toy factories were repurposed
to make weapons, so he fed

his family of five by covertly
making and selling Mickey Mice
while out of earshot the Resistance
built bombs and blew up bridges.

Hop! Click! Hop! And I thought,
yawn. Absent gunpowder,
absent an internal vein of evil,
goodness grows plain,

rural and bland as boiled potatoes.
Only after they died—all of them,
Walt Disney, my grandparents, the Nazis—
did I realize how intense it is

to pull off the pot lid
and stick a fork in, to find that, yes,
the potatoes are ready,
low on scent and spice but dense

with the starch and sugar
that forces one eye to spring,
underground,
from the eye of another.

Ira Sukrungruang

HERITAGE STATEMENT:

Ira Sukrungruang is Thai-American, born in 1976 to two Thai immigrants. His parents—Montri and Chintana—were part of the first wave of Thai immigrants to come to America in the late '60s and '70s. They were responsible for constructing Wat Dhammaram, the Thai Buddhist Temple of Chicago. America, for them, was a workplace and never home. Home was still the familiar heat and humidity of their native land, was still a world scented in jasmine and sprawled in the yawning green of rice fields. Eventually, they would return back to Thailand—divorced, disheartened—and Sukrungruang continues to write about what it means to live in one country but belong in another.

AUTHOR BIO:

Sukrungruang is the author of *Southside Buddhist: Essays* (University of Tampa Press, 2014); *Talk Thai: the Adventures of a Buddhist Boy*; and the poetry collection *In Thailand It Is Night* (University of Tampa Press, 2013). He is co-editor of *What Are You Looking At: The First Fat Fiction Anthology* (Harvest Books, 2003) and *Scoot Over, Skinny: The Fat Nonfiction Anthology* (Mariner Books, 2005). Ira has published his essays, poems, and short stories in many literary journals and anthologies, including *The Bellingham Review*, *Crab*  *Orchard Review*, *Creative Nonfiction*, *Isotope*, *North American Review*, *Post Road*, and *Tilting the Continent: Southeast Asian American Writing*. He has received the New York Foundation for the Arts Nonfiction Fellowship, the Just Desserts Fiction Prize, an Illinois Arts Council Literary Award, and received support from the Blue Mountain Center, Virginia Center for the Creative Arts, and the Writers Colony at Dairy Hollow. He teaches at the University of South Florida and the low-residency MFA at City University of Hong Kong. For more about the author, visit: www.buddhistboy.com.

CHOP SUEY

My mother was a champion bowler in Thailand. This was not what I knew of her. I knew only her expectations of me to be the perfect Thai boy. I knew her distaste for blonde American women she feared would seduce her son. I knew her distrust of the world she found herself in, a world of white faces and mackerel in a can. There were many things I didn't know about my mother when I was ten. She was what she was supposed to be. My mother.

At El-Mar Bowling Alley, I wanted to show her what I could do with the pins. I had bowled once before, at Dan Braun's birthday party. There, I had rolled the ball off the bumpers, knocking the pins over in a thunderous crash. I liked the sound of a bowling alley. I felt in control of the weather, the rumble of the ball on the wood floor like the coming of a storm, and the hollow explosion of the pins, distant lightning. At the bowling alley, men swore and smoked and drank.

My mother wore a light pink polo, jeans, and a golf visor. She put on a lot of powder to cover up the acne she got at fifty. She poured Vapex, a strong smelling vapor rub, into her handkerchief, and covered her nose, complaining of the haze of smoke that floated over the lanes. My mother was the only woman in the place. We were the only non-white patrons.

I told her to watch me. I told her I was good. I set up, took sloppy and uneven steps, and lobbed my orange ball onto the lane with a loud thud. This time there were no bumpers. My ball veered straight for the gutter.

My mother said to try again. I did, and for the next nine frames, not one ball hit one pin. Embarrassed, I sat next to her. I put my head on her shoulder. She patted it for a while and said bowling wasn't an easy game.

My mother rose from her chair and said she wanted to try. She changed her shoes. She picked a ball from the rack, one splattered with colors. When she was ready, she lined herself up to the pins, the ball at eye level. In five concise steps, she brought the ball back, dipped her knees and released it smoothly, as if her hand were an extension of the floor. The ball started on the right side of the lane and curled into the center. Strike.

She bowled again and knocked down more pins. She told me about her nearly perfect game, how in Thailand she was unbeatable.

I listened, amazed that my mother could bowl a 200, that she was good at something beyond what mothers were supposed to be good at, like cooking and punishing and sewing. I clapped. I said she should stop being a mother and become a bowler.

As she changed her shoes, a man with dark hair and a mustache approached our lane. In one hand he had a cigarette and a beer. He kept looking back at his buddies a few lanes over, all huddling and whispering. I stood beside my mother, wary of any stranger. My mother's smile disappeared. She rose off the chair.

"Hi," said the man.

My mother nodded.

"My friends over there," he pointed behind him, "well, we would like to thank you." His mustache twitched.

My mother pulled me closer to her leg, hugging her purse to her chest.

He began to talk slower, over-enunciating his words, repeating again. "We . . . would . . . like . . . to . . . thank . . ."

I tugged on my mother's arm, but she stood frozen.

". . . you . . . for . . . making . . . a . . . good . . . chop . . . suey. You people make good food."

The man looked back again, toasted his beer at his friends, laughing smoke from his lips.

My mother grabbed my hand and took one step toward the man. In that instant, I saw in her face the same resolve she had when she spanked, the same resolve when she scolded. In that instant, I thought my mother was going to hit the man. And for a moment, I thought the man saw the same thing in her eyes, and his smile disappeared from his face. Quickly, she smiled—too bright, too large—and said, "You're welcome."

Natalie Haney Tilghman

HERITAGE STATEMENT:

Although I was not raised by my grandparents, they were integral in my up-bringing and this trip to Italy occurred as part of my Outside Experience while in grad school. It was a life dream to return to my grandparents' birthplace and I now have dual citizenship in Italy and the U.S.

AUTHOR BIO:

Natalie Haney Tilghman was a recip-ient of a 2015 Rona Jaffe Writer's Award. She co-authored *A 52-Hertz Whale*, a Young Adult novel recently released by Carolrhoda Lab (Lerner, 2015). Addition-ally, her work has appeared in *Cicada*, *San-ta Clara Review*, *TriQuarterly,* and *Sudden*
Flash Youth, a fiction anthology by Persea Books. Other honors include first prize for fiction in *The Atlantic*'s Student Writing Contest and a Magazine Merit Award from The Society of Children's Book Writers and Illustrators. She received an MFA from the Rainier Writing Workshop at Pacific Lutheran University. She lives in Glenview, Illinois, with her husband and three children.

PRESENTOSA—TRACING THE GOLD IN MY BLOOD

Roma and Pittsburgh. These were the places where the men in my family—Alfredo and Frank Mastrovincenzo—practiced their craft, sculpting gold by hand into rings, brooches, necklaces, earrings, and bracelets to sell in their jewelry shops. My baby ring and later my wedding rings were made by Bucci's Jewelry Company on Liberty Avenue in Pittsburgh where my great-uncle Frank was once a co-owner. And I've visited my great-uncle Alfredo's home workshop in Roma, lovingly preserved by his widow Rina, several times. But my family's trade actually originated somewhere else entirely—in Castiglione Messer Marino, a tiny town at an elevation of over 1,500 meters, in Abruzzo where my grandmother, grandfather, and great-uncles were born, and where my great-grandfather, Giuseppe, and his brothers first worked as goldsmiths in the early part of the twentieth century. As a third-generation Italian American, I'd always wanted to see the craggy mountains that my great-grandfather scaled by mule on his way to the remote villages where he would vend his art during festivals.

And so, in January of 2010, I set out for my grandparents' birthplace. During my visit, I discovered that it was no coincidence that the goldsmiths in my family hailed from Abruzzo. The region is known for its distinctive jewelry, characterized by filigree work fine as lace. The presentosa, a gold or silver medallion featuring a star and heart, might best represent the local style. Hoping to find my own presentosa, I journeyed to Sulmona, a valley town famous for its candy-covered almond confetti and for being the birthplace of Ovid. A slow train chugged past abandoned shepherds' huts, clay-colored medieval villages, and meadows stubbled with ruins. When I arrived in Sulmona, friendly women in the tourist bureau humored my choppy Italian and directed me to jewelry shops, but because it was the mid-afternoon pranzo, all of them were shuttered.

To pass the time, I perused a bookstore where I found *Amuleti Ornamenti Magici d'Abruzzo* by Adriana Gandolfi. Those pages taught me that, years ago, popular Abruzzese designs included a blindfolded cupid wearing a crown, natural objects, like snakes or horns, and religious subjects. According to local folklore, some kinds of jewelry were traditionally thought to possess magical and curative powers, bringing a wearer fertility, good fortune, or better health. Other charms offered protection from maladies, the evil eye, or witchcraft. Even the materials used to create the decorative arts had symbolic value. Gold represented fire and the sun while silver symbolized the moon and water. The folklore surrounding Abruzzese jewelry probably dated back to pre-Christian times. Jewelry, it seemed, was important not only in the lives of my family, but in the lives of generations of Abruzzese people as well.

As the mountains' shadows swallowed the valley, I left the bookstore. The streets of Sulmona buzzed with people—women linked arms, old men perched on a bench near the drinking fountain, and children darted after soccer balls. My train to Rome was scheduled to leave soon, so I took one last stroll around the piazza. Yellow light warmed one jewelry shop window. I knocked on the door and Alessio Manicelli, the owner, invited me inside. His desk was crowded with works-in-progress and tools. From among his handcrafted jewels, I chose a cupid pendant studded with coral as a souvenir.

While Signore Manicelli wrapped up my treasure, I worked up the courage to tell him about the goldsmiths in my family. I tried to find the words to express that my great-grandfather had been listed among other artists in a museum book on the subject of Abruzzese jewelry. I wanted to say that I had a sense that my family was part of a larger tradition—one that was culturally rich and that I was just beginning to understand. It was hard to shape my feeling of connectedness into English, let alone Italian. But despite the language barrier, Signore Manicelli seemed to understand. Reaching under his desk, he told me he had something for me. A small gift, traditionally worn by people in this part of Italy. Silver flashed in his hand. Signore Manicelli offered me something that I hadn't seen in the store window for sale—something that, since the beginning of my journey, I hoped to find: a presentosa.

Bunkong "BK" Tuon

HERITAGE STATEMENT:

I was born in Cambodia several years before the 1975 Khmer Rouge takeover. I lost my mother to sickness and starvation. In 1979, when the Vietnamese army entered Cambodia, my uncles, aunts, and grandmother took me away from my father and together fled to refugee camps along the Cambodia–Thai border. In 1981, as refugees, we immigrated to the United States. I grew up near the Boston area. While a high school student in Massachusetts, I received a letter from Cambodia informing me of my father's death. I write about memories of Cambodia, life in refugee camps, growing up as a Cambodian refugee in the 1980s, and, with constant difficulty, figuring out my hyphenated identity as a Cambodian American. Because I came to the States around the age of nine (I don't know the exact year of my birth), I belong to the 1.5 generation of U.S. immigrants and refugees—those who were born elsewhere but grew up in the States. Known as the Bridge Generation, we are caught between the world of our elders who came to the States as adults and that of our cousins, nieces, and nephews who were born in the States. Unlike me, both the first and second generations in my family seem confident and assured about their identities, while I struggle to find myself and my place in America.

AUTHOR BIO:

Bunkong "BK" Tuon is an Assistant Professor in Ethnic American Literature at Union College in Schenectady, New York. He received his PhD at the University of Massachusetts and recently completed a book of family poems about Cambodia, America, and that space in between. His poetry collection, *Gruel,* was published by NYQ Books in 2015. His work has appeared in *Genre, In Our Own Words: A Generation Defining Itself, Khmer Voice in Poetry, The Massachusetts Review,* and *The Truth about the Fact: International Journal of Literary Nonfiction.*

LIVING IN THE HYPHEN

Thanksgiving.
Driving home from school with a migraine
I pulled over and vomited on the side of Route 2.
I had been working on an article exploring
the implications of Bhabha's third space, searching
for a theory of an authentic hyphenated, diasporic, trans-national,
(or was it post-national?) trans-global Asian-American identity.

When I arrived at my family's home,
my fifteen-year-old cousin Thearith, the tallest
in our extended family, was having dinner.
Born in the States, he greeted me in his perfect
Bostonian accent. I watched him attack his steak.

On the table, with the dishes
of rice and steak, were two plates:
One contained a Khmer dipping sauce,
made of *prahouk*, lime juice, lemongrass,
grilled peppers, garlic, and Thai chilies;
the other, an A1 Steak sauce
from the local Stop & Shop.

"Thearith, why do you have two sauces for your steak?"

"Well, when I get bored with one sauce, I go for the other.
I choose whatever pleases me at the moment.
It's all good, bro."

PHOTOGRAPH OF MY MOTHER

In the black-and-white wedding photograph
you stand next to your husband—
confident and smiling, looking directly
into the camera lens with jewels glittering around your neck.
That necklace that Grandmother borrowed
from the landowner whose house stood
between the fish market and noodle shops,
where the train snaked alongside the marketplace,
where is it now?

This must be before 1975, before strange cravings,
when your sister, barely a teenager then, barefoot
and tired, waded through muddy rice fields,
on thin, stilted legs, searching for eels,
and you were rib-cage thin, pale,
skin about to burst, eyes bulging,
cold, always cold, waiting for your sister
to bring back lizards, snakes, crickets, and eels;
This must be before Buddhist monks chanting prayers
on our house's veranda, and I was sitting
on your sister's lap, crying under the tamarind tree,
thinking those monks were so rude to you,
bothering your sleep.

Thirty years later, your sisters tell me
that you were beautiful and kind.
As the oldest, you taught them how
to talk softly, to tread gently the dirt
and the bamboo floor, to not look someone
in the eye, but to cast your eyes low,
to be a proper Khmer woman.

Your youngest sister, the one who hunted eels
for you, looked for you
when her first child, a girl, was born in the States.

My fingers trace the worn-out texture, the duct tape
wrapping the photograph's torn corners, and
I am paralyzed. Mother, you smile
so brilliantly at the camera that even your sisters,
who now have children of their own,
would blush at your boldness.

Mother, I am about to marry.
I wish we had a chance to talk.
I have no memory of you;
even a fragment of you angry at me, screaming
at something I did, pulling a nearby branch
to whip me, would help me imagine
what you would say to me now.

EARLY SATURDAY MORNING
IN MALDEN, MA (1986)

Saturday morning
grocery shopping at the only Asian
market in the city;
putting back fish sauce and soy sauce,
picking up milk, bread, and cereal,
I told Grandma to be quiet—
Because Stephanie and her mother were there too.

Itoro Udofia

HERITAGE STATEMENT:

Itoro Udofia was born in 1987 in Houston, Texas, but has spent most of her life growing up on the East Coast. Her parents came to America with the hopes of acquiring Western education during the 1970s and hoped to return to Nigeria. They raised three children born in the United States.

AUTHOR BIO:

Itoro Udofia is a Nigerian-American writer and ed-ucator living in the Bay Area. She has been writing ever since she was a little girl. Itoro's writings can be found on her personal blog, www.thoughtsofmymind-itoro .blogspot.com.

DAUGHTER OF THE DIASPORA

My memories are rooted in stirring fufu in a tiny pot.
Fufu made from jiffy mix
bought at a Price Chopper (exactly 2 dollars and 50 cents)
put it in a pot and stirred till it becomes nice and thick.
"It's supposed to clump together and should be able to form itself into a ball,"
Mama would say. "But remember child . . . real fufu don't really taste that way."
"We're trying to get the flavor I was used to back home," Mama would say.
"Does it come close?" I would ask.
Mama laughs. "Not really."
My memories are rooted in eating fufu when it's 5 degrees out
or singing Nigerian gospel songs quietly instead of singing out loud.
Mama says, "We usually sing these songs out loud till everyone sings . . .
but we'll try to sing these songs more quietly.
Can't wake the neighbors now."
My voice carries little traces from another place.
I'm not anything like Mama.
My memories are rooted in reading Morrison and singing like Nina
and finding any black woman who looks like my image.
Mama says, "Child, you are African but you're different now. You're a child born
in America,
and you'll experience different layers of pain and pressures now. So you can teach
me
and I'll teach you. 'Cause I'm thinking of going back home, but home seems to
be here for you . . ."
Mama's been trying to get me to go back . . . back to her home.
"I'd like us to live there someday,"
Mama says, says to me.
She's speaking as if she's caught in a dream—
"We'll eat *real* fufu, sing Nigerian gospels loudly, and it won't be 5 degrees out,"
Mama says.
I think it would be nice to go . . . and see,

"But I don't think I can stay there Mama . . . I think I'm meant to be here now."
Mama breaks out of her nostalgia.
"True child," Mama says, says to me,
"You live here now. You'll visit but you may not stay . . . guess we'll have to wait and see.
Guess we'll have to wait and see."

Denise S. Valenti

HERITAGE STATEMENT:

My mother came to the United States from Cuba in 1963 after deciding she couldn't live under Fidel Castro's Communist regime. She was twenty-two when she left her widowed mother and five young sisters in the hope of one day helping them to follow her. The Cuban government wouldn't allow her to take anything but the clothes on her back—not even photos—and she spent three months as a refugee in Spain before she was granted entry to the United States. Once in Miami, my mother worked factory jobs while learning bookkeeping. She eventually made her way to New York, where she kept accounts for a manufacturing firm and attended classes to neutralize her Spanish accent. It took several years, but she finally put together enough money to bring her mother and youngest sister to live with her. I was raised in an ethnic Italian and Irish neighborhood in Brooklyn, New York. Even in the world's largest melting pot, I never quite blended, which was painful as a child. As an adult I've found those experiences have only enriched me, and they've certainly fed my writing.

AUTHOR BIO:

Denise S. Valenti is an award-winning journalist and Cuban-Italian-American writer. Her first novel is a work of historical fiction based on her grandfather's struggle with his German-Jewish identity as an émigré to Colombia and Cuba. Denise's work was a finalist in the 2011 and 2012 Brooklyn Non-Fiction Prize and she is the former senior associate editor for *Latina* magazine. She lives in New Jersey with her two children.

SPANISH

"*Dice, 'agua,'*" my mother said to me as she held out a glass. She refused to release it from her grip until I relented, but I walked away with a dry mouth rather than say the word "water" in Spanish. I was about five years old and quickly learned the comeback that was my only sure defense: "You're in America now. Speak English!" It wore my mother down, and eventually, she stopped offering drinks with an accompanying language tutorial.

I had won.

Or so I thought at the time.

Had I grown up a Cuban American in Miami, Spanish would have been an inescapable part of my life. Instead, my mother, a refugee from Castro's rule, settled in Brooklyn, NY, in a primarily Italian, Irish and Jewish neighborhood. I certainly didn't want to be thought of as different in a community where the mere aroma of *arroz con frijoles* might cause "For Sale" signs to spring up three blocks around. And I think my mother never really forced the language on me because she herself worried about how she was perceived. When she came to New York in 1965, she understood that mastering English was her ticket to acceptance and a better way of life. She learned it as quickly as she could and even took classes to eliminate her accent.

What little Spanish I knew was entirely incidental, absorbed from my *abuelita*, who lived in the apartment downstairs from ours. The smell of her Marlboros and the sound of her *telenovelas* would often penetrate the thin floorboards that separated us. Every day she'd come up for a *cafecito* with my mom or to help wash the dishes. If I ventured downstairs, it was usually to admire her collection of elephants and odd figurines. I knew the visit was over when she yelled out, "*No se tocan!*" For a while I thought it meant goodbye.

As a child, I never really connected with her. Maybe it was because I didn't always understand what she was saying. She spoke to me in Spanish, and I responded in English. That was how we communicated, and it worked just fine since neither of us was ambitious enough to clear up any misunderstanding. We'd often exchange embarrassed nods and grins. Whenever we parted, she'd leave me with a single phrase: "*Te veo pronto*." I'll see you soon. I'd return the sentiment with a muffled, "Bye."

Over the years, it was always the same. We spoke far more often with hugs, kisses and awkward smiles than with actual words. As a result, we never really talked. I couldn't ask her what her childhood was like or about life in Castro's Cuba. I'm guessing she knew a lot more about me, having watched me grow up. But I can't remember her ever once asking, "How's school?" or "Do you have a boyfriend?"

Things only got worse when my *abuelita* lost her hearing. It no longer mattered whether I asked her, "How are you feeling?" or troubled with, "*Como te sientes?*" All of a sudden, she couldn't understand anything at all. She was often confused, and when someone spoke to her she'd giggle nervously and shrug her shoulders.

When my *abuelita* fell and broke her hip at age eighty-four, I sat by her hospital bed and watched as my mother and aunt communicated with her by writing words in Spanish on a large pad of paper. She and I, well, we had our system down pat: Winks, smiles, a tight grip of the hand. She seemed to be doing OK, then unexpectedly took a turn for the worse. Over the course of two weeks, I visited her almost daily. Sometimes she'd cry out, "*Ay, que dolor,*" but she didn't have to tell me anything. I knew her body language so well that I could see she was dying. If she realized it, she never told my mother. She never said goodbye. But she did, in a private moment the night before she left us, admit to me, "*Tengo miedo.*" She was afraid. She said other things, too. But that was all I understood. My Spanish wasn't good enough to figure out the very last words she would ever speak to me.

I was never angrier with myself than I was when I left her that evening. And for the rest of my life I'll wonder what she uttered in our final moments together. But I do know this: She loved me, and I'm sure she knew that I loved her. And it was all said in *besitos, abrazos y sonrisas.*

Elisabeth von Uhl

HERITAGE STATEMENT:

My grandmother was a very hard woman. She came from Germany and married another German immigrant in the United States. They then moved to a farm in rural Wisconsin. She had seven children and her husband left her when the oldest was around eighteen years old and shipped off to Vietnam. I never met my grandfather, but I remember my grandmother had thin, yellowed skin that was stretched over her face. Her cheeks drooped down and she had slits in her ear lobes from years of wearing earrings. She spoke German, but never a German I understood. She smoked cigarette after cigarette with her thin, chapped lips and her clothes were always ripped and worn through. Even if new clothes were gifted to her, she always wore a white button-down shirt held together by safety pins. My grandmother used to tell my father that she came to the U.S. from Germany because "in America, the pigs already had forks and knives in them." She was not affectionate with her children or grandchildren. Once, when telling her of a fist fight with my brother and cousin, she simply told me to "hit them back harder."

AUTHOR BIO:

Elisabeth von Uhl earned her MFA from Sarah Lawrence College and has taught composition, poetry, and literature at Fordham University, Montclair State University, and Hostos Community College. Her work has been published in *The Broome Review, The Cortland Review, Cream City Review, CrossBRONX,* and other journals. Her chapbook, *Ocean Sea*—which was a semi-finalist for the Black Lawrence Press Chapbook competition—was published by Finishing Line Press in 2009. She lives in the Norwood area of the Bronx with her husband and son.

CHILD SPEAKS OF GERMAN-IMMIGRANT GRANDMOTHER

I did not know her
before her seven children
were born or before her husband
left. I did not know
her before she broke switches
from the tree to punish
or before she stepped
on the neck of a pinned bird
and took its head off with an axe.

Alexandrine Vo

HERITAGE STATEMENT:

My work is greatly informed by my experiences of growing up in Vietnam and of being a political exile to the U.S. As my father had served in the South Vietnamese Army and was imprisoned for seven years in concentration camps after the War, my family and I were granted permanent residency and later, American citizenship. We settled in Biloxi, Mississippi, where I spent my teen years—a city that was later devastated by Hurricane Katrina, in which we lost our new home. After the South, I went on to live in the Pacific Northwest, the Northeast, and on the West Coast.

AUTHOR BIO:

Alexandrine Vo was born in Quang Nam Province, Vietnam. A Gates Scholar, she holds an MFA from Boston University where she was a George Starbuck Fellow and a Robert Pinsky Global Fellow. Her poems have appeared in *CALYX*, *Poetry Ireland Review*, *Popshot Magazine*, and *The Stinging Fly*, among others. Her first manuscript, *As Though We Are One*, was a finalist for the Kundiman Poetry Prize 2015. Now living in New York City, she is at work on her second manuscript, *The Gallant South*. More info can be found on www.maythefirst.net.

OMPHALOS

in the middle of the body is a door   that opens one way
and locks behind you   adamant as pursed
lips   and suddenly you are there gazing at eternity

with your injured bird's eyes   since the way
back is lost   the tether cut   the vessel hollow—
how?   far from home you seize the first mantle of flesh

put stock in sinews and bones   the shock of air contra blood
and viscera   the hovering in that nothing-wanting dark
so cold the   water now   but it is *may*   may

your father pacing smoking   your sister home to put the pot on
your mother who has this one reason to laugh   on emerald thighs
of mountain   where bees gather   to brew your name

LUCK

When the bombs rained,
my uncle was sneaking out for a smoke
to avoid the eyes of his father
who forbade him from smoking.

And that was how he happened to live. And lived still,
twenty-five years later, though the doctor said he would, in a year or so,
die of stomach cancer.
Maestro! The blood of longevity lives in you.

And grandmother,
not minding the expensive porcelain her husband gave away
in whims of empathy and pain,
or his money from gambling bets

won too easily, wit for wit.
Gambling blood that lives in uncle, my mother, her son.
Poor grandfather, your automatic writer tells us in trances and portents
that you are serving a twenty-year sentence in the land of no name . . .

Blindfolded, he writes in your hand;
he speaks in your voice, you would hardly believe it yourself.
What sins, what crimes? See how your daughter rushes home to fast, pray,
beg deities their forgiveness.

You can tell it to me in the rain,
and I will let it glide through my hands and seep into the brick's bronzed cracks.
Let me speak for you when we are walking together in the yard
in case the others might not hear you.

Whisper it to your wife, and she will pass it to me
in riddles from memory
as she stands still in your green guest room,
her shadow falling like some tree in late afternoon, sun slicing through it.

Bearing the load of living longer, of living too long.
Ninety-four and still talking to silence, to coronations of carambolas
and pommaracs in the yard. To your portrait on the wall,
as if you are there, expecting some reply.

REVISITING

Little city   my city in rustic splendor
under terracotta eaves a wood-framed roof

With your four totems
a bed of planks on which we have slept

How cool beneath us aging in the night
this wood's stern air

   Even the drowse of soot is home
    even the thrum of pig bristles

lulls rustling in the dark while the dirt floor
primps and waits

Fifteen years in exile still every room harbors
a lingering scent of war

This house that empty grieves like a widow
Ribs and skulls sleep soundly in the soil

Ocean Vuong

HERITAGE STATEMENT:

My family immigrated to the U.S. in 1990. I was a year old. We came to the U.S. because my mother is a *con lai* or a half-breed: her father was an unknown American soldier during the Vietnam War and once the U.S. lost the conflict, the Vietnamese government wanted to eradicate its soil of "tainted products of the enemy," and my mother was one of them. Therefore, *con lai*s, as well as their families, were basically deported to the U.S. I was a year old when we left Vietnam, but the immigration took a whole year as we were held up in a Philippines refugee camp for ten months. The story—as well as the story of other *con lai*s and their families—is quite complicated, but this is the abridged version.

AUTHOR BIO:

Ocean Vuong's first full-length collection, *Night Sky with Exit Wounds*, was published by Copper Canyon Press in 2016. He is also the author of two chapbooks: *No* (YesYes Books, 2013) and *Burnings* (Sibling Rivalry Press, 2010), which was an American Library Association's Over The Rainbow selection. A 2014 Ruth Lilly Fellow, Ocean has received honors and awards from Kundiman, Poets House, the Elizabeth George Foundation, the Civitella Ranieri Foundation (Italy), the Saltonstall Foundation for the Arts, the  Academy of American Poets, and a 2014 Pushcart Prize. His poems have been featured in *Best New Poets 2014*, *Boston Review*, *Guernica*, *Harvard Review*, *Kenyon Review*, *The Nation*, *The New Yorker*, *Poetry*, *Tri-Quarterly*, and the *American Poetry Review*, which awarded him the 2012 Stanley Kunitz Prize for Younger Poets. His work has also been translated into Hindi, Korean, Vietnamese, and Russian. Born in Saigon, Vietnam, he currently resides in New York City. More information can be found at www.oceanvuong.com.

RETURNING

Cong Hoa Blvd. lit with traffic, exhaust
from motorbikes, trucks reeking of cod
and shrimp, the sharp wail of a woman
selling coconuts, a schoolboy
in red scarf chanting the names
of girls in an alley the width
of a casket—so much thriving
and yet, I can only think of the body's
ending, how the song can still be heard, even
as the jaw is torn in two. In this city of which
I know only from what is lost, from this flag,
that flag, flags burning, helicopters, people
clinging to helicopters, in this city
whose name written in blood's dialect,
I search the faces for my own and find
those familiar gods: the gentle nose, eyes
creased to see through dust-storms,
cheekbones raised into monoliths.
But all are facing forward, down avenues
paved neon with promise and factories.
Here, every step is a destination's refrain.
And I, with my tattered map,
am still trying to return to that city
where in a dark room at Hung Vuong hospital,
my mother apologized again and again
for letting me leave her womb.

AFTER ALL

the woman blurred on the horizon
is the size of the city
she left behind a hand
brightens the fog
before vanishing
but to say mother
is to name the years between war
and war
the one where you climbed
into the womb to hide
from gunfire
you were calling me
from every window broken
in with rain you
who will not stop
putting rice and fish
at the empty chair
you your face
at the doorway now
is all that's left
of god's thumbprint
hardened with each
darkening year
but mother of all
the mounds of dirt outside
the empty village
of all the rose petals flung
against mourning
which of you
were the sisters who held hands
while soldiers took turns

who fled by closing their eyes
only to find their bodies too cold
to return to mother
I am sorry I wasn't born
to see the girl emerged
from Napalm her pale ankles
dancing beneath a serrated dress
of flames

but mother
which fleck of her ashes
did I bloom from
my hands belonging to no one
reaching for your breast
as father would
for the tops of skulls
or the pearl of milk
like a moon lighting
a mother whose fingers
have named a son
by tracing the curves of bone
in red dust
but mother I ask only to listen
to your silence
like a child learning
how to speak
I ask only
but what good the answer mother
if not to return the want
of knowing nothing
for to even have one

to even write the word
mother
is to carve
a portion of the world
out of a bomb-bright page.

SAI GON, AGAIN

Woke to a soft song
falling through the window.
On the balcony—a woman hanging rags,
her voice delicate, almost fractured
as it weaves through the gray sheet
framing her silhouette.
The lyrics wrap around my tongue
as I am pulled closer to the miracle
of simple things: wind giving life
to laundry, a stranger singing
the only lullaby I know by heart.
I want to complete our song, see
her shadow freeze as I finish the verse
where the mother carries her son
across the broken bridge of childhood.
But when I open my mouth, the sound
is impossibly small—a moan wilting
into whisper. The voice is someone else's
screaming
from across the earth.

Kristy Webster

HERITAGE STATEMENT:

My father was born in 1919 in Helena, Montana. His parents were farmers as well as zealous Jehovah's Witnesses ministers. At the age of forty, my father relocated to Barranquilla, Colombia, to preach and make converts. He worked as a taxi cab driver to support himself as he received no payment from the church for his religious work. There he met my mother, who at age seventeen began studying with Jehovah's Witnesses, converting from Catholicism by the time she was nineteen. Earlier in life she aspired to become a nun. When she and my father met she was twenty. They married six months later and remained in Colombia for two more years, diligent in their ministry work. After those first two years my father brought my mother to the United States for what was supposed to be a visit. It turned out to be over fifty years. My mother has visited Colombia only a handful of times since then due to economic difficulty. She was a stay-at-home mother her entire life while my father worked in the orchards and fields, usually the only Caucasian working among Mexican migrant farm-workers. Both my parents are fluently bilingual and are still carrying on their ministry work among the Spanish-speaking community in Eastern Washington.

AUTHOR BIO:

Kristy Webster was born in Prosser, Washington, in 1975. Kristy is the author of *The Gift of an Imaginary Girl: Coco & Other Stories* published in 2015 by A Word With You Press. She earned her MFA in creative writing from the Rainier Writing Workshop at Pacific Lutheran University and her BA from the Evergreen State College where she majored in creative writing, visual arts, and feminist studies. Her work has appeared in several online journals such as: *Connotation Press, The Feminist Wire, A Fly in Amber, Lunch Ticket, The*  *Molotov Cocktail, Pacifica Literary Review, Pithead Chapel*, and *Shark Reef Literary Magazine*. Her work is also featured in two print anthologies by GirlChild

Press, *A Woman's Work* and *Just Like a Girl*. Her short fiction has been published in two anthologies as well as several online journals. She lives in Port Townsend, Washington, with her two sons and too many cats. To learn more about Kristy go to www.kristywebster.com.

MOTHER FIRE, FATHER ICE

As a child, I used to put my dark hand over my sister's porcelain skin and think of Neapolitan ice cream. I'd think how her hands reminded me of the vanilla and strawberry, and our mother's hand reminded me of the chocolate, and I was somewhere in the middle. If my sister was vanilla-strawberry-cream, I was chocolate-vanilla creamy cream.

Our home, our childhood, was made of fire and ice. Our father, a flaxen-haired, blue-eyed Depression-era child twenty years our mother's senior, has a past made up of horses, of rural Montana in the 1920s. It's seasoned with near-death experiences in coal mines and driving taxis in Bogota. His weathered face and hands are testaments of a life spent in the orchards, working in the beating sun, the relentless winds. My father's calluses and scars are his medals. Focused, resilient and stoic, our father taught us a silent regard for hard work and sacrifice. He didn't give hugs and kisses, or play catch, but he was always watching us, observing from an emotionally safe distance the four children he never planned on having. My father, the unknowable. My father, the ice.

My raven-haired, brown-skinned, Colombian-born mother spoke of servants, waxed poetic about the mango tree in her front yard, the public market, and *platanos* fried to a golden brown. Early on, it became apparent that Colombia was her first love, the lover she'd left behind when she married my father and moved to the States. Her eyes filled with tears when she spoke of the streets of Barranquilla, the ocean, the parrots in the public parks, her mother, her father, and her brothers. The opposite of my father's cool, collected nature, my mother's erratic moods, from her explosive outbursts to her overbearing coddling, were both terrifying and exhilarating. My mother, the volcano. My mother, the fire.

When I was ten and my sister was thirteen, my mother sat with us under a yellow-leafed tree that reminded me of tiny fluttering. My mother asked us if she should divorce our father. My only question was, "Do I still get to live with you?" They both looked at me in disbelief. My only concern was keeping my matching mother. At that time, I believed that my mother equated my entire world, my whole identity.

My two sisters have my father's ivory, rose-colored skin and one of them even had flaxen blonde hair when she was very young. They fit in well with our father's English/German/Swiss family. But I stood out like a dark-faced sunflower among pale pink carnations. *One of these things is not like the other, one of these things is not the same . . .* A blonde cousin approached me and my sister at a family reunion when I was about eleven. She said, "I don't mean to be rude, but, which one of you is adopted?" My older sister and I exchanged looks and she explained for us as she always did, that we had the same parents and neither of us were adopted: Our mother is Colombian and our father is white.

One time my father's sister insisted I had brown eyes while looking directly into my undeniably blue irises. Her granddaughter, my cousin, corrected her, "No grandma, she has blue eyes! See?" But my aunt Mora insisted that since I had dark brown hair and dark olive skin, there was no way that I had blue eyes. My eye color rarely escaped some type of commentary when I was little. At school, my blue eyes kept Mexican-American classmates skeptical of my ethnicity, the genetic tattle-tale that I wasn't all brown. In my freshman year, two girls were making fun of my clothes in Spanish assuming I couldn't understand. When I turned around and spoke to them in their native tongue, their eyes widened. "My blue eyes don't mean what you think they mean," I wanted to say. From that day on I sat with those girls during lunch. Eventually we became friends.

As a child I'd stare at the mirror to find the places where I diverted from my mother's template, the blue eyes being the most obvious. But then I also took notice of my fuller lips, lips nothing like my mother's. I have my father's lips, his mouth, and his nose, the "Webster" nose. Beyond that, I have my father's love of solitude, and also his hands, hands made for making.

I asked my sister once what she puts on forms that ask for her ethnic identity. My blonde, blue-eyed sister looked at me incredulously, "Caucasian, of course." Yet, I've always identified with my mother in every way; skin color, hair color, even culture, though I've never been to Colombia. Had I not earned the right to circle Latino/Hispanic?

When I moved away from Eastern Washington, to the abundantly Caucasian and virtually sunless Olympic Peninsula, it seemed as though I was losing some of my brownness. I had a hard time finding Spanish-speaking people. I grew paler and paler every year. My teenage son took Spanish from a blonde, blue-eyed teacher whose Spanish was far superior to mine. What happened to me? Get some miles between me and my dark-skinned mother, live in a town that's 98 percent white and English-speaking and my chocolate cream melts? What does this mean for me? Does it mean I should start circling the same ethnic identifier as my sister?

It turns out though, there's a more fastidious, impenetrable chord that's kept me connected to my mother's land and her roots: her story. When my mother told me stories about growing up in Barranquilla I didn't just listen to them, I devoured them, I asked for seconds and thirds. *Tell me again, about the Colombian rains, those tropical storms that make Pacific Northwest rain look like cheap drizzle. Tell me about the time your mother, my Abuela Magola, left you in charge of killing your first chicken. Tell me how you tortured that thing, taking the knife all slow and delicate, thinking you were being kind. Tell me how you used to write poetry and maybe this time you'll answer why you stopped.*

Why did you stop? Should I stop? Am I yours, that much? Tell me about the kidnappers again, that's my favorite! They had the little boy and guns, and you spied on them, you and your brothers laid out on your bellies on the rooftop just watching, waiting . . . Did they get him back? They did. Were you scared? You weren't. At least you don't remember. Tell me again how long it was before you got to see your native country again? Twenty years. You went twenty years without going home? That's why you asked us about a divorce all those years ago? Yes. That's why. You wanted permission to return home and not come back. You weren't meant for this country, this language, you said, you didn't belong. Will you be okay without me, is what you were really asking?

My parents have now been married for over fifty-six years. The under-the-tree talk a residual childhood hiccup weaved through our new narrative as adults, as wives, as mothers. The color of my heart still leans towards, and still identifies with, my mother. My skin is paler now, and I fumble over Spanish prepositions and yet it runs deep in my blood. I have my mother's proficiency for mischievous mimicking, for high-highs and low-lows. I have her drama in my bones, her country's essence sailing through my cells. I don't know how it hasn't capsized in all this whiteness, but somehow it sails on, the unsinkable ship that is my mother's DNA.

People ask me all the time, "What are you?" Usually I don't mind so much. I want to tell them that my mother's face radiates like a mocha-skinned moon and that my father's crystal blue eyes sparkle on like little pools flashing their depths. My father has a silly white man dance and never leaves home without his fedora. My mother sings, and when she sings I feel the ghosts of her country rising.

I am my father's daughter and my mother's song.

Chris Wiewiora

HERITAGE STATEMENT:

My father grew up speaking Polish and English in Chicago, and then majored in Russian at college. He was born in England, but his mother was born in the southwest of Poland (now in Ukraine). They immigrated to the States in the '50s. My mother is an American and born in West Virginia. I was born in West Virginia, but grew up in Warsaw, Poland, because both my parents were missionaries with Campus Crusade for Christ under the Iron Curtain in the '80s. I grew up speaking English, while surrounded by Polish.

AUTHOR BIO:

Chris Wiewiora is a half–Polish American who lived in Warsaw from 1987 to 1996. In the summer of 2008, he and his father visited the country again. He still doesn't speak Polish too well. Currently, he lives in Ames, Iowa, where he is a graduate student in Iowa State University's MFA in Creative Writing and Environment program. He mostly writes nonfiction, which has appeared on *Huffington Post, nerve.com,* and *theRumpus.net.* Also, he regularly contributes to the *Good Men Project.* Read more at www.chriswiewiora.com.

M-I-S-S-I-S-S-I-P-P-I

We are our own the way a river swallows
itself. The need that need follows follows.
— John Poch, "Lullaby"

In kindergarten, I sat on gray carpet. Cutout letters of the alphabet strung above the blackboard. The other kids repeated after the teacher, "Ah."

I knew that the sound wasn't the one that connected to the letter. The teacher made a noise like the one I heard Mom make at home when she lowered herself into the bathtub. The only reason Mom said we could ever disturb her was if we were bleeding or dying.

"Eh," I made the correct sound like the Canadians at the International Church said at the end of their sentences when they wanted clarification or for someone to agree with them.

The teacher ignored me.

"Bi," she said.

The other kids repeated her.

I said "Be" and held it. I let the E elongate and buzz around the room. I thought of the TV show *Maya and the Bee*. Each night, Joe and I got to watch the half-hour of *Dobranoc/Goodnight*. When the VCR blinked 20:00, us brothers already sat in front of the blank screen, one of us pressed the "on" button and then we sang to the theme songs of the cartoons that were kept in English, but then turned down the volume when the Polish narrator dubbed over the English voices. In kindergarten, I ran out of breath.

The teacher looked at me.

"Sa," she said.

If I knew anything, then I knew how to say the first letter of my name.

"Cee," I said. It sounded the same as see. I wanted to shout SEE! Couldn't she see I was an American? It didn't matter if Mom and Dad brought our family to Poland, because they were missionaries. I was born in America. And even if Dad was Polish, Mom wasn't, and I wasn't going to speak Polish.

"Da," the teacher said, looking at me.

I stared down at the gray carpet. I plucked the pilled-up bunches of woven material. I tore the pieces out until the teacher was done saying the wrong sounds.

The lesson ended and then the other kids took out their plastic bags while the others lined up at the door. I followed them, led by our teacher down the hallway.

I felt small. It didn't matter if I was a loudmouth. I couldn't be understood. I didn't ask where the kids were going, I just followed.

I walked at the back of the line. We went down a staircase into a basement. The windows let in a pale, white light from the outside. Kids grabbed bowls and then had something that looked like cabbage and broth plopped into them. At the end, a table held a stack of pastries made of spirals of browned dough with flakes of sugary glaze and a yellow dollop of custard or a scoop of candied fruit.

I didn't have any *zloties*. I only had the lunch Mom packed for me. I went back to the classroom with nothing.

I took my Teenage Mutant Ninja Turtles lunchbox out of a cubby. I walked over to a corner and sat with my back to the wall. I opened up the clasps of the lunchbox.

On top was a note: *As long as I'm living my baby you'll be.* I could already read somewhat and the sentence was from a book she loved to read to me before bed as I cuddled in her lap. The story followed a mother who would cradle her son each night and sing the words of a lullaby.

I shoved the note in my pocket and wiped my nose with the cuff of my sleeve. Mom had made me a peanut butter and jelly sandwich. Wedged next to the PB&J was a box of California raisins.

I couldn't understand most of what the other kids were saying as they ate and played. They weren't all Poles. Many of them were Indian kids chattering away and a few Asian kids that Mom had told me were Thai.

A Thai girl walked over to me. She waved her hand. I opened up the box of raisins and chewed one. I wasn't that hungry. I opened my hand and dumped some of the raisins out and then offered them to her, saying, "Raisin." She smiled and took them. When she ate them all, she said, "Raisin." I shook the rest of the raisins into my hand and offered them to her. She took them and then finished again. "Raisin," she said. I shook my head and showed her the empty box. She walked away.

The film of water on top of the puke-green tiles was cold. I walked up on my toes trying to touch the least amount of water. A huddle of boys in Speedos stood by the edge of the indoor pool. I was the only one with trunks. The school required swimming lessons since they had a pool right there.

The swim teacher's belly hung down and a necklace nestled in the hair on his chest. He blew a whistle. I followed the other boys putting in their nose plugs. We jumped into the pool. I got water in my ears but didn't shake it out.

I held onto the pool's edge and kicked. I wanted to swim up and out of the pool onto the tile and through the halls and across the parking lot and then plunk into the Wisla River near the zoo. We flew home each summer across the Atlantic, but I would swim it now. I couldn't wait through winter and spring. I needed to go to America. I would go up the Mississippi.

Up was the same as north. I would go up, and then right. Right would be to West Virginia. Almost heaven, away from Poland. I would swim down the hills to my grandparents' house in Buckhannon with strawberry patches across the road. I would choose to live with Mom's parents, not Dad's mom, grandma in Chicago where they spoke Polish. I would swim to my Grandma and Grandpa Almond. Home.

When I got there I would ask Grandpa Almond to fix me. He had been a doctor. He knew when things were wrong and he could cut out the Polish.

In the pool, I breathed in water. I choked, and then gulped down more on purpose. If I filled my body with water, then maybe I could become a fish and I could swim back to America.

I felt two hands haul me up and out of the pool. I thrashed. The water foamed. My body slapped against the tiled deck and a hand smacked between my shoulder blades. I couldn't keep the water down. I threw up.

Mom and I had walked past the Marines guarding the door of the American School. The kids and their parents hugging on their way inside all spoke English. We sat in the principal's office, because she had called Grandma Almond who then sent money.

Mr. Roland, the principal, wore a white button-up shirt, a red tie, and pants. He reminded me of my Grandpa Almond. Mr. Roland had reddish hair. Grandpa Almond was called Doc or Red around town, even though he had retired and his hair was white.

The secretary made a copy of my American passport with my blonde mop in the photo that didn't match my hair anymore. It had begun to turn brown since going to the other school. I swung my feet, slung over the chair, imagining pumping my legs out on the swings I saw in the playground.

"Your mom says you can read a little already," Mr. Roland said.

"A lot," I said. My voice sounded loud. I was beginning to be the boy I had been. Mom was always reminding me to use my inside voice again.

"Alright now," Mr. Roland said. He nodded at Mom. "There's one question for new students to get into the American School of Warsaw. You have to spell something." He held up his finger.

"Okay," I said. I could spell my name.

"Spell *Mississippi*," Mr. Roland said.

I stared at him.

"It's a river," Mr. Roland said.

Of course I knew it was a river. I knew it was a state, too. I knew it was in America. I knew about steamboats and the water's flow south and that it cut the country in half, but I didn't know how to spell it.

I felt dunked underwater and was gulping for air, but I swallowed water. Grandma had already paid all the money. I wanted to speak English. I was an American. I wanted to say I was Mississippi!

But I was Polish and I felt dumb. I couldn't speak Polish and couldn't spell English. I didn't belong at either school.

"Nothing to get in a huff about," Mr. Roland said. He waved his hand.

Mom placed her hand on my shoulder. It felt like being pulled from the pool. I held down the urge to throw up.

"Em, eye, s, s, eye, s, s, eye, pee, pee, eye," Mr. Roland sung the spelling. "You'll never forget it. Welcome."

Aida Zilelian

HERITAGE STATEMENT:

I am a first-generation American-Armenian born in Queens, New York, in 1973 and raised by parents whose families were victims of the 1915 Armenian Genocide. It took me many years to appreciate my culture, and this story provides a small glimpse into my struggle of living in America while being raised by immigrant parents. My father came to America in 1968 and my mother in 1967.

AUTHOR BIO:

Aida Zilelian is a New York writer and English teacher. Her debut novel *The Legacy of Lost Things* was released in March 2015 (Bleeding Heart Publications) and was the recipient of the 2014 Tololyan Literary Award. Her work has been published in several anthologies and over twenty-five literary journals including *Per Contra*, *Red Fez*, *Theurgy*, *Wilderness House Literary Review*, and others. She has read her work at various reading series in Queens and Manhattan including Sunday Salon; Phoenix Reading Series; Gartal; REZ Reading Series; Oh, Bernice!; and First Tuesdays. She is the curator of Boundless Tales, a reading series in Queens, New York. In 2011, her first novel *The Hollowing Moon* was one of four semi-finalists in the Anderbo Novel Contest. She is currently working on her third novel. Find out more at www.aidazilelian.com.

THE ART OF TRYING

My hand began to ache as I held the blunt knife in my hand and pressed into the slab of plaster to create a new, clean line. One would expect that perhaps we would have been provided with a more pliable material, one that didn't need the force and brutality with which I tackled this piece of cement-like clay. I was nine years old and in Armenian Saturday school. Me and seven other students were in the art studio standing behind a desk, our knives in one hand and a picture of an intricately designed cross next to our empty rock-like canvas, each of us emitting small, angry grunts as we thrust our knives against the surface only to realize we were creating pathetic little scratches instead of deep, curved grooves. We were all assigned the task of creating a *khachkar*. Literally translated, it means "cross stone," and carries the weight of hundreds of years of Armenian history and tradition dating back to the twelfth century.

The weeks progressed and the grey rectangular slab became my mortal enemy as I attempted to carve into it and create a *khachkar* masterpiece. We were given four weeks to complete it with the expectation that we would also be taking it home and working on it during our leisure time. I would put mine on a table in the basement, where it would remain untouched until the following Saturday morning when I would hoist it under my arm and feel the weight of it pressing on my lap as my mother drove me to school. My only relief was the knowledge that my classmates also hadn't made much progress. However, the anxiety of having to complete the project in less than a week began to prey on my nerves.

The art teacher, Mr. Samosian, walked around the room, quietly evaluating our work as a curator would walk through a museum. I could only assume he was disappointed considering he hadn't uttered one encouraging word. Instead, he clicked his tongue against his teeth, which created a sharp sucking noise and made our hearts wearier.

"None of these look like anything close to becoming a cross," he said.

We all put down our knives and listened.

"Aida," he said. "You barely have the shape of a cross on there. Have you been working at home? It doesn't look like it," he said, answering for me.

"It's very tough," I said honestly, hoping my classmates would chime in. All I heard was a stray cough and the tinkering of someone's knife against the stone.

"We are displaying these at the church festival next Sunday," he said, his voice full of warning. "Do what you can with the remainder of the period and then finish the rest at home."

It was then and there that I decided to feign illness and not go to the festival at all. I wasn't ashamed of how little I had produced, but furious with this impossible and sophisticated project that would have been better suited for a professional sculptor, someone of the likes of Rodin, for instance. It also echoed the role that my culture and upbringing would resonate throughout my childhood and adolescence. Everything about being Armenian felt like a hindrance from living my idea of a normal life. I wouldn't be able to marry someone unless he was Armenian. My mother never made Brussels sprouts. I wasn't allowed to watch *Different Strokes* or *Three's Company*. I was forced to wear skirts that hung below my knees and wearing a bikini was out of the question no matter how old I was. And I couldn't have a boyfriend. Being Armenian felt as if I had been permanently cursed with no reprieve in sight.

My parents had enrolled me in St. Illuminator's Armenian Day School since the first grade, when the school first opened. My father had been one of the founders of the school and my mother was the head of the PTA. The school offered a Saturday program, and for reasons I could not fathom, my mother had insisted I attend on Saturdays as well. Never mind the fact that the next day I would have to sit through a two-hour Sunday school lesson at the Armenian Church in the city. Perhaps my mother thought that keeping me occupied among my peers would help preserve in me a sense of my culture. As I grew up, I was discouraged from having friends who were American, despite the fact that I had very few Armenian friends and little interest in belonging to such a small, clannish culture.

I realized that it wasn't only a generational gap that made it difficult to have a healthy relationship with my parents, but also a cultural one. My father's family had fled to Bucharest, Romania during the Armenian massacre, and he had lived there until he came to America during his early adulthood. My mother's family, also originally from Armenia, had gone to Beirut for the same reason. I was too young and self-absorbed to appreciate how their lives had shifted so drastically when they moved to this country. I was more concerned about how insulated I felt, existing and growing in a small bubble that did not extend itself to the real world.

"I don't feel well," I said.

It was Saturday evening and we were sitting at the dinner table.

"What's the matter?" my mother asked. She didn't look concerned. I knew I had to be more convincing.

"My throat," I said, resting my hand beneath my chin. "It hurts."

"When did it start hurting?" she asked. She had a way of finding me at fault regardless of the circumstances.

"Just a little while ago," I said. "After I came home from school."

"Why didn't you say something then?" she asked. She was irritated.

"I thought it would go away," I said, "but it got worse."

She snorted. "You thought," she said. "You and your thinking." Unexpectedly, she reached over and put her hand on my forehead. "You don't have a fever," she said. "Go to your room and lie down."

I lay down on my bed with a newfound terror. When I had made up my mind that I was going to fake being sick, I had also stopped trying to work on the *khachkar*. It was as I had left it—practically blank with some faint marks that resembled more of a geometric exercise than a detailed cross.

I was consumed in my thoughts until I noticed my father in the room.

"There's a piece of cement on the table in the basement," he commented.

I didn't say anything.

"Is it yours?" he asked.

I nodded. "It's supposed to be a *khachkar*," I said, bursting into tears, and covered my face with my arms.

"Do you want me to help you with it?" he asked.

I nodded again. It hadn't occurred to me to ask for help. Although my parents spoke English well, I knew they hadn't graduated from high school and their reading and writing was poor. I had always done my homework by myself, knowing that I could never turn to them.

I held the knife in my hand and felt my father's grip on top of mine, his hand strong and steady. He helped press deeply into the surface and my hand moved through the rough sketch I had wanted to draw. It took a long while, or at least it seemed to, and finally we stopped. It wasn't close to the picture that Mr. Samosian had given us as inspiration, but I knew I could bring it to the festival to have it put on display. On the bottom right hand corner there are two initials: AZ and HZ. The first one is mine that my father carved in for me. The second one is his and much less noticeable. When we were finished he went upstairs. I knew I would always remember that he had helped me with it, but his initials HZ—Harutiun Zilelian—felt significant. I would like to believe that his fatherliness had taken precedence over his nationalism, and that he helped me with it because he knew I needed him. My *khachkar* had preserved that moment in time. It was far more than I had hoped for.

ACKNOWLEDGMENTS

"A Situation for Mrs. Biswas" appears in the collection *Undergloom* by Prageeta Sharma (Fence Books, 2013). "Alaska," "My Father in the Night," "The Immigrants' Son," and "The Red Sweater" appear in the collection *Imago* by Joseph O. Legaspi (CavanKerry Press, 2007). Used by permission. "An American" appeared in *The New Republic*. "AMÉRICA" appears in *City of a Hundred Fires*, by Richard Blanco. Copyright © 1998. All rights are controlled by the University of Pittsburgh Press, Pittsburgh, PA 15261, upress.pitt.edu. Used by permission of University of Pittsburgh Press. "An Echo" is part of the larger piece entitled "Because a Wall Fell Down" and previously appeared in *Michigan Quarterly Review*. "Arise, Go Down" appears in *The City in Which I Love You* by Li-Young Lee (BOA Editions, Ltd., 1990). "Blood" appears in *19 Varieties of Gazelle: Poems of the Middle East* by Naomi Shihab Nye (Greenwillow Books, 2002). Originally published in *Yellow Glove* by Naomi Shihab Nye (Breitenbush Books). Copyright © 1986 by Naomi Shihab Nye. Reprinted by permission of the author. All rights reserved. "Half-and-Half" appears in *19 Varieties of Gazelle: Poems of the Middle East* by Naomi Shihab Nye, published by Greenwillow Books (2002). Reprinted by permission of the author. "Caffeine" and "The Day John Lennon Died" appear in *The Gravedigger's Archaeology* by William Archila (Red Hen Press, 2015). "Cartography" appeared in *Tigertail: A South Florida Poetry Annual*. "Chop Suey" appeared in *Brevity*. "Cuts and Folds" appeared in *Drunken Boat*. "Cuando sueño con Arizona" appeared in *Off the Coast*. "Dirty Dancing, János, with You" appeared in *Passager*. "Finite Love" appears in the collection *Sauce Robert* by F.J. Bergmann (Pavement Saw Press, 2003). "Home" appears in the collection *Bright Felon*. Copyright © 2009 by Kazim Ali. Reprinted by permission of Wesleyan University Press. "House Rules" originally appeared in *The Asian American Literary Review*. "House Rules" and "Ancestry" appear in the collection *Day of Clean Brightness* by Jane Lin (3: A Taos Press, 2017). Reprinted by permission. "I Ask My Mother to Sing" appears in the collection *Rose* by Li-Young Lee (BOA Editions, Ltd., 1993). "Inheritance" appeared in *Salamander*. "Laying a Foundation" appeared in *Wisdom of Our Mothers Anthology* (Familia Books, 2010) and *Arkina Magazine*. "Legacy" appeared in *Prairie Schooner* and the collection *Another Rude Awakening* by Dori Appel (Cherry Grove Collections, 2008). "Letter from Mother" and "Thread Rite" appeared in *Bellingham Review*. "Letter to Baghdad" appeared in *World Literature Today*. "Looking for the Gulf Motel" appears in *Looking for the Gulf Motel* (University of Pittsburg Press) by Richard Blanco. Copyright © 2012. All rights are controlled by the University of Pittsburgh Press, Pittsburgh, PA 15260. Used by permission of the University of Pittsburgh Press and Stuart Representation for Artists. "In Defense of Small Towns" and "Meditation with Smoke and Flowers" appear in the collection *Requiem for the Orchard* by Oliver de la Paz (University of Akron

Tina Schumann, Ed.

EDITOR BIO:

Tina Schumann is author of three po-
etry collections: *As If* (Parlor City Press,
2010), which was awarded the Stephen
Dunn Poetry Prize; *Requiem: A Patrimo-
ny of Fugues* (Diode Editions), winner of
the Diode Editions Chapbook Contest for
2016; and *Praising the Paradox* (Red Hen
Press, 2019). Her work received the 2009
American Poet Prize from *The American
Poetry Journal*, a Pushcart nomination and
finalist status in the National Poetry Series,
Four Way Books Intro Prize and the New

Issues Poetry Prize. Her poems have appeared in publications and anthologies
since 1999, including *The American Journal of Poetry, Ascent, Cimarron Review,
The Human, Midwest Quarterly, Nimrod, Parabola, Palabra, Terrain.org*, and
Verse Daily. www.tinaschumann.com